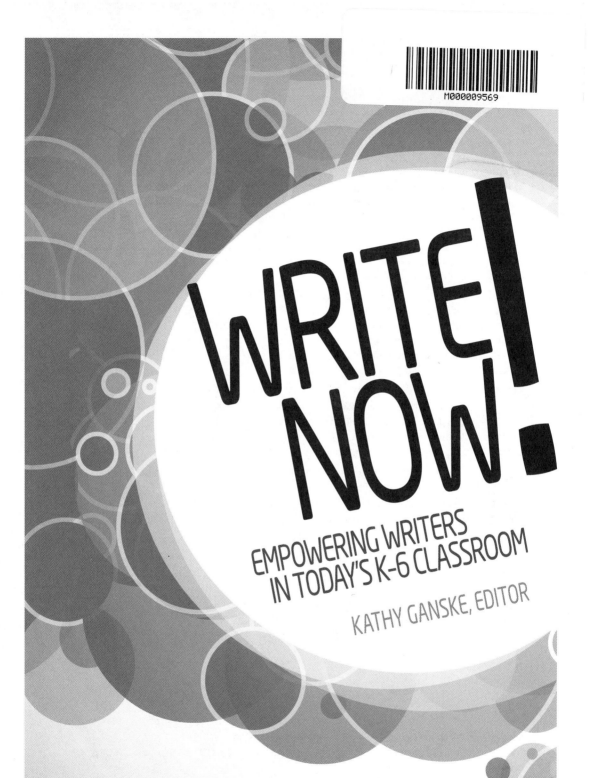

WRITE NOW!

EMPOWERING WRITERS IN TODAY'S K-6 CLASSROOM

KATHY GANSKE, EDITOR

INTERNATIONAL
Reading Association

800 BARKSDALE ROAD, PO BOX 8139
NEWARK, DE 19714-8139, USA
www.reading.org

The International Reading Association attempts, through its publications, to provide a forum for a wide spectrum of opinions on reading. This policy permits divergent viewpoints without implying the endorsement of the Association.

Executive Editor, Publications Shannon Fortner
Acquisitions Manager Tori Mello Bachman
Managing Editors Susanne Viscarra and Christina M. Lambert
Editorial Associate Wendy Logan
Creative Services/Production Manager Anette Schuetz
Design and Composition Associate Lisa Kochel

Cover Design, Lise Holliker Dykes; art, © Shutterstock/mona redshinestudio

Library of Congress Cataloging-in-Publication Data

Write now! empowering writers in today's K–6 classroom / edited by Kathy Ganske.

  pages cm

 Includes bibliographical references and index.

 ISBN 978-0-87207-353-1 (alk. paper)

 1. Language arts—United States. 2. English language—Composition and exercises—Study and teaching (Elementary)—United States. I. Ganske, Kathy.

 LB1576.W733 2014

 372.6—dc23

                              2014018363

Suggested APA Reference

Ganske, K. (Ed.). (2014). *Write now! Empowering writers in today's K–6 classroom*. Newark, DE: International Reading Association.

*For Donald Murray, whose work inspired so many of us
to be better teachers of writing*

CONTENTS

. . . .
PART I
. . . .
What Does the Research Tell Us About Student Writing in Our Schools?

· · · · · · · · · · ·
PART III
· · · · · · · · · · ·

How Do We Get Kids Excited About Writing?

ABOUT THE EDITOR

 **Kathy Ganske** is a professor of the practice of literacy at Peabody College, Vanderbilt University, in Nashville, Tennessee, USA, where she teaches courses in literacy development, theory and practice of writing, language arts, and literacy for diverse learners; directs the Graduate Elementary Education Program; and works with school partnerships. She is the author or coauthor of several books, including *Word Journeys: Assessment-Guided Phonics, Spelling, and Vocabulary Instruction* (2nd ed.; Guilford, 2000), *Word Sorts and More: Sound, Pattern, and Meaning Explorations K–3* (Guilford, 2006), *Mindful of Words: Spelling and Vocabulary Explorations 4–8* (Guilford, 2008), and *Supporting Struggling Readers and Writers: Strategies for Classroom Intervention 3–6* (Stenhouse & International Reading Association, 2002). In addition, Kathy is a coeditor with Douglas Fisher of *Comprehension Across the Curriculum: Perspectives and Practices K–12* (Guilford, 2010), as well as the author of numerous articles and book chapters. Her current research interests include meeting literacy needs in high-needs schools; promoting discussion and academic vocabulary, especially during small-group word study instruction; and literacy teacher preparation.

Kathy's work draws on more than 20 years of elementary classroom teaching experience. She has taught in open and self-contained classrooms in Iowa, Colorado, Wyoming, and Virginia and across the spectrum of grades. She continues to be active in schools through consulting and research work. Kathy is a fellow of the National Writing Project, which she, like many, describes as a life-changing experience. In her spare time, she enjoys writing poetry and taking in the wide assortment of music and outdoor opportunities available in Nashville, among other things. She is currently in the process of developing a personal website (www.kathyganske.com), so stay tuned.

CONTRIBUTORS

Rose Cappelli
Literacy Consultant
Pennsylvania Writing & Literature
  Project
West Chester, Pennsylvania, USA

Amber B. Chambers
Doctoral Student
Arizona State University
Tempe, Arizona, USA

Lynne R. Dorfman
Literacy Consultant
Pennsylvania Writing & Literature
  Project
West Chester, Pennsylvania, USA

Kathy Ganske
Professor of the Practice of Literacy
Director of Graduate Elementary
  Education
Vanderbilt University
Nashville, Tennessee, USA

Matt Glover
Author/Consultant
Cincinnati, Ohio, USA

Steve Graham
Warner Professor of Educational
  Leadership and Innovation
Arizona State University
Phoenix, Arizona, USA

Dana L. Grisham
Adjunct Professor
National University
San Diego, California, USA

Karen R. Harris
Warner Professor of Educational
  Leadership and Innovation
Arizona State University
Phoenix, Arizona, USA

Julia D. Houston
Doctoral Student
Arizona State University
Tempe, Arizona, USA

Jon-Philip Imbrenda
Doctoral Student
Temple University
Philadelphia, Pennsylvania, USA

Carol Jago
Associate Director
California Reading and Literature
  Project
University of California, Los Angeles
Los Angeles, California, USA

Karen A. Pelekis
Elementary Classroom Teacher
Greenacres Elementary School
Scarsdale Public Schools
Scarsdale, New York, USA

Carole C. Phillips
Library Media Specialist
Greenacres Elementary School
Scarsdale Public Schools
Scarsdale, New York, USA

Timothy Shanahan
Distinguished Professor Emeritus
University of Illinois at Chicago
Chicago, Illinois, USA

Linda Smetana
Professor
California State University, East Bay
Hayward, California, USA

Michael W. Smith
Associate Dean for Faculty
   Development and Academic
   Affairs, College of Education
Temple University
Philadelphia, Pennsylvania, USA

Jeffrey D. Wilhelm
Professor of English Education
Director, Boise State Writing Project
Boise State University
Boise, Idaho, USA

Thomas DeVere Wolsey
Adjunct Professor
University of Central Florida
Orlando, Florida, USA

INTRODUCTION

Write Now! Empowering Writers in Today's K–6 Classroom evolved from an institute in which most of the contributors participated as part of the 2013 International Reading Association's annual preconference program. Spurred by the renewed emphasis on writing brought about by the Common Core State Standards (National Governors Association Center for Best Practices & Council of Chief State School Officers [NGA Center & CCSSO], 2010) and other state standards, the institute grew out of a sense of urgency to ensure that teachers, administrators, and others who work with students have the necessary explicit support and research grounding to effectively teach writing in grades K–6.

Although writing was not one of the National Reading Panel's five pillars (National Institute of Child Health and Human Development, 2000), its role in the Standards is significant: For example, in the Common Core (NGA Center & CCSSO, 2010), writing encompasses literacy learning, content learning, evaluation of student reading performance, and in some states, evaluation of content knowledge, such as mathematics. Expectations are rigorous, and no wonder, as writing is critical for success in the academic and workplace worlds. Yet, according to the summary report of the National Assessment of Educational Progress (National Center for Education Statistics, 2012), some two thirds of the students in the United States fail to become proficient writers. For over a decade, concerns have been expressed about students' achievement in writing and the impact of low achievement on their lives and ultimately on society as a whole (e.g., Graham & Hebert, 2010; Lee, Grigg, & Donahue, 2007; National Commission on Writing for America's Schools and Colleges, 2003; Yancey, 2009). This volume, like our institute, provides an avenue for teachers and educational leaders to expand their expertise by delving into the following questions:

1. What does the research tell us about student writing in our schools?

2. How do we encourage developing writers?

3. How do we get kids excited about writing?

Write Now! Empowering Writers in Today's K–6 Classroom, edited by Kathy Ganske.
© 2014 by the International Reading Association.

These three questions provide the organizational structure for *Write Now!* Knowing research that grounds an issue or a teaching technique is empowering. It affords the tools by which you can advocate for better practices if they are not in place, or understand why a particular strategy or approach is beneficial if best practices are being used. I can't imagine teaching without some knowledge of research. Research aids one's ability to make informed decisions, rather than decisions based on hunches or trust. To develop writers, whether young or old, typical or struggling, it is also essential for teachers to have a working repertoire of strategies and to know how to capitalize on exemplary texts to model the way real authors write, a notion advocated by such writing giants of the 1970s as Elbow, Emig, Graves, and Murray. Finally, getting kids excited about writing is all about motivation. We've all seen the unmotivated writer—unlikely to take any risks in writing, may not put pencil to paper or writes only the barest of minimums, and often complains bitterly. If students are going to improve as writers, they need to write—a lot. Therefore, in addition to effective instruction, writers need to be engaged. Digital media have the potential to engage both the novice and the more advanced writer. They can also be tapped to benefit boys whose interests outside of school often have no outlet for expression in school. Students are also typically motivated by multigenre projects, which have the capacity to not only engage but also develop and reinforce writing skills across genres and deepen content knowledge.

Our journey to expand your writing expertise of both typical and challenged learners includes many tips, strategies, techniques, and concrete examples. Our perspectives vary—researchers, educators who prepare teachers, practicing teachers, and writing consultants—but we all highly value writing and are invested in helping teachers develop motivated, competent, and confident writers in grades K–6. Although *Write Now!* is not intended to be all encompassing in addressing the three questions, we believe these three topics, and the chapters they include, provide a well-balanced diet for growing proficient writers A brief synopsis of the content of each chapter follows.

What Does the Research Tell Us About Student Writing in Our Schools?

In "Writing About Reading: Writing Instruction in the Age of the Common Core State Standards," Timothy Shanahan identifies the types of writing required by the Writing and Reading Standards and focuses on demands of the latter. Students must be able to summarize key ideas and details of the texts; conduct evidence-based analyses and evaluations of the information, craft, and structure of texts; and synthesize information from multiple texts or distinct sections of single texts. He reviews specific instructional issues and provides practical advice for addressing them.

In Steve Graham and Karen Harris's "Six Recommendations for Teaching Writing to Meet the Common Core," the recommendations are evidence-based practices that have been tested scientifically and shown to be effective. Graham and Harris also draw from the writing instructional practices of exceptional literacy teachers.

How Do We Encourage Developing Writers?

In "Moving Student Writers Forward With Mentor Texts," Lynne Dorfman and Rose Cappelli describe how to use children's literature as mentor texts to teach narrative and informational writing skills. They describe techniques to help students strengthen their word choice and voice and to develop quality ideas through the use of rich descriptions and anecdotes, using a gradual release of responsibility model.

Matt Glover examines the roles of vision and choice and how they positively affect young writers in his chapter, "Vision and Choice in the K–3 Writing Workshop." He describes how choice of topic, choice of genre, and the organizational decisions that student writers make result in an increased energy for writing. When these novice writers also have a vision for what they will be creating, their writings are further enriched.

Carol Jago takes the production of opinion writing to a new level in "Growing Writers: Teaching Argumentative Writing Through Evidence-Based Thinking." Students are keen to assert what they think but are often less than scrupulous in their presentation of supporting evidence for their claims. This chapter describes classroom protocols for helping young writers develop the tools they need to craft persuasive—and artful—arguments.

In "Turning Broccoli Into Ice Cream Sundaes: Self-Regulated Strategy Development for Persuasive Writing Using Informational Text," Karen Harris, Steve Graham, Amber Chambers, and Julia Houston describe self-regulated strategy development (SRSD), an evidence-based strategy that has been shown to be effective with struggling writers, students with learning and other disabilities, and average and above-average writers. The authors guide readers through the process of using SRSD with a focus on strategies for persuasive writing using informational text.

How Do We Get Kids Excited About Writing?

Michael Smith, Jon-Philip Imbrenda, and Jeffrey Wilhelm argue that a close analysis of the texts that boys embrace outside school can be used to understand how those texts can be used to foster boys' academic writing and why the texts are important as ends in themselves. In "Boys and Multiplicity: Expanding the Writing and Writers That Count in School," the authors describe instructional strategies for building on students' interests in nontraditional texts such as comic books and video games.

Karen Pelekis and Carole Phillips show us the potential of technology for creative expression, increased access to developmentally appropriate resources, and collaboration in "Teaching Digital Writing in K–3." This chapter addresses the what, why, and how of meaningfully incorporating digital tools for writing in the primary grades. The authors share a wealth of examples of projects that have been successfully used in classrooms from kindergarten to third grade.

In "Multigenre Projects: Building Knowledge, Motivation, Collaboration, and Writing Expertise in Grades 4–6," Kathy Ganske explores the concept of multigenre projects that integrate social studies or science with the language arts. Multigenre writing can be highly engaging and serve as a way to develop and reinforce students' writing in different genres, while connecting writing to texts and building content knowledge. The why and how of implementing multigenre projects are discussed in the context of numerous examples and suggested resources.

Finally, in the last chapter, "Supporting Writers in Grades 4–6 With Digital Media and Sources," Thomas DeVere Wolsey, Dana Grisham, and Linda Smetana explore the complications and opportunities that digital environments afford young authors. To write opinion, informational, and literary texts, students must learn new content, concepts, vocabulary, and the most appropriate style of writing to share their knowledge. The authors describe ways to help students work nimbly and accurately with sources found in digital and traditional environments.

Kathy Ganske

REFERENCES

Graham, S., & Hebert, M. (2010). *Writing to read: Evidence for how writing can improve reading.* Washington, DC: Alliance for Excellent Education.

Lee, J., Grigg, W., & Donahue, P. (2007). *The Nation's Report Card: Reading 2007* (NCES 2007-496). Washington, DC: National Center for Education Statistics, Institute of Education Sciences, U.S. Department of Education.

National Center for Education Statistics. (2012). *The Nation's Report Card: Writing 2011* (NCES 2012-470). Washington, DC: National Center for Education Statistics, Institute of Education Sciences, U.S. Department of Education. Retrieved from nces.ed.gov/nationsreportcard/pdf/main2011/2012470.pdf

National Commission on Writing for America's Schools and Colleges. (2003). *The neglected "R": The need for a writing revolution.* New York, NY: College Board.

National Governors Association Center for Best Practices & Council of Chief State School Officers. (2010). *Common Core State Standards for English language arts and literacy in history/social studies, science, and technical subjects.* Washington, DC: Authors.

National Institute of Child Health and Human Development. (2000). *Report of the National Reading Panel. Teaching children to read: An evidence-based assessment of the scientific research literature on reading and its implications for reading instruction* (NIH Publication No. 00-4769). Washington, DC: U.S. Government Printing Office.

Yancey, K.B. (2009). *Writing in the 21st century: A report from the National Council of Teachers of English.* Urbana, IL: National Council of Teachers of English.

PART I

What Does the Research
Tell Us About Student Writing
in Our Schools?

CHAPTER 1

Writing About Reading

Writing Instruction in the Age of the Common Core State Standards

Timothy Shanahan, *University of Illinois at Chicago*

As of this writing, 45 states and the District of Columbia have adopted the Common Core State Standards for the English Language Arts (National Governors Association Center for Best Practices & Council of Chief State School Officers [NGA Center & CCSSO], 2010). Although all the states had been working toward educational standards since the early 1990s, never before had such a large proportion of states agreed to aim at the same educational goals. That is remarkable enough, but independent analyses show that these new standards are markedly higher than what the states were committed to previously (Carmichael, Martino, Porter-Magee, & Wilson, 2010).

Since the Common Core came onto the scene, my colleagues who are particularly knowledgeable about writing instruction have told me how pleased they are that writing will finally be accorded the attention they think it deserves. I agree with them as to the importance of writing, but I'm not sure that it is actually emphasized any more in these standards than in previous ones. Nevertheless, I believe that the Common Core is changing the equation in important ways that could lead to more writing instruction and to a greater emphasis on how writing should connect to reading, two things we would all like to see.

Changing Emphasis on Writing

Although all states required writing instruction prior to the Common Core—just look at your previous state standards—schools had,

Write Now! Empowering Writers in Today's K–6 Classroom, edited by Kathy Ganske. © 2014 by the International Reading Association.

nevertheless, drifted away from writing instruction over the past decade. The place of writing in the school curriculum in the United States had always been fraught (Clifford, 1987), but this had improved quite a bit during the past generation. In the 1970s and 1980s, the influence of James Moffett, Donald Graves, and Lucy Calkins began to be felt. Many elementary teachers had not emphasized writing because they didn't know how to teach it, and these experts and others provided valuable guidance on how children could be writers in the classroom (Shanahan, 1979, in press). Additionally, there was generous federal support for these efforts: The feds supported a national center to encourage research on the teaching of writing and provided funding for the National Writing Project, which offered extensive professional development on writing instruction. This was the time when state-testing programs began including writing, which also had a powerful impact on the curriculum (Cooper, 1984). Finally, because of the increased awareness of reading–writing relationships, commercial reading programs began incorporating writing, grammar, and spelling supports in their curricula.

These supports sound formidable, yet writing's foothold in the classroom has proved to be startlingly tenuous. In 2002, No Child Left Behind became law. It required that the states test reading and math skills in grades 3–12, but writing was not included in these accountability requirements. Although teachers were supposed to continue to teach their state's educational standards—standards that included writing—instead there was a narrowing of the curriculum. Some of the states even dropped their writing assessments, and the amounts of writing research eroded throughout the 1990s (Shanahan, 2012). The lack of an infrastructure emphasizing writing has apparently led many teachers to divert their gaze from writing instruction.

In that context, the Common Core's rearticulation of the writing standards appears to some to be an increase of emphasis on writing. What they have really done is to *continue* to include writing in educational standards—remember, such standards were already there—and to remind us of the important role that writing plays in college and career readiness. Additionally, the new testing consortia (the Partnership for Assessment of Readiness for College and Careers and the Smarter Balanced Assessment Consortium) have included writing in their plans for evaluating student progress in the English language arts.

In many ways, the new writing standards aren't that different from the old ones. The Common Core still encourages teachers to teach students to write narratives and expository/explanatory pieces, and to emphasize the writing process (e.g., planning, drafting, revising, editing). Many states required the teaching of research writing, and that continues to be emphasized as well.

Writing About Reading

That is not to say that there are no changes. Past standards have called for the teaching of persuasive writing, and the Common Core has broadened this to argument. That means students need to learn to use evidence in support of their positions and to try to consider and refute potential counterarguments. Likewise, the research requirements in the Common Core are more fully articulated than those in at least some of the past state standards and more inclusive of the various technological tools needed for research and writing. Perhaps the biggest change in the writing goals is that they have been more closely linked to reading. Research has shown that reading and writing share underlying knowledge bases (Tierney & Shanahan, 1991) and that writing about reading can have important impacts on both writing quality and reading development (Graham & Hebert, 2010). Accordingly, the Common Core requires that students write less about their own experiences and knowledge and more about the ideas expressed in texts (and other sources).

The Common Core emphasizes this idea of writing about text in two distinct ways: In the primary-grade standards, they either make "writing about text" ideas an option or imply that students are to write about something that they have learned through reading. For example, kindergarten students are "to compose opinion pieces in which they tell a reader the topic or the name of the book they are writing about and state an opinion or preference about the topic or book" (NGA Center & CCSSO, 2010, p. 19). For grade 1, students are to "write informative/ explanatory texts in which they name a topic, supply some facts about the topic, and provide some sense of closure" (p. 19). In neither example are students explicitly required to write about text or the information drawn from text, although it is an explicit option in the first example and a clear possibility in the second.

However, by grade 4—and from that point on—a second approach is used, and the matter becomes unambiguous. In addition to the seemingly optional or implicit mentions apparent throughout the primary-grade standards, the upper-grade standards also state that students are to "draw evidence from literary or informational texts to support analysis, reflection, and research" (NGA Center & CCSSO, 2010, p. 21), and the Common Core document goes on to explain that this means students are to "apply" the Reading Standards for Literature and Informational Text through their writing. In other words, to determine what students are to write about and how they are to write, teachers must turn to the Reading Standards.

There teachers will find 10 standards for each grade level, and each of these Reading Standards is explained for both literary and informational texts. The Reading Standards are organized into four functional categories: three that are relevant to using writing to explore text and one that is not (the fourth category, "Range of Reading and Level of Text Complexity"). Let's explore the kinds of writing about text that the Common Core encourages.

The first reading category, "Key Ideas and Details," requires students to answer questions about what they read, summarize or retell the information, and describe connections among the ideas or characters in texts—by identifying themes, recalling sequences of events, or making causal links. Writing assignments aimed at these particular standards would require that students be able to summarize what they read, identifying the key ideas and their major supports.

"Craft and Structure," the second reading category, emphasizes an awareness of the author's point of view and how texts work to support or extend the author's ideas or purposes. This category is less about what texts say and more about why and how texts say what they do. Accordingly, readers are asked to distinguish the points of view of authors, narrators, and particular characters or to determine the differences in what an author or illustrator contributes to a text. Readers who are considering such issues need to become adept at recognizing the structure of the information (e.g., chronological sequence, comparison, cause/effect, problem/solution), the significance of how information is juxtaposed or compared, and the role that word choices play (e.g., why did the author tell us that the character "whispered" in this scene?).

Finally, the Reading Standards emphasize a third category, "Integration of Knowledge and Ideas." For the most part, these standards reemphasize either skills mentioned explicitly in the Writing Standards or skills that may be underlying these. For example, the Writing Standards require that fifth graders "conduct short research projects that use several sources to build knowledge through investigation of different aspects of a topic" and that they "gather relevant information from print and digital sources" (NGA Center & CCSSO, 2010, p. 21), while on the reading side, they are to "integrate information from several texts on the same topic in order to write or speak about the subject knowledgeably," or "draw on information from multiple print or digital sources" (p. 14). Basically, these standards are asking that students learn to access multiple sources of information and to synthesize that information in their own writing, such as by writing a report. Furthermore, to enable such full-blown syntheses, the Reading Standards encourage lots of comparative judgment across texts about what is being read. For example, "compare and contrast the themes, settings, and plots of stories written by the same author about the same or similar characters" (p. 12). This category might also require such comparisons across different parts of a single text, such as comparing a table with the information stated in prose or comparing two chapters from a text.

It should be clear from this that a major emphasis of the Common Core Writing Standards is that students be able to write about what they read. That is, the Writing Standards expect students to be able to summarize in writing the key ideas and details of a text; to analyze in writing how texts work—in terms of word choices, text structures, and point of view; and to synthesize information in writing from multiple texts, including making evaluative comparisons of the information drawn from those texts. This is strikingly different from past standards or from past writing assessments that have encouraged students to write about what they already know (Shanahan, in press).

Why the shift? One obvious reason is that in college and the workplace, few assignments require writing about one's personal experiences, but there are many tasks that require summarization, analysis, evaluation, and synthesis of information. Another reason has to do with the benefits of writing about reading. Research shows that writing about text is a particularly powerful way of improving student reading achievement

(Graham & Hebert, 2010); that meta-analysis of 50 studies showed that writing about text has a bigger impact on reading comprehension than reading alone, reading and rereading, or reading and discussing the information. Furthermore, this analysis showed positive learning outcomes at a variety of ages from both summarization and from more extensive writing, including analysis and synthesis. However, summarization tended to have a bigger impact on the comprehension of younger learners, while more extended forms of writing paid off to a greater extent as students moved up the grades, a pattern consistent with the writing demands of the Common Core in which summarization and simple analyses and syntheses are the initial emphasis. The point is that the Common Core emphasizes the kinds of writing that students need to learn, and it does so in ways that are consistent with the relevant research findings.

There are good reasons why writing about text has such powerful impacts on students' reading ability. Each way of writing about text requires them to read the texts carefully. If you want to write a summary, then you need to pay particular attention to the main idea of the text and to consider which key details are essential. Text comparisons work pretty much the same way, whether one is comparing some aspect of an author's message or how the author expresses it; to compare texts, it is necessary that you first abstract that information from the text, which requires an especially careful reading. Writing also requires, by its very nature, that readers express this information explicitly. By getting your ideas about a text outside your head, it becomes possible to recognize unclear thinking and omissions in your understanding. Building such awareness allows the writer to go back to the text to figure out the immediate problem, but more importantly, it also likely sensitizes students to such information in future reading.

Teaching Students to Write About Text

The Common Core State Standards tell what students need to learn, but they are silent about how to accomplish those goals. That is up to the teachers. Elsewhere, I have explained how teachers might teach students to summarize, analyze/evaluate, and synthesize what they read through writing (Shanahan, 2013). The remainder of this chapter provides basic guidance in how to make such "writing about text" instruction effective.

Write About High-Quality Texts

As already discussed, writing about text requires that readers pay particularly close attention to the text content or craft, and such writing will require, by its very nature, repeated review of the information. For example, let's say students are to read two science articles, one about frogs and one about toads, and the idea is to have students use the information to compare the two types of organisms. Obviously, to do this, students will have to read each of the texts, which is the first examination of the information. Then, it would be necessary to summarize and organize the information; this might be done with a chart such as the one in Figure 1.1. To do that, the reader would reexamine the text to figure out what characteristics could be used and how these characteristics distinguish these particular animals (e.g., frogs' skin is smooth and moist, toads' skin is bumpy and dry). That would be a second review of the information. Finally, students would include this information in their own texts, creating well-formed and accurate comparisons of these two types of animals, as a third analysis of this content. (A fourth review may be possible if the students revise their texts, which would be especially true if the revision pushed them back into the original texts to verify the accuracy of the information.)

If students are going to read and reread a text in that fashion, then it is essential that the text be worth reading. Writing about text is partly about communicating what we know to others, but it is even more about gaining extensive and deep knowledge about what one writes (Shanahan, 2004). That means the texts that students write about have to contain sufficient amounts and quality of information to merit this kind of investment of time and effort. This is true for both informational and literary texts. Literature

Figure 1.1. Comparison Chart

	Frogs	Toads
Skin	Moist and smooth	Dry and bumpy
Teeth		None
Eyes		
Hind legs	Long and powerful	
Eggs		

does not usually contain much in the way of facts about the social or natural world, yet some literature is so widely known that it, in itself, represents important cultural knowledge (e.g., fairy tales, classics). Even when literary texts don't carry that kind of information, they can, if their quality is high enough, provide students with important opportunities to understand how literature works or to gain insights about human emotions and relationships.

Introduce Students to Appropriate Text Models

The texts that students write about are only one part of the "writing about text" equation. Another has to do with what students' visions are of what it is that they are being asked to produce. Teachers might have very clear ideas of what a good text summary would look like or how to organize a good report that synthesizes information from multiple texts, but that doesn't mean students do. It's hard to replicate something that you don't have a mental image of in the first place.

One way to guide students to produce the kinds of writing that can deepen their reading and writing skills is to have them read model texts and then imitate some aspects of the model through their own writing. There are few published studies of this approach (only two with elementary students), but those studies suggest that reading appropriate models can have a positive, albeit small, impact on student learning (Graham & Perin, 2007). However, these studies did little more than have students read the text models—nothing like the kind of thorough guided analysis usually recommended for teaching with text models (Cramer & Cramer, 1975; Dorfman & Cappelli, 2007). The idea of text modeling is to get students to carefully and analytically read texts to identify the key features to be imitated in their own versions of that kind of text. That means students need to engage in such reading with an eye aimed specifically at identifying features of craft and structure, something not likely to happen when students read without any or much explicit guidance.

To make modeling work effectively, teachers should select appropriately salient texts that provide clear examples of the language or structures that students are to mimic. It also might be important to offer more than a single example (Charney & Carlson, 1995). Then, students need to read the texts or listen to the teacher reading them, which would be followed by some kind of guided analysis—breaking the texts down into their key elements. Thus, if students were to use the chart in Figure 1.1, then it would make sense to have them read some texts that make these kinds of comparisons (e.g., a text that compares alligators and crocodiles, or lions and tigers). Student attention would be drawn to how the author organized the information, and the kinds of language that were used to make the comparisons and to link the various parts of the comparison. Once students are conversant with these essential features or characteristics of such text, then they are ready to attempt to compose their own comparisons. Teachers might even scaffold the students' initial efforts by providing a template for the students to fill in or complete with information that they have found in their own reading or research: "There are several ways that frogs and toads can be compared. One important difference has to do with their ___. Frogs' ___ is ___, while the ___ of toads is ___. Then, there is ___." Over time, such scaffolding can be reduced, and students can write their own comparisons.

Provide Explicit Instruction

Often, teachers assume that writing about text simply requires assignments in which students will read texts and write about them: "Read this story and summarize its key events in a paragraph," or, "Read this article and evaluate the author's argument." Such assignments certainly should engage students in the right kinds of cognitive activities, yet they are not likely to support much learning—except, perhaps, for those students who are already adept at that kind of writing. Explicit instruction is the most effective approach to guiding students to produce high-quality examples of such writing (Graham, McKeown, Kiuhara, & Harris, 2012; Graham & Perin, 2007).

Explicit teaching requires explaining to students what it is that they need to learn. For example, the Common Core calls for students to "describe in depth a character...in a story..., drawing on specific details in the text (e.g., a character's thoughts, words, or actions)" (NGA Center & CCSSO, 2010, p. 12). What is it that students are supposed to learn, and why? It would be a good idea not only to give this kind of an assignment but also to explain it to students:

Stories focus on characters' goals, their efforts toward those goals, and how those efforts might conflict with the efforts of others. As such, stories can be valuable in helping people understand how to live and work together. To really understand a story, it is necessary to develop a clear understanding of what kind of character someone is and what it is that they are trying to accomplish or what goals they are trying to reach. When you read a story, it is imperative that you engage in such analysis, and when you write about a story, it is important to explain such a character in a clear way, including what they want and why they want it. These lessons are going to guide you to think and write about such characters more effectively.

Additionally, explicit instruction will give students overt guidance in what to do, although over time, this guidance should be reduced or dropped altogether. As such, the activity illustrated in Figure 1.1 is not a beginning-level illustration but a midlevel one. If I were starting students out with such a task, I would probably fill in some of the open spaces as examples, particularly if I thought any of these might be hard to extricate from the original texts. The idea, initially, would be to teach students how to fill in the chart, and it wouldn't be necessary to fill in all the spaces to do that. Once students had experience with such instruments and were becoming adept at identifying key features of comparison, then they might be given a form that looks like the one pictured in Figure 1.1. This example has already been started, but over time, as students demonstrate that they can successfully complete such a chart, they could be given one that is totally blank. Eventually, the teacher should even be able to leave out some or all of the categories. The idea is, through a series of smaller steps, to guide students to locate the key information (and even to construct such charts entirely on their own).

Similarly, it was earlier suggested that teachers provide students with a template or frame that they could use to insert the ideas into a partially well-formed composition. As students become proficient at inserting the correct information, then the teacher needs to withdraw some of this support. To do this, it would be helpful to explain to students what it is that is being provided. Figure 1.2 provides a brief template for writing a comparison of frogs and toads, based on some of the information included in the comparison charts. This template provides an introduction and a conclusion to this kind of paper. Then, it requires students to fill in some blanks for the first comparison (that frogs have teeth and toads do not), which is followed by a sentence that explains why this matters (teeth allow

> **Figure 1.2. Template for Writing About Similarities and Differences**
>
> Frogs and toads are both amphibians, and they look very similar. But if you study them closely, you will find many important differences. For example, frogs have ___, but toads do not. This difference is important because it allows frogs to eat harder food such as snails. Another difference is that frogs ___, but toads ___. This matters because ___. A third difference is ___. This is important because ___. Just because two animals look very much alike doesn't make them the same.

frogs to eat different foods than toads can eat). The next comparison is more up to the students. The template requires that some feature that frogs and toads differ on be described, and that its significance be explained in a follow-up sentence, but there is less guidance here. The choice of comparison features to focus on is up to the students. The third comparison is even sketchier, as students have to now recognize that they need to tell about that feature for both the frog and the toad.

As with the chart in the previous example, teachers need to remove such explicit guidance gradually, as students show that they can compose such an essay without so much support. This might eventually lead to the use of a template in which specific sentences are not included, but the key information might be functionally described: introduction, comparison 1, explanation of comparison 1, transition to comparison 2, comparison 2, and so forth. The idea is to provide enough scaffolding so most students can carry out the task successfully, and then to continually withdraw the amount of support while maintaining a high level of success—until eventually there is no support at all. Thus, the "writing about text" assignment that is to be completed independently by students should not be a starting point but the result of a series of explicit instructional steps. This approach would be the same whether students were writing summaries, analyses/evaluations, or syntheses, although the guidance and activities relevant to each would differ in their particulars.

Finally, explicit instruction requires forthright feedback. Students need to be able to access honest and helpful evaluative information about how successfully they have accomplished the task. That means the teacher has to have a clear idea of what quality writing looks like, suggesting that the value of the models described earlier is not just for students. Teachers who can see the differences between the text models and the ones written by students are the ones who will be able to give students incisive feedback and who will have a great sense of what to do next:

> Look at the introduction in your synthesis. When you just had to fill in the key information to the introduction, you did well, but look at your introduction and this model. What's the difference? I think you left out a key explanation that would allow your readers to know why you were comparing these species. Reread the model, and let's see if you can find that kind of explanation. Where would you add that information to your writing?

Explicit teaching should give students a clear idea of what it is that they are trying to do and an explanation of the reasons why. It should provide students with a clear set of steps that, if negotiated successfully, will result in successfully accomplishing the task: writing a clear summary, analyzing or evaluating a text, or writing a report that synthesizes the information effectively from multiple sources. Finally, explicit teaching provides students with specific evaluative feedback that offers both a clear idea of where they stand and what they need to learn and that builds their ability to conduct similar self-evaluations.

Increase the Challenge Levels of the Assignments

When trying to learn something, it is important to proceed from simpler versions of the task to more complex ones. There are several ways that teachers can take students along such a complexity continuum when it comes to writing about text. Texts vary in complexity, as measured by Lexiles and other readability measures, and it is easier to write about a text that can be read easily. Thus, teachers might start out with texts that don't place much language demand on students (e.g., using a text that is relatively easy for students to read or by reading it to them). But once students can write about such texts effectively, teachers need to ramp up the difficulty level of the texts used as the basis of writing—shifting to students doing the reading and shifting to texts that will be more challenging for them. (It's better for students to confront such demands when teachers are available to provide helpful guidance than when students are on their own.)

Another feature of "writing about text" activities that can be controlled in this way has to do with how many text features are to be the focus of attention. Emphasizing how to describe and explain a single comparison is likely to be somewhat easier than doing this with two or three comparisons, if only because of the need to make transitions across the multiple comparisons. Similarly, writing a multifeature comparison without an appropriate introduction or a useful conclusion is usually easier than writing one that includes those text features. It is not that teachers should ignore the importance of coordinating and connecting all of these features, just that they need to take the long view, aiming to develop this kind of proficiency through a series of incremental steps. Assignments that both emphasize the development of proficiency with particular aspects of writing and expressly guide students to connect these proficiencies into a more successful and complete whole are needed.

Conclusions

The Common Core State Standards appear to be reenergizing teachers to address writing instruction in their classrooms and are encouraging a strong emphasis on writing about text. Generally, this means that the Standards are encouraging the teaching of summarization, analysis/evaluation, and synthesis of information from texts and other sources. Students are to do each of these things through writing, and the Writing Standards themselves tell teachers to look to the Reading Standards to identify specifically what it is that students need to write about when writing about texts.

To make such assignments work effectively, teachers will need to select high-quality texts (in terms of content and style) for students to write about and text models that exemplify what effective summaries, analyses, and syntheses should look like. Teachers will also need to provide explicit instruction in both how to read texts effectively—that is, to read with an eye to the content or text elements to be written about—and how to write effectively about the texts. Finally, it is essential that teachers assign reading/writing tasks that guide students along a progression of learning that goes from simple to complex. Providing students with many opportunities to read and study high-quality texts and to write about those texts with the kinds of supports described herein should prepare students to be truly college and career ready.

REFERENCES

Carmichael, S.B., Martino, G., Porter-Magee, K., & Wilson, W.S. (with Fairchild, D., Haydel, E., Senechal, D., & Winkler, A.M.). (2010). *The state of state standards—and the Common Core—in 2010.* Washington, DC: Thomas B. Fordham Institute. Retrieved from www.edexcellence.net/publications/the-state-of-state-of-standards-and-the-common-core-in-2010.html

Charney, D.H., & Carlson, R.A. (1995). Learning to write in a genre: What student writers take from model texts. *Research in the Teaching of English, 29*(1), 88–125.

Clifford, G.J. (1987). *A Sisyphean task: Historical perspectives on the relationship between writing and reading instruction* (Technical Report No. 7). Berkeley, CA: National Center for the Study of Writing and Literacy. Retrieved from www.nwp.org/cs/public/print/resource/593

Cooper, P.L. (1984). *The assessment of writing ability: A review of research* (GRE Board Research Report No. 82-15R). Princeton, NJ: Educational Testing Service. Retrieved from www.ets.org/Media/Research/pdf/RR-84-12-Cooper.pdf

Cramer, R.L., & Cramer, B.B. (1975). Writing by imitating language models. *Language Arts, 52*(7), 1011–1014.

Dorfman, L.R., & Cappelli, R. (2007). *Mentor texts: Teaching writing through children's literature, K–6.* Portland, ME: Stenhouse.

Graham, S., & Hebert, M. (2010). *Writing to read: Evidence for how writing can improve reading.* Washington, DC: Alliance for Excellent Education.

Graham, S., McKeown, D., Kiuhara, S., & Harris, K.R. (2012). A meta-analysis of writing instruction for students in the elementary grades. *Journal of Educational Psychology, 104*(4), 879–896. doi:10.1037/a0029185

Graham, S., & Perin, D. (2007). A meta-analysis of writing instruction for adolescent students. *Journal of Educational Psychology, 99*(3), 445–476. doi:10.1037/0022-0663.99.3.445

National Governors Association Center for Best Practices & Council of Chief State School Officers. (2010). *Common Core State Standards for English language arts and literacy in history/social studies, science, and technical subjects.* Washington, DC: Authors.

Shanahan, T. (1979). The writing crisis: A survey and solution. *Phi Delta Kappan, 61*(3), 216–217.

Shanahan, T. (2004). Overcoming the dominance of communication: Writing to think and to learn. In T.L. Jetton & J.A. Dole (Eds.), *Adolescent literacy research and practice* (pp. 59–74). New York, NY: Guilford.

Shanahan, T. (2012). Writing research [Section introduction]. In P.J. Dunston, S.K. Fullerton, C.C. Bates, K. Headley, & P.M. Stecker (Eds.), *The 61st yearbook of the Literacy Research Association* (pp. 100–102). Oak Creek, WI: Literacy Research Association.

Shanahan, T. (2013). Best practices in writing about text. In S. Graham, C.A. MacArthur, & J. Fitzgerald (Eds.), *Best practices in writing instruction* (2nd ed., pp. 334–350). New York, NY: Guilford.

Shanahan, T. (in press). Common Core State Standards: A new role for writing. *The Elementary School Journal.*

Tierney, R., & Shanahan, T. (1991). Research on the reading–writing relationship: Interactions, transactions, and outcomes. In R. Barr, M.L. Kamil, P. Mosenthal, & P.D. Pearson (Eds.), *Handbook of reading research* (Vol. 2, pp. 246–280). Mahwah, NJ: Erlbaum.

Timothy Shanahan is a distinguished professor emeritus of urban education at the University of Illinois at Chicago, USA, where he is the founding director of the UIC Center for Literacy. He also is an honorary research professor at Queen's University in Belfast, Northern Ireland. He served as the director of reading for the Chicago Public Schools and is an author or editor of more than 200 publications. Timothy is a past president of the International Reading Association and received the William S. Gray Citation of Merit for his contributions to the field of reading. He received a presidential appointment to serve on the National Institute for Literacy Advisory Board, served on the National Reading Panel, and helped author the Common Core State Standards. He was inducted into the Reading Hall of Fame in 2007 and is a former first-grade teacher. His blog, Shanahan on Literacy (www.shanahanonliteracy.com), is widely read.

CHAPTER 2

Six Recommendations for Teaching Writing to Meet the Common Core

Steve Graham & Karen R. Harris, *Arizona State University*

Good writing is essential to success. At school, writing is used to assess and promote students' learning (Writing Study Group of the NCTE Executive Committee, 2004). At home, writing connects us to our friends and the world at large, thanks to e-mail, blogs, texting, and other forms of digital composing (Hillocks, 2002). At work, writing is increasingly part of the everyday fabric of white-collar jobs as well as blue-collar positions (National Commission on Writing for America's Families, Schools, and Colleges, 2004, 2005, 2006).

Despite the obvious importance of acquiring strong writing skills, little attention is devoted to teaching writing in most U.S. schools (Applebee & Langer, 2011; Brindle, 2013; Gilbert & Graham, 2010). The typical student spends little time writing, and much of what is written involves activities such as completing worksheets, making lists, and writing single-sentence responses to homework questions. Although there are notable exceptions, teachers commonly report that they spend little time teaching writing and that they are not adequately prepared to teach this complex skill. It is not surprising, therefore, that only about one third of students in the United States become proficient writers (National Center for Education Statistics, 2012).

Although its scope is broader than writing, the Common Core State Standards, an effort led by the National Governors Association Center for Best Practices and the Council of Chief State School Officers (2010), address these issues head on by making writing a central part of the

Write Now! Empowering Writers in Today's K–6 Classroom, edited by Kathy Ganske.
© 2014 by the International Reading Association.

school reform effort in the 45 states that have adopted the Common Core, along with Washington, DC. Even in states that have not adopted these standards, such as Texas (see Graham & Associates, 2013), writing and writing instruction are receiving new emphasis.

The Common Core sets a challenging agenda for the teaching and use of writing in schools, emphasizing four basic applications of writing skills (see Table 2.1):

1. Learning to write for multiple purposes
2. Producing and publishing well-organized text that is appropriate to the task and purpose by planning, revising, editing, and collaborating with others
3. Using writing to recall, organize, analyze, interpret, and build knowledge about a topic or materials read
4. Applying both extended and shorter writing tasks to facilitate learning of content material

Table 2.1. Writing Applications in the Common Core State Standards

Application	Benchmarks
1. Text type and purposes	• Write supported opinions on specific topics or texts. • Write informative and explanatory text that clearly conveys information about the topic. • Write narratives that develop imagined and real events or experiences.
2. Production and distribution of writing	• Produce writing in which the development and organization of ideas is appropriate to the writer's task, purpose, and audience. • Develop and strengthen writing by flexibly using planning, revising, editing, and rewriting processes and strategies. • Use digital technology, including the Internet, to produce, collaborate, publish, and share writing with others. • Develop keyboard skills.
3. Research to build and present knowledge	• Use writing to carry out short research projects to build knowledge about a topic. • Use writing to facilitate recall and understanding of information. • Use writing to draw information/evidence from different sources to support analysis, reflection, and research (grades 4 and 5 only).
4. Range of writing	• Use shorter and extended writing tasks to facilitate content learning.

These applications are interdependent, and the skillful execution of each depends on students' facility and mastery of a range of other writing skills (see the Language Standards in the Common Core document), including handwriting/typing, spelling, conventions, grammar, word choice, and sentence construction. These foundational writing skills make it possible for students to transcribe, sculpt, and convey their meanings and intentions (Graham, 2013), with an increased emphasis on using writing to learn starting at grade 4.

Although the Common Core establishes grade-level objectives for the four writing applications and for a variety of foundational writing skills, it is purposefully silent about instruction, leaving it to teachers and schools to decide how these goals are best met. Although we believe that teachers are the ones who should make such decisions, this is not an easy task, as writing is an extremely challenging and complex skill that is not easily mastered (Graham, 2006). Good writing depends on the writer's ability to regulate a variety of processes, strategies, and mental operations to plan, draft, evaluate, and revise text. Additionally, good writing depends on the writer's ability to access different types of knowledge, such as knowledge about the topic, the intended audience, and the genre. Writers must further apply a variety of transcription and translation skills, such as handwriting, typing, spelling, and sentence construction, to realize their intentions. Writing also requires engagement and persistence and is shaped by the writer's motivational state, as attributes such as efficacy, anxiety, and attitudes can enhance or impede its execution. Finally, the writer must intelligently apply these resources across situations, occasions, and contexts over time.

So, how should teachers and schools go about providing effective writing instruction to students so they master the Writing Standards specified in the Common Core? One approach is to use evidence-based writing practices as a means to meet these goals. We examine why this is a good idea next.

Why Should I Use Evidence-Based Writing Practices?

Advice on how to teach writing is readily available (Graham, 2011). One source of advice is professional writers, who draw on their own writing experiences and insights. Other sources are those who teach writing and those who observe and study writing teachers in action. Professional writers, writing teachers, and those who observe writing teachers surely possess considerable wisdom about how best to teach writing, but their recommendations often lack essential elements of trustworthiness. First, when drawing from personal experience or observing the experiences of others, it is difficult to separate the wheat from the chaff. In other words, it is difficult to know with any certainty what practice out of the many used should be recommended for application by other teachers. Second, there is often no direct evidence that the recommended practice has made a difference. When evidence is provided, it often takes the form of testimonials or the presentation of selected students' writing, making it difficult to determine if the evidence is representative or atypical. Third, if the recommendation is based on the experiences of a single professional writer or teacher (or even a few of each), there is no way to predict whether the practice will be effective for other teachers. Consequently, advice on how to teach writing based solely on the experiences, insights, or observations of skilled writers, teachers, or experts is a risky proposition, as the validity, reliability, and generalizability of such recommendations are uncertain.

A more trustworthy approach for making recommendations on how to teach writing involves the use of scientific methods to systematically test the effectiveness of a particular intervention (Graham, 2011). Intervention studies that test the effectiveness of a specific teaching procedure provide evidence on whether the procedure produced the desired impact, whether the observed effects are representative (replicated across students and situations), and how much confidence can be placed in them (via statistical analyses). Because such studies quantify the observed impact of the intervention, it is possible to determine the direction (positive or negative) and relative strength (in comparison to the control condition) of the writing intervention across investigations.

In this chapter, we draw on scientific testing of specific writing interventions to make recommendations for teaching writing, placing these recommendations within the context of the Common Core. Before proceeding to these, several caveats are in order. First, the recommended practices presented here should be viewed as "potentially" effective. Just because a practice was effective in multiple research studies does not guarantee that it will be effective in all other situations, including your classroom. The safest course of action is for you to monitor the effects of the recommended practice to be sure it works in your class with your students.

Second, the number of research-validated writing practices is rather slim. Thus, an evidence-based practice for each Writing Standard in the Common Core does not exist. The practices presented here provide more general instructional guidelines for addressing the four applications and the fundamental writing skills mandated by the Common Core.

Third, just because a writing practice is not identified here as evidence-based does not mean that it is not effective. Many writing practices have not been tested at all, much less repeatedly tested. In this chapter, we focus primarily on writing practices that have been scientifically tested in at least four studies.

To help better round out our recommendations for teaching writing, we draw on qualitative studies of exceptional literacy teachers to identify the practices that they commonly apply when teaching writing. Although such an analysis cannot establish that a specific practice was responsible for improving students' writing performance, it is reasonable to assume that practices employed by exceptional teachers across most studies are potentially more important than those that are idiosyncratic to a specific teacher or school.

Source for the Recommended Writing Practices

The evidence-based writing practices presented next were identified in a meta-analysis conducted by Graham, Harris, and Santangelo (in press). In a meta-analysis, an effect size measuring the impact of the intervention on the outcome measure is computed for each study, and the resulting effect sizes are averaged across studies testing a specific intervention. Graham and colleagues identified 21 previous meta-analyses of writing practices conducted since 1986. The researchers recomputed an effect size for each study in these meta-analyses for students in grades K–8 and then computed an average weighted effect size (weighted by size of study) for each writing intervention. In this chapter, we present practices that were scientifically tested for improvement in writing quality in four or more studies in which students in the writing intervention group were compared with students receiving an alternative intervention or no intervention. Instead of reporting the average weighted effect size from Graham and colleagues, we report how many percentile points an average student (i.e., at the 50th percentile) improved as a result of each writing practice.

Graham, Harris, and Santangelo (in press) further reexamined qualitative studies examining the writing practices of exceptional literacy teachers (from Graham & Perin, 2007), identifying procedures for teaching writing that were consistently used by these teachers. These practices are also included as part of our recommendations.

Recommendations for Teaching Writing

1. Establish Writing Routines That Create a Supportive Writing Environment

Although the Common Core establishes specific Writing Standards that students are expected to master at each grade, it is silent about the context in which writing and writing instruction take place. This should not be overlooked, however, as writing is a social activity, and students are more likely to learn, enjoy, and apply writing if it occurs in a pleasant, motivating, and supportive environment. Exceptional literacy teachers make establishing such an environment a key ingredient of their writing programs. Practices that they consistently apply to achieve this objective are presented in Table 2.2.

The same practices that exceptional literacy teachers apply to create a supportive and motivating writing environment are also part of the process approach to writing instruction that is so popular with U.S. teachers. This approach emphasizes creating a pleasant and positive writing atmosphere, promoting high levels of student interactions to support writing, writing for real audiences and authentic purposes, stressing personal responsibility and ownership of writing projects, and encouraging self-reflection and self-evaluation. The process approach also supports students in at least three additional ways by (1) providing students with extended opportunities to write; (2) creating routines in which students are asked to plan, draft, revise, and edit their text; and (3) offering personalized individual assistance and feedback, as well as brief instructional lessons, as needed. This model's emphasis on the writing process, peer and teacher support of these procedures, and extended opportunities to compose are consistent with

Table 2.2. Creating a Pleasant and Motivating Writing Environment

- Establish a stimulating mood during writing time (e.g., make your excitement visible to students) and make it clear that you enjoy writing and teaching it.
- Make students' writing visible by having them share it with others; by displaying it on the wall; and by publishing it in anthologies, books, or other classroom collections.
- Create a positive classroom environment, where students are encouraged to try hard, believe that the writing skills and strategies they are learning help them write well, and attribute success to their effort and the tactics they are learning.
- Develop classroom routines, such as sharing in-progress writing and completed papers with peers, that promote positive interactions among students.
- Set high but realistic expectations for students' writing, encouraging them to exceed their previous efforts and accomplishments.
- Adapt writing assignments and instruction so they are appropriate to students' interests and needs.
- Keep students engaged by involving them in thoughtful activities (e.g., discussing ideas for their papers) versus less thoughtful activities (e.g., completing a worksheet).
- Encourage students to act in a self-regulated fashion, doing as much as they can on their own (e.g., instead of spelling a word for a student, provide hints that help the student spell the word).

the Common Core's focus on developing and strengthening writing via planning, drafting, revising, and editing (see Table 2.1, application 2), as well as writing routinely over extended time frames (see Table 2.1, application 4). Scientific tests of the process approach found that it resulted in a 14 percentile point increase in writing quality for average writers (Graham, Harris, & Santangelo, in press).

2. Teach Foundational Writing Skills

The Common Core's Language Standards emphasize the mastery of a variety of fundamental writing skills, including handwriting, spelling, grammar, usage, and vocabulary. The development of keyboarding skills is also emphasized in the Writing Standards (see Table 2.1, application 2).

Handwriting, keyboarding, and spelling skills are the means by which students transcribe their ideas onto paper or into digital text. Such skills need to be automatized so they can be executed quickly, correctly, and with little thought; otherwise, they interfere with other aspects of the writing process (Graham, 2006). Slow handwriting/keyboarding or having to think about how to spell a word while writing can lead students to forget ideas or plans held in working memory. In addition, readers are more negative about a writer's ideas if words are misspelled or handwriting is difficult to read (Graham, Harris, & Hebert, 2011).

Before students transcribe an idea into text, they must first transform the idea into the words and syntactic structures that will convey their intended meanings. This involves constructing a sentence(s) for the idea, using appropriate grammar, and selecting the right words. This process of constructing sentences is a thoughtful and highly effortful process, which cannot and should not be automatized, but teachers can help children become more facile in carrying out this translation process (Graham, 2006).

Scientific studies of writing interventions support the practice of directly teaching handwriting, keyboarding, and spelling skills to elementary-grade students (Graham, Harris, & Santangelo, in press). Average students in grades 1–3 who were taught these skills evidenced a 21 percentile point increase in writing quality as a result of such instruction. Further, across the elementary grades, the spelling of average students who were taught this skill increased by 21 percentile points, whereas handwriting instruction resulted in a 20 and 23 percentile point jump in legibility and fluency, respectively (Santangelo & Graham, 2013). Table 2.3 provides several examples of successful practices for teaching text transcription skills.

Table 2.3. Examples of Teaching Text Transcription Skills

- Teach students how to form individual letters (e.g., *l, i, t*) via modeling and guided practices (moving from learning the letters as an individual unit to writing them in a word; e.g., *little*). Have students practice increasing their letter-writing fluency by writing a sentence neatly and quickly, including the target letters (e.g., "It got littler and littler.") for three minutes, with the goal of gradually increasing the number of letters written during the next two sessions (no more than a 10% increase in each session).
- Use a word sorting activity to help students learn the underlying structure for two or more spelling patterns (e.g., CVC vs. CVCe). With traditional study practices as well as collaborative games, help students learn how to spell eight high-frequency words that fit the target patterns and that students cannot currently spell correctly. Provide additional practice with the target spelling patterns by having students construct words (with a partner) that fit each pattern. Ask students to use words that fit these patterns to produce a short piece of text that they will share with a classmate.

In contrast, the scientific evidence does not support teaching grammar skills via traditional methods, such as defining a grammar term and practicing its application on a worksheet, or using sentence diagramming to learn about grammar (Andrews et al., 2006). Rather, the evidence supports the use of sentence combining as a means for helping students develop more sophisticated sentence construction skills, including sentences that are more grammatically correct (Andrews et al., 2006). Sentence-combining instruction involves modeling how to combine two or more simpler sentences into a more complex one. Students then practice combining similar types of sentences and are encouraged to practice applying the newly learned skill in their writing. Average students taught such sentence-combining strategies evidence a 21 percentile point increase in the quality of their writing (Graham, Harris, & Santangelo, in press).

Although the construction of a good sentence involves selecting just the right words, teaching students about new words to use in their writing appears to be a promising practice, but not an evidence-based one as defined here, as Graham, Harris, and Santangelo (in press) located only three studies that scientifically tested this practice. Nevertheless, when average students were taught words to use in their writing (e.g., words about space for a space story), they evidenced a 28 percentile point jump in writing quality.

3. Teach Students About Different Types of Text and Their Purposes

The Common Core emphasizes that elementary-grade students need to learn to use different types of text for a variety of purposes (see Table 2.1, application 1). This includes using writing to support a point of view, writing text that clearly conveys information or explains an idea, and creating narratives about real or imagined experiences. With the Common Core, each of these genres of writing becomes progressively more complex from one grade to the next, as one or more new elements are added to the description of the desired product. These added elements are specific to the genre emphasized (e.g., support reasons with facts and details at grade 4).

There are several evidence-based practices for helping elementary-grade students acquire the knowledge about text structure that is emphasized in the Common Core. This includes directly teaching students about the different elements included in a specific type of writing. To illustrate, the teacher might describe a story element (e.g., the setting), point out the element in several stories, ask for other examples from students, present and discuss nonexamples of the story element, and ask students to generate their own examples of the element within and outside the context of a story. Scientific tests of this and similar practices demonstrated that the writing quality of an average student for the instructed genre increased by 16 percentile points (Graham, Harris, & Santangelo, in press).

Another evidence-based practice for improving students' skills at producing different types of text is to provide them with a model text and ask them to emulate it. This can—and should, in our opinion—include discussion about the characteristics of the model text. This is one of the oldest techniques for teaching students about different types of writing, and scientific testing of this procedure showed that it resulted in the same percentile point jump in the quality of text produced by average writers as did directly teaching text structure (Graham, Harris, & Santangelo, in press).

An additional approach for teaching students about different types of text and their purposes is strategy instruction. We included this evidence-based practice in our next recommendation because it primarily focuses on teaching students strategies for planning, editing, and revising. Nevertheless, this approach often teaches students strategies that are specific to a particular type of text (e.g., opinion essays), resulting in writing improvements in the targeted genre (Graham, Harris, & Santangelo, in press).

4. Enhance the Planning, Revising, and Editing of Text

The Common Core stresses more than just the creation of specific types of products, emphasizing that students become adept at applying the processes used to create such text. This includes developing and strengthening writing through planning, revising, and editing, as well as producing text in which the development and organization of ideas is appropriate to the writer's task, purpose, and audience (see Table 2.1, application 2).

One way to help students employ these processes in an effective manner is to directly teach strategies for how to plan, revise, and edit text.

Such strategies can be more general, such as brainstorming or semantic webbing, or tied to specific types of text, such as creating a story or writing a persuasive text (see Table 2.4 for an example of genre-specific strategies). Collectively, scientific tests of this and similar practices demonstrated that the writing quality of an average student increased by 34 percentile points as a result of learning planning, revising, and editing strategies (Graham, Harris, & Santangelo, in press).

At the most fundamental level, teaching planning, writing, and editing strategies involves describing a strategy and establishing its rationale, modeling how to apply it, and providing students with assistance in applying the strategy with the goal of independent and effective use of it. One approach that built on and added to this basic instructional model was particularly effective: the self-regulated strategy development (SRSD) model (Harris et al., 2008; see also Chapter 6 of this volume). With SRSD, any knowledge or skills needed to effectively use the target writing strategy are taught (typically before the teacher models strategy use). Students are made aware of their writing gains through self-evaluation and are encouraged to attribute these gains to their own effort and strategy use. Students are taught to use other self-regulation procedures (e.g., goal setting, self-instructions, self-reinforcement) to regulate the use of the strategy, the writing process, and/or their own writing behavior. SRSD resulted in a 39 percentile point increase in writing quality for average writers, whereas other approaches to teaching writing strategies netted a 20 percentile point gain (Graham, Harris, & Santangelo, in press).

Another evidence-based practice that can not only facilitate the process of writing but also enhance the creation of genre-based text is

---

Table 2.4. Example of Genre-Specific Strategies for Story Writing

- Before drafting a story, students generate possible ideas for their narrative by thinking about and recording ideas regarding characters, the setting, the main character's goals, actions to achieve those goals, characters' reactions, and how the story ends.
- After producing a first draft, students evaluate each of these elements in their story to determine what revisions they need to make to improve it.

Note. Other examples of writing strategies can be found in *Writing Better: Effective Strategies for Teaching Students With Learning Difficulties,* by S. Graham and K.R. Harris, 2005, Baltimore, MD: Paul H. Brookes; and "Powerful Writing Strategies for All Students," by K.R. Harris, S. Graham, L.H. Mason, and B. Friedlander, 2008, Baltimore, MD: Paul H. Brookes.

the establishment of specific goals for writing. For instance, teachers can ask upper elementary–grade students to address both sides of an argument, providing three or more reasons to support their point of view and countering with at least two reasons supporting the opposing view. Goals can be more general, however, and focused on a specific process (e.g., "Add three new ideas to your paper when revising it"). Scientific tests of these types of teacher-established goals found a 29 percentile point increase for an average writer (Graham, Harris, & Santangelo, in press)— quite a jump for a practice that is relatively easy to implement.

A third evidence-based practice for facilitating the process of writing is to have students work together as they plan, draft, revise, or edit their text. This approach involves teaching students what to do as they work together on a specific process. For example, the teacher might provide instruction to pairs of students on how to apply the strategies in Table 2.4 conjointly and in a productive and cooperative manner. Scientific testing showed a 31 percentile point jump in the quality of average students' writing through the use of such approaches (Graham, Harris, & Santangelo, in press).

An additional evidence-based practice for facilitating the writing process is to put into place practices that help students acquire information to write. Such prewriting activities involve locating possible writing content via brainstorming, reading, drawing, the Internet, and/or using graphic organizers. In scientific tests, the application of these procedures resulted in a 21 point percentile point jump in the quality of text produced by an average writer (Graham, Harris, & Santangelo, in press).

Finally, students' writing is improved if they receive feedback from the teacher or peers, are taught to self-evaluate their writing, and/or receive feedback from a computer. Scientific testing demonstrated that together such feedback resulted in a 23 percentile point increase in the quality of writing produced by average students (see Graham, Hebert, & Harris, in press).

5. Use 21st-Century Writing Tools

The Common Core recognizes that using digital tools, such as word processing, is now an essential part of writing (see Table 2.1, application 2). Students are expected to use these tools as they produce, collaborate on, publish, and share their writing with others. Over the past several decades, numerous scientific studies have tested the effectiveness of using word processing as a stylus for writing. When compared with writing by hand, average students who used word processing as their primary tool for composing evidenced an 18 percentile point increase in writing quality (Graham, Harris, & Santangelo, in press). This was not surprising, as word processors provide several tangible advantages over writing by hand, such as (1) producing legible text that can easily be deleted, added, rewritten, or moved; (2) bundling with other software, such as spell checkers or speech synthesis, that support the writer; and (3) connecting to the Web and other programs, allowing students to gather material for what they write and to share their text with others.

6. Have Students Write and Use Writing to Promote Understanding and Learning

With the Common Core, students are expected to write frequently and use writing as a tool to support their understanding and learning of content material presented in text and the classroom (see Table 2.1, applications 3 and 4). A basic assumption underlying writing instruction is that students must write frequently if they are to develop as writers. This proposition is supported by scientific evidence obtained from studies in which the amount of writing that students undertook was increased. This simple strategy resulted in an 8 percentile point increase in writing quality for average writers (Graham, Harris, & Santangelo, in press).

Writing about material read or presented in class is deemed to be advantageous for several reasons. First, writing can force students to decide what ideas are most important and how they are related to one another. Second, the permanence of writing allows students to review, reexamine, critique, and even construct new understandings of the extracted material. Third, writing forces students to put the ideas of others into their own written language, making them think more carefully about what the ideas mean. Scientific testing supports the beneficial effects of writing on comprehension and learning, as average students evidenced a 24 percentile point jump in reading comprehension when asked to write about text read, and a 9 percentile point increase in learning when asked to write about material presented in class (Graham, Harris, & Santangelo, in press). Table 2.5 provides examples of practices for supporting students' understanding and learning of content material.

> **Table 2.5. Writing Activities That Promote Students' Comprehension and Learning**
>
> - Writing short answers to questions about the content
> - Creating written questions about material read or presented
> - Taking notes about material read or presented
> - Writing a summary of material read or presented
> - Writing more extended responses, such as explaining how something learned can be applied or relates to one's own life

Concluding Comments

If our students are to meet, and hopefully exceed, the Writing Standards set forth in the Common Core, they need and deserve a strong writing program at every grade level. We think that the proven practices presented herein should be part of that program. Of course, the success of these evidence-based practices depends on them being applied judiciously and with good common sense, as their application requires multiple decisions about how to use them in tandem, how to make them work within your current approach to writing instruction, or both. In essence, the success of these practices depends on your skills as a professional teacher, as they are just tools and you are the master.

REFERENCES

Andrews, R., Torgerson, C., Beverton, S., Freeman, A., Locke, T., Low, G., ... Zhu, D. (2006). The effect of grammar teaching on writing development. *British Educational Research Journal, 32*(1), 39–55.

Applebee, A.N., & Langer, J.A. (2011). A snapshot of writing instruction in middle schools and high schools. *English Journal, 100*(6), 14–27.

Brindle, M.E. (2013). *Examining relationships among teachers' preparation, efficacy, and writing practices* (Unpublished doctoral dissertation). Vanderbilt University, Nashville, TN.

Gilbert, J., & Graham, S. (2010). Teaching writing to elementary students in grades 4–6: A national survey. *The Elementary School Journal, 110*(4), 494–518. doi:10.1086/651193

Graham, S. (2006). Writing. In P.A. Alexander & P.H. Winne (Eds.), *Handbook of educational psychology* (2nd ed., pp. 457–478). Mahwah, NJ: Erlbaum.

Graham, S. (2011). Teaching writing. In P.C. Hogan (Ed.), *The Cambridge encyclopedia of the language sciences* (pp. 848–851). New York, NY: Cambridge University Press.

Graham, S. (2013). Writing standards. In L.M. Morrow, K.K. Wixson, & T. Shanahan (Eds.), *Teaching with the Common Core Standards for English language arts, grades 3–5* (pp. 88–106). New York, NY: Guilford.

Graham, S., & Associates. (2013). *Get it in writing: Making adolescent writing an immediate priority in Texas*. Atlanta, GA: Southern Regional Education Board. Retrieved from publications.sreb.org/2013/GetItInWriting_TX_Final.pdf

Graham, S., & Harris, K.R. (2005). *Writing better: Effective strategies for teaching students with learning difficulties*. Baltimore, MD: Paul H. Brookes.

Graham, S., Harris, K.R., & Hebert, M. (2011). It is more than just the message: Presentation effects in scoring writing. *Focus on Exceptional Children, 44*(4), 1–12.

Graham, S., Harris, K.R., & Santangelo, T. (in press). Research-based writing practices and the Common Core: Meta-analysis and meta-synthesis. *The Elementary School Journal*.

Graham, S., Hebert, M., & Harris, K.R. (in press). Formative assessment and writing: A meta-analysis. *The Elementary School Journal*.

Graham, S., & Perin, D. (2007). What we know, what we still need to know: Teaching adolescents to write. *Scientific Studies of Reading, 11*(4), 313–335. doi:10.1080/10888430701530664

Harris, K.R., Graham, S., Mason, L.H., & Friedlander, B. (2008). *Powerful writing strategies for all students*. Baltimore, MD: Paul H. Brookes.

Hillocks, G., Jr. (2002). *The testing trap: How state writing assessments control learning*. New York, NY: Teachers College Press.

National Center for Education Statistics. (2012). *The Nation's Report Card: Writing 2011* (NCES 2012-470). Washington, DC: National Center for Education Statistics, Institute of Education Sciences, U.S. Department of Education.

National Commission on Writing for America's Families, Schools, and Colleges. (2004). *Writing: A ticket to work...or a ticket out*. New York, NY: College Board.

National Commission on Writing for America's Families, Schools, and Colleges. (2005). *Writing: A powerful message from state government*. New York, NY: College Board.

National Commission on Writing for America's Families, Schools, and Colleges. (2006). *Writing and school reform*. New York, NY: College Board.

National Governors Association Center for Best Practices & Council of Chief State School Officers. (2010). *Common Core State Standards for English language arts and literacy in history/social studies, science, and technical subjects*. Washington, DC: Authors.

Santangelo, T., & Graham, S. (2013, February). *Meta-analyses of handwriting and spelling instruction*. Paper presented at the 21st annual Pacific Coast Research Conference, San Diego, CA.

Writing Study Group of the NCTE Executive Committee. (2004). *NCTE beliefs about the teaching of writing*. Retrieved from www.ncte.org/positions/statements/writingbeliefs

ABOUT THE AUTHORS

Steve Graham is the Warner Professor of Education at Arizona State University in Phoenix, Arizona, USA. He is the former editor of *Exceptional Children, Contemporary Educational Psychology*, and the *Journal of Writing Research* and the incoming editor of the *Journal of Educational Psychology*. Graham served as a coeditor of the *Handbook of Learning Disabilities* (2nd ed., Guilford, 2013), *Handbook of Writing Research* (Guilford, 2008), and *APA Educational Psychology Handbook*

(American Psychological Association, 2012). He also coauthored three Carnegie Corporation reports, all published by the Alliance for Excellent Education: *Writing Next: Effective Strategies to Improve Writing of Adolescents in Middle and High Schools* (2007), *Writing to Read: Evidence for How Writing Can Improve Reading* (2010), and *Informing Writing: The Benefits of Formative Assessment* (2011).

Karen R. Harris is the Warner Professor in the Division of Educational Leadership and Innovation at the Mary Lou Fulton Teachers College, Arizona State University, Phoenix, Arizona, USA. Before earning her doctoral degree, she taught kindergarten and fourth-grade students and then elementary and secondary students in special education. Her research focuses on children's writing. She developed the SRSD model of strategies instruction, and her current research focuses on professional development for SRSD for teachers working in general and special education. A former editor of the *Journal of Educational Psychology*, she also served as lead editor of the *APA Educational Psychology Handbook* (American Psychological Association, 2012) and has authored more than 200 peer-reviewed publications. She is the president of the Division for Educational Psychology of the American Psychological Association and has served as the president of the Division for Research of the Council for Exceptional Children and as an officer for the American Educational Research Association.

PART II

How Do We Encourage Developing Writers?

CHAPTER 3

Moving Student Writers Forward With Mentor Texts

Lynne R. Dorfman & Rose Cappelli,
Pennsylvania Writing & Literature Project

Yes, it is important to show students how the teacher writes, but it is also of paramount importance to provide students with mentor texts so they can see how other writers compose. It is critical that my students be able to move beyond simply telling me what a text says; I want them to begin to recognize *how* the text is constructed. (Gallagher, 2011, p. 20)

It was November, and the third graders were working on a "sharing a secret" lead for their informational piece about the Pilgrims for social studies class. Lynne (first author) decided to ask Danny, a reluctant writer, if he would like to have a conference, and was surprised when he readily consented, presenting her with a four-paragraph text. Lynne noticed the unique structure that Danny chose to hold his piece together and was even more surprised by his explanation.

Danny, the lead you chose for this piece is very effective and shares a secret! I didn't realize that the Mayflower was built to carry cargo. But what really interests me is your organization of this entire piece. How did you decide to talk about the good things and the bad things the Pilgrims faced because of this fact?

"Mentor texts!" he exclaimed proudly. "I'll show you." Danny walked to his desk and returned with a copy of *That's Good! That's Bad!* by Margery Cuyler. Slightly crumpled and stained with pencil marks (or could that be chocolate?), the book held the secret to Danny's success. He had found a mentor text on his own to imitate for its organizational scaffold in his piece about the Mayflower. It was so perfect. Danny understood how to use a mentor text to help him with this piece of writing, and he had navigated through this process without Lynne's or his teacher's help. Lynne marveled at the potential use for mentor texts.

What Is a Mentor?

Through the influence of Greek mythology, the term *mentor* has come to mean someone who shares wisdom and knowledge with a less accomplished colleague. A mentor provides gentle nudges to help a student or colleague take a risk and try something new. A mentor serves as a guide or facilitator who is always ready to step back and allow the protégé to take on greater independence. This is not a new idea. Students of the arts study the masters to learn techniques and try them out. Throughout the ages, apprenticeship has been an integral part of learning a trade or a profession. Today, university students spend a year with mentor teachers to experience the rigors of classroom instruction and management. The mentees take away many valuable skills—even whole systems—during their internship. Most of these are adapted and changed slightly for an individual fit.

This concept of mentorship can also be applied to our work with young writers as we help them study mentor texts. A mentor text can be a book, a newspaper article, a song, a poem, or even a travel brochure. The text is used to try out a genre or a writer's craft. Its job is to move a writer forward through close imitation. A student who plays it safe and doesn't experiment with sentence patterns, word placement, figurative language, and various punctuation marks will become stagnant in his or her writing. The student's voice will not mature, and by middle school, he or she may lack a sophistication that should have been acquired earlier by studying and imitating authors and genres.

When writers explore mentor texts, they must be ready to do the hard work of an apprentice. They must be willing to closely read to discover how the author created an effective piece of writing that moves readers to think, consider possibilities, and ultimately imitate the author's craft and organizational structure. Student writers must learn to make good decisions about when and where to use the craft or organizational structure of the mentor text.

Finding Mentor Texts

Good writing is all around us. Teachers may choose a set of books to designate as mentor texts that will be used over and over again throughout the course of a year. These texts should help the students at this grade level gain insight and maturity. Teachers may start with books that are familiar and loved. They need to give these books a close read to determine what secrets their pages can share with the young authors. Most of the time, these texts should be able to be used independently by the students or with guidance or collaboration. When students understand the concept of imitating real-world writing, they can begin to find their own mentors and share their new learning with their peers.

For us, *Painting the Wind* by Patricia and Emily MacLachlan (2003) is a gold mine for focused lessons in writing workshop, especially for the intermediate grade levels. Rose (second author) was first drawn to this book because of the author (that's always a good place to start). She was familiar with the work of Patricia MacLachlan and knew this book would be a good read and offer many possibilities for studying craft. A first reading convinced her that this was a text to add to her collection because it tells the story of a young painter who learned a new skill by imitating the work of others. On subsequent readings, she started to focus more on the craft of the authors. Rose was always looking for good examples of specific word choice to use with her students. In *Painting the Wind*, she noticed that the authors use specific names of flowers (e.g., larkspur, poppy, cosmos) and colors (e.g., Scarlet Lake, Cadmium Red, Terracotta). She was also particularly struck by the many ways that Patricia and Emily MacLachlan use listing: with semicolons and commas, using a sentence fragment, with a dash, without the use of a conjunction (traditional listing), with the use of a repeated conjunction (*and*), and with a colon—all this within the span of a picture book! Within the pages, Lynne found even more uses for her students. She noticed that the writing is in the present tense, just like the novel *Shiloh* by Phyllis Reynolds Naylor that so many of her students read and *Where I Live* by Eileen Spinelli. She liked the idea of revisiting these texts in several focus lessons to help her students "be in the moment" when they are writing. In *Painting the Wind*, Lynne also noticed the use of hyphenated adjectives (e.g., *coffee-colored*, *sweet-faced*), the effective use of dialogue, and the use of epithets to name the painters (e.g., "the painter of flowers," "the painter of still lifes," "the painter of landscapes").

We still continue to discover new ideas for lessons and ask questions of each other about the authors' choices. For example, we wonder why the authors chose to name the dogs but not the main character or the painters. We model our thinking aloud for our students so they can understand and imitate how we process text. Returning to a mentor text is like watching a movie for a second or third time: You start to notice things that you never really paid attention to the first time because you were too busy trying to follow the story. As we used *Painting the Wind* with our students, they noticed things, too: strong verbs, character snapshots, variations in print, and effective repetition.

One day, Lynne noticed that Patricia and Emily MacLachlan had placed two adjectives out of their traditional order in this sentence: "The paintings are on the walls: the faces, young and old, the bowl of tulips, the full moon over a quiet sea, a red poppy that fills a canvas" (n.p.). Although we couldn't find another sentence that uses adjectives after the noun that they described in *Painting the Wind*, we decided to investigate other texts by Patricia MacLachlan. In *Sarah, Plain and Tall*, she writes, "There will be Sarah's sea, blue and gray and green, hanging on the wall" (MacLachlan, 1985, p. 58). We laughed when we both realized that even in the title of the book, MacLachlan places adjectives after the noun. In *Skylark*, we found this sentence: "And then there was only smoke, the grasses all black and smoldering" (MacLachlan, 1994, p. 33). After we discovered these examples in her books, we started to search for adjectives after the noun in other texts as well. We returned to a classic, *Owl Moon* by Jane Yolen (1987): "We reached the line of pine trees, black and pointy against the sky, and Pa held up his hand" (n.p.). In *Prairie Summer* by Nancy Hundal (2003), we found this example: "And the heat, high and still. The insect drone, still and high" (n.p.). *Anna's Table* by Eve Bunting (2003) provided a treasure trove of examples. In this book, we meet Anna, who collects objects from nature. Many of the descriptions include this same adjective placement:

> On it I have a seahorse, elegant and small. (n.p.)
>
> I have a pomegranate, hard and dry. (n.p.)
>
> I have a caterpillar, curled and mummy black,
> a lizard, thin and wide, run over by a car. (n.p.)

We noticed (and wanted our students to notice, too) that adjectives after the noun interrupt the flow of the sentence, causing the reader to slow down and actually notice the impact of the adjectives. For example, in *Harry Potter and the Chamber of Secrets*, J.K. Rowling (2000) uses ordinary adjectives that become quite extraordinary because of what they are describing. By placing the adjectives after the noun, the reader doesn't simply zoom by and miss the significance of the author's adjectives: "Not only were there a dozen frost-covered Christmas trees and thick streamers of holly and mistletoe crisscrossing the great hall, but enchanted snow was falling, warm and dry, from the ceiling" (p. 212). We noticed that Rowling does place one important adjective before the noun (*enchanted*) and is able to stack her sentence with two more important adjectives by placing them after the noun. This technique helps the reader visualize, pause, and wonder.

Consider this sentence from the last page of *Fireflies!* by Julie Brinckloe (1985): "I held the jar, dark and empty, in my hands" (n.p.). One astute fifth grader in Lynne's class noted that at that moment in time, the boy in the book was feeling as dark and empty as his jar, his efforts to catch hundreds of fireflies released in one small moment. Another fifth grader understood that this sentence sounded more like poetry than prose. Lynne rewrote the sentence in the traditional pattern: "I held the dark, empty jar in my hands." She had her fifth graders read her sentence several times aloud and then reread Brinckloe's sentence. They talked about what fits best in the text and unanimously agreed that the adjective placement after the noun makes a significant difference. Although we know that well-placed adjectives enhance a description, too many adjectives in a single sentence can be ineffective. Placing adjectives after the noun helps the writer avoid the kind of sentence that appears to be overloaded with adjectives before the noun appears.

Writing With Students: The Your Turn Lesson

Writing takes time, and to learn something well also takes time. Sometimes as we confer with students in writing workshop, we'll use a mentor text to help a particular student learn something new. But sometimes we may want to slow things down a bit and offer all of our student writers the chance to discover and imitate the craft of an author. We call this a Your

Turn lesson. It begins by returning to a mentor text, guiding students to notice what an author has done, and encouraging them to form an idea about why the author has used this technique in this particular location in the text. Next, we invite students to explore other texts by the same author and different authors to find additional examples that can be used for close imitation. We set a purpose for our young writers by explaining to them exactly what it is we are going to do. In the case of adjectives after the noun, we might say something like, "Writers, today we are going to try using well-chosen adjectives as interrupters that slow the rhythm of the sentence and help the reader to linger on its meaning." Because writers need a storehouse of words and ideas from which to pull, the next step is to do some brainstorming. In this example, we could just brainstorm adjectives in general, but it will be more effective for the shared and individual writing experiences for the class to brainstorm around a specific noun or nouns, such as *weather, day, night, winter, summer, Halloween, dog, cat,* or *classroom.* In the fifth-grade class where Lynne was working, she had the students brainstorm adjectives to describe themselves in anticipation of their field day. The list included words such as *happy, excited, elated, anxious, hungry, nervous, silly, eager, chatty, quiet, noisy, jumpy, reluctant, athletic, strong, sleepy,* and *energetic.* She placed them on an anchor chart so the writers could refer to the list while composing.

Before asking students to try something, the teacher must try it out first. Modeling writing in front of your students achieves many goals. First of all, it puts the teacher in the game. That is, the teacher becomes a part of the writing community and can talk to his or her students as writer to writer. Writing in front of students also aids the teacher during conferences and while offering feedback. If the teacher is writing often and trying out the same skills and strategies—the same craft that he or she hopes the students will use—then the teacher will have to problem solve, experiencing the same difficulties or obstacles that the student writers face as they draft and revise. The teacher will, in fact, be able to provide more effective feedback to every student. If we want our students to view themselves as writers, then we, as teachers, must also view ourselves as writers. In our work around the country, we have learned that many teachers do not feel comfortable with their own writing or with the teaching of writing. Many of them have never had a writing course. If you are reluctant to write in front of your students, try it out first in private to reach an acceptable comfort level. But remember that showing students a piece of writing that has possibly been revised several times is not the same as demonstrating the drafting process while you think aloud. There's nothing better than recruiting your students to help you if you get stuck. (They love to do that!) In Lynne's class, she asked the students for help with describing rain. She used their words to model the use of adjective pairs as interrupters:

> The August rain, angry and merciless, pelted the young
> cornstalks into the soggy earth.
> The April rain, sweet and nurturing, soaked the rich soil
> to awaken the flowers.

Then, she returned to the anchor chart and asked students to use the following template to describe how they might feel on the morning of field day:

> The children arrived, ___ and ___, at the field day.

The students worked in small groups to produce some sentences. The adjective pairs included *cold/hungry, excited/eager, happy/carefree, nervous/chatty,* and *anxious/quiet.* This shared experience is an important part of the Your Turn lesson model. It is especially important for struggling writers, nonwriters (those who can write but choose not to), and English learners because they need that safety net for some support before venturing out on their own. Students can work as a whole class, in partnerships, or in small groups (alone or with the teacher). This social dimension of writing workshop cannot be omitted. This experience allows students to listen to their peers while they problem solve and try out different strategies. The shared or guided experience helps writers notice and appropriate the writing behaviors of their classmates. They will grow in confidence, self-esteem, and ability.

When students are ready, they can try the technique on their own. We encourage our students to try it out in a piece that they are currently working on, or return to a previously published piece and do some revision. In this way, students begin to realize that a piece of writing is never truly finished. Another place to try it out is in the writer's notebook, where students can continue to write more examples, or find a short description, poem, or anecdote that can be enhanced by the particular craft being studied.

Last but not least, a Your Turn lesson culminates in reflection. Student writers gather to share their work, discuss, and receive feedback. They should come to this final reflection prepared, so sometimes it's best to pose a question that they can be thinking about (and sometimes writing about) before they join their classmates in a specified location. It is never inappropriate for students in grades 3 through middle school to gather their chairs in a circle or sit on a rug the way primary-grade writers do to share their thinking and writing. The closeness of the community electrifies the atmosphere. Here are some possible questions to use:

- How did this [technique/craft/structure] work for you?
- How will it affect the reader?
- How will it help you as a writer?
- When is it appropriate to use [exclamation marks/metaphors/ parentheses/contractions/adverbs/fragments/lists/proper nouns/ adjectives after the noun/etc.]?

The Your Turn lesson was named to indicate to teachers that this type of lesson gives both the teacher and the students the chance to work through the gradual release of responsibility (I do/we do/you do) slowly and methodically to try out something that is worth trying out. Although some writing lessons may be fairly short, a Your Turn lesson can often extend over a two-day period. Your Turn lessons should be saved for those writing competencies that will move your writers forward at the particular grade level you teach. These lessons will nudge your writers to take risks and write differently today than they did yesterday.

Building Content With Rich Description

Effective writing is about the development of quality ideas. Good writing is a balance of fast and slow; that is, there are moments when the writer chooses to linger or dwell. These moments are often created through rich description. At other times, the writer moves quickly with little detail to either move through time or get to the essence of the piece. One way that all writers in all genres build content within a piece of writing is to write descriptions of characters, settings, events, objects, and even emotions. To do this, writers show the reader how something looks, smells, sounds, tastes, and/or feels. Using the senses is a powerful strategy to help the reader experience the text as if he or she is a part of it, leading to an empathetic response.

> Writers use all the senses to give us a concrete, physical experience....If we want our readers to remember what they've read, to linger over passages where they can close their eyes and imagine what it would be like, how they would feel, what they would do,...then we must provide them with details to give them this concrete experience. (Dorfman & Cappelli, 2007, p. 75)

Most of us take in our world through our eyes. We rely heavily on this one sense, sometimes to the exclusion of the others. However, it can be appropriate to create a description employing only one sense. Well-chosen adjectives and figurative language, such as similes and metaphors, can help the writer paint a vivid picture with words. Consider Robert Burleigh's (2009) description of the moon in *One Giant Leap*: "It is gray, it is brown, it is blue-edged. / Its billion-year-old landscape is cracked and scarred, / Its surface gouged and cratered and pitted with tiny holes, / Like a battlefield from some ancient war" (n.p.). The most effective descriptions are ones that are unique and easily understood. Everyone should be able to comprehend the passage, but something there forms a lasting impression that sticks with the reader long after the words have been consumed. The use of proper nouns will help the writer pack a powerful punch by using fewer words to conjure up an image. For example, when we think of New York City, our mind sees something totally different than if we think about the Florida Everglades. Stephen Swinburne's (2006) *Wings of Light: The Migration of the Yellow Butterfly* opens with a description of a particular butterfly that he wants his readers to follow throughout his text. He calls our attention to one particular butterfly by giving his readers a telling detail:

> It is a summer morning on the rain forest floor in the Yucatan Peninsula. A yellow butterfly with a notch in its wing, sliced by a bird's beak, flutters across the sunbeams. The butterfly spirals upward and weaves around moss and orchid-covered branches. (n.p.)

Swinburne's description is built around specific nouns, a telling detail, and strong verbs (*flutters*, *spirals*, *weaves*), giving this description specificity and establishing the author's expertise.

Good writing will often employ two or more senses, such as sight and smell, or sight, taste, and sound. Just the addition of one more sensory experience will improve a piece of writing. In *Charlotte's Web*, E.B. White (1952) brings us into Wilbur's barn with the sense of smell:

> The barn was very large. It was very old. It smelled of hay and it smelled of manure. It smelled of the perspiration of tired horses and the wonderful sweet breath of patient cows. It often had a sort of peaceful smell—as though nothing bad could happen ever again in the world. (p. 13)

Alice Schertle uses sight and sound in her lead sentence in *Down the Road*: "Hetty lived in a little gray house with a big stone chimney and a screen door that squeaked in a friendly way for comings and goings" (n.p.).
In *Rachel: The Story of Rachel Carson*, Amy Ehrlich (2003) writes,

> The woods near Rachel's cottage were shadowed with spruce trees, but in the open patches, reindeer moss grew and the pines smelled sweet in the sunshine. If you were lucky, you could sometimes hear the silvery song of a hermit thrush. (n.p.)

Students and teachers can have a discussion about how Ehrlich masterfully creates a unique description. She appeals to our senses of sight, sound, and smell. You can almost feel the sunshine and the softness of the moss. When a community of writers becomes a collective think tank, their curiosity is often aroused. Lynne's fourth graders wanted to know exactly what reindeer moss looks like, and because Lynne couldn't answer their questions, she set them off to do some research. The fourth graders could have used a simile to help them envision reindeer moss because it looked to them like heads of broccoli.

Debbie Miller (2002) understands the importance of sensory description for keen observations of the world. In *Reading With Meaning: Teaching Comprehension in the Primary Grades*, she states, "Children everywhere know that the secret of wisdom is to be curious about the world, to open up their senses and see, hear, taste, touch, and smell life's treasures" (p. 149). However, it's important to note that we should not expect our writers to always employ all five senses. Good writing is honest and sincere and should never sound phony or plastic. Writing rich description involves a sense of knowing what fits for each particular description within a particular genre.

Description can evoke a strong emotion. In *Amber on the Mountain*, Tony Johnston (1994) helps us feel Amber's loneliness through her description of the sparse population on the mountain where she lives. Jen

Bryant's (2013) choice of a strong verb (*itched*) in *A Splash of Red: The Life and Art of Horace Pippin,* helps readers feel Pippin's burning desire to paint: "As he walked along the streets of West Chester, his fingers itched to draw all the colors and textures he saw" (n.p.).

After students spend some time studying the craft of writing a good description and have many opportunities to practice, we are often rewarded by seeing the tracks of our teaching in their writing. Allison, a fifth grader, captured her readers with a description of her uncle's cat in her story "Gaining Her Trust." She used color words, a simile, and a telling detail and created a contrast between the physical description and the intense emotion the cat was feeling at that moment in time:

> I stared softly at her almond-shaped eyes glimmering brown with charcoal pupils. They glared back instead. They were clouded with raging temper and held no trust. Yes, her fur was silky and soft. The dark muddy-colored fur was highlighted with interesting splashes of brown and beige. Her long, fluffy tail waved in the air like a proud flag. The one spot on the tip of her left ear—the only white she wore anywhere—made me think that she must have been kissed by a beautiful angel.

Building Content With Anecdotes

Story is a powerful vehicle for delivering information, persuading someone to think or feel a certain way, and helping us more deeply understand characters and events. An anecdote is a short, interesting, and sometimes amusing story or account of a particular incident or event. We often find anecdotes in personal and biographical accounts because they help explain some aspect of a person's character, motivations, or inspirations.

> Authors use anecdotes for many reasons. Besides illustrating a point or illuminating a character trait, an anecdote provides a breath of fresh air. Nonfiction text can become heavy and complex. We know that we slow down as readers when we read informational writing. The anecdote provides a break for the reader. (Dorfman & Cappelli, 2009, p. 49)

Sometimes authors are inspired to build an entire book around an anecdote. *Hanukkah at Valley Forge* by Stephen Krensky (2006) is based on a story of George Washington's encounter with a Jewish soldier at Valley Forge. The book suggests that reflecting about the miracle that is celebrated at Hanukkah gave Washington hope that the Continental Army could also overcome a great tyrant. Jen Bryant (2009) built *Abe's Fish: A Boyhood Tale of Abraham Lincoln* around an anecdote found in the first official biography of this president. Her book tells the story of Lincoln's chance meeting with a soldier during the War of 1812 and how it may have deepened Lincoln's understanding about freedom. Books such as these can be used to introduce anecdotes to our student writers.

Anecdotes can be used throughout a text to develop ideas and understandings about characters, real or imagined. By using primary source documents, such as journals, diaries, pamphlets, and newspapers, history can be rewritten to help negate biases and offer truths. In *Independent Dames: What You Never Knew About the Women and Girls of the American Revolution*, Laurie Halse Anderson (2008) used anecdotes to help us understand that women at this time played an integral part in the fight for independence:

> Sixteen-year-old Elizabeth (Betty) Zane saved an entire fort full of people when it was attacked by British and Native American forces. The Americans in Fort Henry quickly ran out of gunpowder. Elizabeth slipped out of the fort and sprinted sixty yards to her brother's cabin where the gunpowder was stored. She filled her apron with the gunpowder and raced back while all the enemy guns were shooting at her. (p. 35)

Other books that use anecdotes throughout the text are *My Brother Martin: A Sister Remembers Growing up With the Rev. Dr. Martin Luther King Jr.* by Christine King Farris, *Bully for You, Teddy Roosevelt!* by Jean Fritz, and *Talkin' About Bessie: The Story of Aviator Elizabeth Coleman* by Nikki Grimes.

Sometimes anecdotes can be used to begin a piece of writing in an interesting way. One morning Rose was working with some second-grade struggling readers. She was using an article from a *National Geographic* magazine about bones to help them practice strategies for understanding nonfiction text. Rose noticed that the author began the piece by telling his readers about when he broke his arm and how this led to his interest in learning more about bones. Using this story as an example, she quickly explained what anecdotes are to her students. Modeling with her own writing, she recounted an anecdote about a bird stealing a watch that was lying on a beach blanket. She explained that this anecdote might serve as an introduction to a research piece about what kinds of nesting materials birds use or how to attract birds. She helped her students brainstorm shared experiences that happened at school and other small stories that were part of their individual memories. Michael recalled a story about finding an unexpected sunflower growing in his garden, John talked about getting to feed a giraffe at the zoo, and Andrew told about finding a snake in his family's canoe. The boys then discussed what topics for research these anecdotes could lead to. Andrew wrote,

> Once I went to my uncle's house. All my cousins were there. They were lifting a canoe and there was a snake. It was black and had a yellow stripe down its back. Charlie got bit. We had fun except for Charlie.

He decided that this small anecdote could possibly be used as an introduction to a piece about snakes or first aid for snake bites. For these students, the magazine article became a mentor text. Often, we can connect the work we do in reading to the work we do in writing as we move students forward as readers and writers.

Using Writer's Craft to Reach Reluctant Writers and English Learners

Writers are people who love words. We want to create that love of words with our students by introducing them to the numerous sentence structures and word combinations in the English language. Sometimes a writer's craft can help our most struggling writers be successful and have fun at the same time. Consider how adjective placement after the noun (discussed previously in this chapter) adds a distinctive rhythm and emphasis to a sentence. This structure helps writers understand the importance of using well-chosen adjectives, as well as the role of commas in slowing the rhythm of the sentence.

In her book *I Love the Night*, Dar Hosta (2003) uses a craft that employs adverb/adjective pairings to describe how the different nocturnal animals feel about nighttime: "superbly superb," "gloriously glorious," and "splendidly splendid." Students in all the elementary grades can sprinkle this craft into a story, a poem, or even an opinion piece.

One craft to use with writers of all ages is highlighting a verb. Sharon Creech (2001) uses this unique craft throughout *Love That Dog*:

Some of the tiger sounds
are still in my ears
like drums
beat-beat-beating. (p. 9)

My brain was pop-pop-popping
when I was looking at those poems. (p. 35)

Katherine Hannigan (2004) also used this structure in *Ida B...and Her Plans to Maximize Fun, Avoid Disaster, and (Possibly) Save the World*: "Daddy'd hand me a dish, I'd sprint to the cupboard and put it away, race back again, and put my hand out for the next one, with my right foot tap, tap, tapping the seconds that were ticking by" (p. 2).

This strategy will help writers focus on the verbs that they are using, sometimes choosing to replace a verb for a stronger one. Verbs that have more than one syllable can be altered for originality and for rhythm. Here are some examples from a fifth-grade class written during a shared experience:

I stam-stam-stammered my way through the speech.

The butterfly flut-flut-fluttered through the garden.

The church bells bing-bang-bonged the news.

The Your Turn lesson in Figure 3.1 provides a guide for teaching this craft. Emphasis on the shared and guided experiences will help struggling writers and English learners move toward their target skills.

Figure 3.1. Your Turn Lesson: Highlight a Verb

Hook: Return to the mentor text, *Love That Dog* by Sharon Creech, and read parts where the author uses the craft "Highlight a Verb." Here is an example:

We think maybe you did
because
you were
smile-smile-smiling
all over the place. (p. 82)

Options: *Ida B...and Her Plans to Maximize Fun, Avoid Disaster, and (Possibly) Save the World* by Katherine Hannigan or a variation in *Saturdays and Teacakes* by Lester L. Laminack.

(continued)

Figure 3.1. Your Turn Lesson: Highlight a Verb (*Continued*)

Purpose: Explain to your students what it is you are going to teach them. You might say something like this:

> Writers, today I will show you how you can highlight a strong verb in your writing to add song and poetry to your piece and emphasize a thought or feeling. This strategy will help you become more aware of the verbs you use and may even lead you to make better verb choices. It will let your readers know more about the action you are describing.

Brainstorm: Create a list of verbs with your students using the plain form of the verb, such as *run, sleep, love, write, read, climb, kick, ski, trudge, hop, slide, peck, dart, dodge, squeeze, jump, slip, pace, dash, trot, jog, wade, dive*, and *laugh*. Make sure this list is recorded in a permanent place, such as an anchor chart, a computer file that can be displayed on a whiteboard, or as notes in a reference section of an individual notebook.

Model: Using some of the verbs from the list, create sentences in front of your students. Use both hyphens and commas to model this craft. Be sure to think aloud to help make your process visible to your students. Here some examples from Lynne's notebook:

- I laugh, laugh, laughed until my face was wet with tears.
- We dash-dash-dashed across the yard on our new bikes.
- Jamal was slip, slap, sliding across the frozen lake, trying to control the puck.
- Sammy pad-pad-paddled the kayak out into the blue-green ocean.

Note: Try to create at least one example that uses a two-syllable verb.

Shared/Guided Writing: Ask students to use one or several of the verbs from the brainstormed list to write some sentences in their writer's notebook to practice this craft. Simply repeat the verb one time in its plain form and finish with the *-ed* or *-ing* form. The verbs can be separated with commas or hyphens. Students can do this with a partner or in a small group. Share some of these sentences with the whole group and post them on a bulletin board or chart.

Example: We trudge, trudge, trudged through the deep snow.

Independent Writing: Ask students to search their writer's notebook for a sentence where they want to really emphasize the action. They can return to a piece of writing that they have already published, or use the piece that they are currently drafting and revise it using this technique.

Reflection: After students have the opportunity to revise or write, ask them to share with the whole class or a small group. The following questions can help guide their thinking:

- How did your sentence's meaning change by highlighting a verb?
- Was this technique difficult or easy to do? Explain.
- Did you substitute any verbs for stronger ones? How did the substitution(s) improve your piece of writing?
- Did this technique help you create a stronger emotion?
- When do you envision using this craft again?

In Conclusion

Mentor texts help teachers and students return to a text to reread for many different purposes. Mentor texts serve as models so students can try out new strategies and formats and become different writers than they were yesterday. Although picture books can serve as perfect mentor texts for modeling punctuation, craft, and structures, mentor texts include all genres and can be found everywhere.

REFERENCES

Dorfman, L.R., & Cappelli, R. (2007). *Mentor texts: Teaching writing through children's literature, K–6.* Portland, ME: Stenhouse.

Dorfman, L.R., & Cappelli, R. (2009). *Nonfiction mentor texts: Teaching informational writing through children's literature, K–8.* Portland, ME: Stenhouse.

Gallagher, K. (2011). *Write like this: Teaching real-world writing through modeling and mentor texts.* Portland, ME: Stenhouse.

Miller, D. (2002). *Reading with meaning: Teaching comprehension in the primary grades.* Portland, ME: Stenhouse.

CHILDREN'S LITERATURE CITED

Anderson, L.H. (2008). *Independent dames: What you never knew about the women and girls of the American Revolution.* New York, NY: Simon & Schuster Books for Young Readers.

Brinckloe, J. (1985). *Fireflies!* New York, NY: Aladdin.

Bryant, J. (2009). *Abe's fish: A boyhood tale of Abraham Lincoln.* New York, NY: Sterling.

Bryant, J. (2013). *A splash of red: The life and art of Horace Pippin.* New York, NY: Alfred A. Knopf.

Bunting, E. (2003). *Anna's table.* Chanhassen, MN: NorthWord.

Burleigh, R. (2009). *One giant leap.* New York, NY: Philomel.

Creech, S. (2001). *Love that dog.* New York, NY: HarperCollins Children's.

Ehrlich, A. (2003). *Rachel: The story of Rachel Carson.* Orlando, FL: Harcourt.

Hannigan, K. (2004). *Ida B…and her plans to maximize fun, avoid disaster, and (possibly) save the world.* New York, NY: HarperTrophy.

Hosta, D. (2003). *I love the night.* Flemington, NJ: Brown Dog.

Hundal, N. (2003). *Prairie summer.* Markham, ON, Canada: Fitzhenry & Whiteside.

Johnston, T. (1994). *Amber on the mountain.* New York, NY: Dial Books for Young Readers.

Krensky, S. (2006). *Hanukkah at Valley Forge.* New York, NY: Dutton Children's.

MacLachlan, P. (1985). *Sarah, plain and tall.* New York, NY: Harper & Row.

MacLachlan, P. (1994). *Skylark.* New York, NY: HarperCollins Children's.

MacLachlan, P., & MacLachlan, E. (2003). *Painting the wind.* New York, NY: Joanna Cotler.

Rowling, J.K. (2000). *Harry Potter and the chamber of secrets.* New York, NY: Scholastic.

Schertle, A. (2000). *Down the road*. New York, NY: Voyager.

Swinburne, S.R. (2006). *Wings of light: The migration of the yellow butterfly*. Honesdale, PA: Boyds Mills.

White, E.B. (1952). *Charlotte's web*. New York, NY: Harper & Row.

Yolen, J. (1987). *Owl moon*. New York, NY: Philomel.

ABOUT THE AUTHORS

 Lynne R. Dorfman is currently a codirector of the Pennsylvania Writing & Literature Project at West Chester University in West Chester, Pennsylvania, USA, and an adjunct professor for Arcadia University in Glenside, Pennsylvania, USA. She served as a classroom teacher and writing coach for 38 years in the Upper Moreland School District in Pennsylvania. Lynne is a coauthor of *Mentor Texts: Teaching Writing Through Children's Literature, K–6* (Stenhouse, 2007), *Nonfiction Mentor Texts: Teaching Informational Writing Through Children's Literature, K–8* (Stenhouse, 2009), and *Poetry Mentor Texts: Making Reading and Writing Connections, K–8* (Stenhouse, 2012). She often facilitates staff development workshops and loves to present at local, state, and national conferences. Lynne lives in Pennsylvania with her husband and three Welsh corgis and spends the summer months on Long Beach Island in New Jersey.

 Rose Cappelli is a literacy consultant and serves as a teacher consultant for the Pennsylvania Writing & Literature Project at West Chester University in West Chester, Pennsylvania, USA. She worked as a classroom teacher and reading specialist for more than 30 years. Rose is a coauthor of *Mentor Texts: Teaching Writing Through Children's Literature, K–6* (Stenhouse, 2007), *Nonfiction Mentor Texts: Teaching Informational Writing Through Children's Literature, K–8* (Stenhouse, 2009), and *Poetry Mentor Texts: Making Reading and Writing Connections, K–8* (Stenhouse, 2012). Rose lives in Malvern, Pennsylvania, with her husband. In addition to reading and writing, she enjoys gardening and golfing.

CHAPTER 4

Vision and Choice in the K–3 Writing Workshop

Matt Glover, *Author/Consultant*

As a first grader, Andrew was relatively new to writing workshop. Each day throughout the year, he had opportunities to make books and to make key choices in how to make books. Late in the year, Andrew created *How to Make a Book* (see Figure 4.1).

In his book, Andrew shows much of what he had learned about book making. In addition to realizing that there has to be content (starting with the pages he advises), he shows us that he knows features of books by including a glossary. He solves problems as he writes by using a sticky note to add text to the bottom of a page when he runs out of space. He names various crafting techniques a writer might use, such as bold-faced words and speech bubbles, and uses them in his book. The illustration on the second page shows him hard at work on a book (notice the stack of pages he's finished), and some of his other illustrations show what he's illustrating (a knight and a princess). Andrew even knows how to create a bit of suspense, as we can tell when he writes on one page, "Oh don't forget the best part of every single book is the.............get redy for it!" and then ends the suspense on the next page with, "HAPY ENDING!"

As you read his book, you get the sense that Andrew enjoys writing. His bold-faced print, words written in all capitals, and use of ellipses almost command the reader to pay attention and share in his enthusiasm for all he has learned about composing a picture book.

In this chapter, I focus on two of the underlying instructional decisions that influenced Andrew as a young writer: vision and choice. Throughout the year, his teacher has been using picture books in writing workshop, so students have also been making picture books. Andrew's teacher has helped

Write Now! Empowering Writers in Today's K–6 Classroom, edited by Kathy Ganske.
© 2014 by the International Reading Association.

Figure 4.1. Andrew's Book *How to Make a Book*

How to make a book

writin and illustrated by Andrew

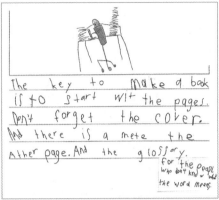

The key to make a book is to start wit the pages. Don't forget the cover. And there is a mete the Ather page. And the glossory.

for the peopl who don't know what the word meons.

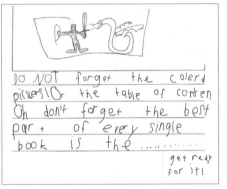

DO NOT forget the colerd picters! Or the table of conten. Oh don't forget the best part of every single book is the...........

get redy for it!

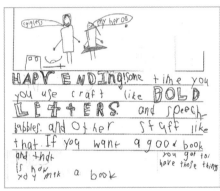

coigless my her oll

HAPY ENDING!some time you you use craft like BOLD LETTERS. and speech babbles. and Other staff like that. If you want a good book and that is how xd y mek a book

you got to have those thing

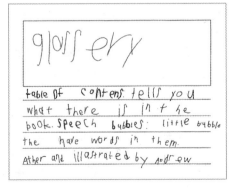

glossery

table of contens tells you what there is in t he book. Speech bubbles: little babble the have words in them. Ather and illastrated by Andrew

him learn ways to study a stack of picture books and learn from mentor authors how to write well. Because of his strong familiarity with books, Andrew has an understanding and vision for what it means to create a book.

What's as important but slightly trickier to see is the issue of choice. As in most units of study, for this piece of writing, Andrew had the opportunity to choose his topic. In other units, he also had the opportunity to choose which genre would best fit his audience and purpose. Learning to study a stack of mentor texts and find good topics has empowered Andrew and strengthened his image of himself as a writer.

Vision and choice aren't new ideas. Writing experts such as Katie Wood Ray (2004, 2006), Penny Kittle (2008), Ralph Fletcher (1993), and Carl Anderson (2000) have been talking about these ideas for years. They know that a key way that young writers learn is to study what other authors do. They know that choice increases students' ownership and engagement. Yet, increasingly in today's classrooms, I see students who are engaging in types of writing for which they have no vision. I see students who are writing to prompts, and students who go through year after year of writing instruction without ever having the opportunity to choose their topics or genre. But in the educational environment that we live in, it appears that some schools interpret high standards to mean conformity in instruction, and strive to have all students learn the same thing on the same day at the same time. This often leads to students engaging in formulaic writing that only exists in the world of school, often with little authentic choice, rather than seeing how standards can encourage authentic writing. So, while the ideas of vision and choice aren't new, they are more important than ever as we consider how to support young writers.

Using Mentor Texts: The Importance of Vision

In writing workshops that nurture students like Andrew, teachers use mentor texts (real-world pieces of published writing). Even though there is a long tradition of mentor texts in writing workshop, in classrooms I work in across the country, I often see several common issues. I sometimes see teachers who aren't using mentor texts, and students who don't connect the writing that they are doing to published writing. I also see teachers who use one or two mentor texts but do not provide enough examples to help students inquire deeply enough into how writers produce a type of writing to be able to try those techniques on their own. I also see classrooms where teachers have a misalignment between their mentor texts and what students are writing. In each of these situations, without effective use of mentor texts, it is difficult for a teacher to support students' ability to notice what authors do and then try it out in their own writing.

Some Terms to Consider

Before we look at the advantages of having a stack of mentor texts, I want to clarify how we'll think about mentor texts and mentor authors in this chapter. There are three different mentors that teachers can use in writing workshop. Teachers and students can study published authors and the writing they create. Teachers can also act as mentors by sharing their own writing. Additionally, students can become the mentor when teachers, or the students themselves, share student writing. Any writer you learn from is a mentor, but for the purpose of this chapter, our focus will be on published authors and their writing.

I'll also refer to a *stack* of mentor texts. A stack of texts basically represents the 5–10 books that a teacher decides to use in a unit of study. Sometimes teachers call this a set or a collection of books, but for me, a set starts to sound like a prepackaged set of books that comes with a unit. Although resources like that are helpful to have, teachers are the ones who ultimately need to decide which books to put in their stack. Teachers, not program writers, should decide which mentor texts to use. Ray has talked about stacks of texts for years, and the word *stack* seems to fit best. For me, it creates an image of a teacher sitting on the floor of a library, pulling books off the shelf, and deciding which ones to put in his or her stack for that unit. Whether we call it a stack, a set, or a collection, there are advantages to using examples published in the real world of writing to help students learn what authors do.

Finally, the use of the word *make* is also intentional. As Ray (2004) says, writing workshop is "a happy place where we make stuff" (p. 1). The word *make* implies so much more than just writing. It refers to the entire composition of a piece of writing, pictures and words included. It conveys the project-like sense of creating something rather than just writing. Whether students are making a book, an article, or a poem, they use all they know about composing to create a piece of writing for others to read.

Helping Students Develop a Vision for What They Will Make

Considering that studying a stack of published mentor texts can provide students with a clear vision for what they're going to create, one of the fundamental questions in the teaching at any grade becomes, What are students reading or studying that's similar to what they're going to write? (Ray, 2006). There are two important parts of that question. The first part, "what are students reading or studying," refers to what's in your stack of real-world samples of writing. The second part, "that's similar to what they're are going to write," is just as important. It's not enough to study a stack of mentor texts if students aren't making the same thing. Students need to be making the same thing that they're studying (or studying the same thing that they're making) to maximize the impact of the stack.

What do students have the most vision for in preschool through second grade? Picture books. Ray (2004) examines the importance of making picture books in *About the Authors: Writing Workshop With Our Youngest Writers*, and others have built on this idea over time. Primary-grade teachers read picture books frequently and, in the process, help students discover what authors do so these young writers have a clear vision for making picture books. Picture books, whether narrative or informational, answer both parts of the question. Therefore, the main type of writing that primary-grade students would be making throughout the year would be picture books.

Teachers sometimes assume that students graduate out of picture books when they're in first or second grade, but the issue isn't one of graduating out of these types of books. I know many fourth and fifth graders who make extremely complex picture books as part of a study of historical fiction or biographies. The question isn't when students should graduate out of picture books but when your stack of texts should change.

Often, that stack changes in third grade. Grade 3 is when teachers often start using types of writing such as feature articles, short stories of realistic fiction from children's magazines, or short stories from a collection of memoirs. Third graders can make picture books and often do so early in the year, but usually they have a different stack of mentor texts and produce pieces of writing based on that stack. For example, if students are studying realistic fiction, teachers might use short stories from *Highlights* and *Boys' Life*. *Ranger Rick* and *National Geographic Kids* would be great sources for a unit on feature articles, and memoir collections such as *Marshfield*

Dreams: When I Was a Kid by Ralph Fletcher or *Knucklehead* by Jon Scieszka for writing life stories. If students are studying commentary, they can study commentaries from newspapers and magazines. Dorfman and Cappelli offer additional mentor text ideas in their chapter in this volume.

Having a stack of texts other than picture books might happen in first or second grade as well. If second graders are studying reviews, for example, then they need a stack of published reviews to study. Second graders might also study, and then make, feature articles. But in grades K–2, the stack is most often picture books, with students using text and pictures to compose their own.

When teachers start thinking about having students make picture books, some natural questions arise. Figure 4.2 gives some practical tips regarding the logistics of book making.

Regardless of how appropriate the mentor texts are in the stack, just having and reading a stack isn't enough. For a stack to influence their

Figure 4.2. Practical Book-Making Tips

When teachers decide to start having students make picture books, there are some questions that pop up. Here are some quick practical thoughts on the logistics of book making.

1. *Number of pages:* At the beginning of the year, I start the students off with four to six sheets of paper each. Some teachers start with three-page books because they want students to write a story that has a beginning, a middle, and an end. As you'll see later, I'm not recommending that students start with any particular genre, so I don't need three pages for a story. Also, even later in the year when we study stories, three pages won't be enough because we'll want more than one page for the middle.

2. *Loose paper or prestapled:* I prestaple the books, at least at the beginning of the year, because I want to give students something that looks like a book. It doesn't make sense to a student if we say, "Go make a book. Here's one sheet of paper." It's also easier for many students to receive a prestapled book than to say, "Go get the number of pages that you think you'll need, keep them organized, and then staple them when you're done." That's what you'll want young students to do eventually, but you don't have to start there.

3. *Paper size:* I use 8½ × 11 paper instead of paper folded in half. Kindergartners draw and write fairly big, and half-size paper isn't big enough. We want first and second graders to write a lot for each illustration, and half-size paper isn't big enough for an illustration and a lot of writing. So, we just go ahead and use full-sized paper right from the beginning and on up through the grades.

writing, students must know how to study the stack. They need to know how to read like a writer.

Reading Like a Writer

Another benefit of studying with students those craft moves that an author makes to create a text is that it strengthens a student's self-image as a writer. Students should see themselves as creating the same type of writing as published authors. Basically, we want them to be like 4-year-old Molly. I've shared this story numerous times with teachers because it's still my best example of a student having a strong self-image as a writer:

One day, I was in Molly's preschool class reading the book *Silly Sally* by Audrey Wood. We were talking about how Wood uses pictures and words in her book. After a while, Molly said, "That Audrey Wood, she's just like me." What Molly was essentially saying was, "Yeah, Eric Carle, Donald Crews, me, Audrey Wood—we all do the same thing. We all make picture books." Molly saw herself as no different from Carle or Wood. That's the image that we want all students to have. We want third graders to say, "Ralph Fletcher, Jon Scieszka, me—we all write memoirs."

Having an image of yourself as a writer is crucial because as soon as you see yourself engaging in the same process that published authors use, you start to read that type of writing differently. As soon as you know that you are going to make a picture book, for example, you read picture books differently. You start to read like a writer.

Here's a quick example of this: Not too long ago, I was asked to write a blurb for the back cover of a friend's book. I thought it would be easy. Blurbs are short, and I've read a lot of blurbs in my life, so no problem. I sat down one day to write the blurb and was quickly stuck. I found that I had no idea how to write a blurb. The problem was that even though I had read a lot of blurbs in my life, I had only read them like a reader. When I read a blurb on the back of a book, I was only interested in what it said about the book. I didn't pay attention at all to how it was written.

So, now that I was stuck, what did I do? I pulled a bunch of books off my shelf, turned them over, and basically created a stack of blurbs to study. This time, I didn't read them like a reader. Instead, I read them like a writer, like someone who was going to write his own blurb. I didn't care at all about what was said about the books. All I cared about was how the blurbs were written. Did they mention the title of the book? Were they written in first person? How formal or casual was the voice? After studying my stack of blurbs, I could more easily write my own.

Having the ability to study a stack of texts to figure out how to write one's own texts is a lifelong skill in being a writer. Over the past several years, I've heard or read numerous interviews of authors who were asked some version of the question, What advice would you give to writers who are just starting out? Invariably, they answer that they would have them read and read and read. If teachers actively support students in developing the ability to study what published authors do, the students will thereafter have a skill that they can use anytime that they're presented with a new writing challenge.

When students have a stack, an opportunity to study the stack, and a teacher as a guide, their abilities as writers increase. Here are four ways teachers often use mentor texts to support their young writers:

1. *Designing a unit of study:* When teachers are designing or projecting a unit of study in writing workshop (Glover & Berry, 2012), the starting point is usually to gather and study their stack of mentor texts for teaching possibilities. These potential teaching points are sources for what will be taught in minilessons and conferences throughout the unit.

2. *Immersion:* Most units of study start with immersing students in the stack of texts. Over the first few days of the unit, teachers and students do the work of writers by inquiring into the craft and techniques that the authors used to create the texts. Teachers model their noticing of what authors do, and support students in noticing on their own.

3. *Minilessons:* Many minilessons start with helping students notice a particular technique that an author has used and then consider and practice how they can try this out in their own writing.

4. *Conferring:* In writing conferences, the goal is to help students become better writers rather than just fixing writing. One effective strategy is to have several mentor texts on hand during conferences so you can use them to show students what an author did, and to help them understand how they can try it out on their own.

Teaching students to have a vision for what they're making and to read like a writer increases their compositional thinking. When we add choice to the mix, students' engagement and energy for writing increase as well.

Choice

The issue of choice impacts our energy and motivation throughout our lives. The things we choose to do reflect our interests and passions. Although children and adults often have to engage in tasks that they have no choice over, the choices they *do* make reveal significant information about their motivations and interests. Although students make numerous different choices when writing, choice of topic and genre in particular affects their energy and motivation for writing. Let's look at choice of topic first.

Choice of Topic: Almost Always

There are two main reasons why it is important for students to choose their own topics. One is that the ability to choose your topic has an impact on your motivation and energy for writing. Students will write with more stamina when they have a topic that they care about. Think of it like this: If someone were to ask you right now to spend the next 30 minutes writing, none of you would choose a topic that you don't like. None of you would say, "I really want to write about my daughter, but instead I'll write about baseball." What would be the thought process behind choosing a topic you don't like? It's true for adults, and it's also true for children. Essentially, if we give students topics, we're communicating that topic doesn't matter and that they will have equal levels of energy regardless of the topic (Ray & Glover, 2008). When students have choice of topic, and especially when they find topics that they care deeply about, their energy for writing increases.

The second reason why we want to consider giving students choice of topic is that the ability to find good topics is an important skill in being a writer. Students don't learn how to find topics by having teachers give them one. Like any skill, to become proficient at it, you need practice. Students need self-images as individuals who can generate topics and who have ideas that are worth writing about. If we give students topics all the time, we're essentially saying that they can't find topics on their own.

Of course, there are instances when teachers must assign a topic or prompt. For example, some state or district assessments require students to write to a prompt. It would be unfair if a student's first experience with a prompt were on a high-stakes assessment. It would be just as unfair to give students a steady diet of prompt writing, never allowing them to develop the skill of finding good topics. Rather than constantly giving students prompts, we can teach them how to write to a prompt when needed. Teachers do this by teaching students how to identify what type of writing the prompt is asking for and then to think about what all they know about that type of writing. For example, if the prompt asks students to write about a time when they were excited, they need to be able to tell that the prompt is asking them to write a story. Students then have to think about what they know about good story writing. If they can already write well, they can handle prompt writing.

Another reason why teachers might limit topic choice is to integrate writing and a content area. For example, a first-grade teacher might want his or her students to write informational books about animals because they are doing research and learning about animals in science. It makes sense that if students are already thinking and talking about particular animals, students will be interested in writing about those animals. This can also help the teacher see what the students have learned about the animals. Therefore, limiting the topic in this situation makes sense. However, even in situations like these, teachers can provide a degree of choice. Allowing students to choose which animal to write about or to determine the focus for what they want their readers to learn about the animal still allows for a degree of choice, even though the topic is limited. Authentic choices provide students with greater ownership over their writing, so teachers should allow for as much choice as possible and also teach students strategies for finding good topics.

There is a caution with narrowing the range of topics when integrating with a content area. It is important for the teacher to decide when during the unit students will write about a predetermined topic. For instance, it is important that students know how to write the genre of informational text. Their learning of this can happen with topics of choice, although topic limits may be used for portions of the study. For example, I recommend that students' first several books in an informational writing unit be made on topics of their choice. Their first books can be about football or dancing or dogs or any other topic that they know about and are interested in. Then, toward the end of the unit, they may write their books about a more limited topic, such as an animal of their choosing. By contrast, if a student is writing about penguins (something the student may not know very much about) in a new genre (informational writing, which the student may not know very much about either), then we are asking the writer to do two new things at once. Instead, if we save the animal book for the last two weeks of the unit, at which point the students will know much more about informational writing, then their animal books will be easier to write and written at a higher level and will show more of what they know about informational writing.

Barriers to Choice of Topic

When I talk with teachers about choice of topic, one of the questions that usually comes up is, What about students who write about the same thing over and over and over again? Often, the topic is one that might not be the teacher's favorite, such as video games or superheroes, but sometimes it's just students who write over and over about their family or their dog.

I'm not overly concerned about students who have a favorite topic that they write about over and over. First, I'm more concerned about students who have a hard time finding topics than the students who have favorite topics. Students are more likely to be self-directed and write with more stamina when they have a favorite topic, even if it's one that they've written about before.

Second, just because a student has written about this topic before doesn't mean that as the teacher, I've run out of things to teach the student. Let's say a 6-year-old boy loves writing about Star Wars. We would expect his 10th Star Wars book to be better than his fifth, which was better than his second. Because the chosen topic doesn't affect what you want students to learn, the topic in essence doesn't matter. For his next Star Wars book, I can teach him how to use dialogue. For the one after that, I can show him how to illustrate a setting. For yet another Star Wars book, I can show him how to use ending punctuation. There's always something new to teach a student, so the topic does not dictate what we can teach.

Third, even though the topic doesn't influence what I'm going to teach, genre does. So, when we're in a genre study, the student should be writing in that genre. For example, Paul loved writing about Pokémon. He had written tons of Pokémon stories in kindergarten, but when his class started a study of informational writing, Paul needed to write in that genre to show what he had learned. Unsurprisingly, his first informational topic was Pokémon. Paul had to think very differently in this new genre even though he had a familiar topic. He had to decide what sections he was going to include. He used labels and diagrams to teach about Pokémon. He even had a conclusion that read, "To learn more about Pokemon, read other Pokemon books in stores, now!" This new genre was actually easier for him to tackle with this favorite topic.

Finally, we can help students choose new topics without banning their favorite topic. I can imagine that I might get to the point when I would say, "OK, Paul, 43 Pokémon books is enough. Let's try something else." But as soon as I took away his favorite topic, I'd run the risk of decreasing Paul's energy for writing. Instead, I'd use every strategy I have for helping him choose a new topic.

Another barrier that teachers often encounter is the student who can't find a topic. I sometimes hear from teachers, "My students can't find topics, so I have to give them one." When else in students' lives at school do we just do the work for them? If a student said that he or she didn't know how to do a math problem, the teacher's response wouldn't be to do the problem for the student. Instead, the teacher would teach a strategy or process for solving the problem. The response should be the same when a student can't find a topic.

Here are some quick strategies for helping students find topics:

- *Find topics outside of writing workshop:* For many teachers, it's more difficult to help a student find a topic when the clock is ticking during a writing conference. It's often much easier to find a topic during conversations at other times of the day. When a student arrives in the morning, or as we're talking with that student on the way to lunch, we can look for writing topics. We should be able to say 20 times a week, "You could write a book about that." They obviously won't write about all the topics we suggest, but the more we suggest naturally, the more likely we are to find one that they will care about.

- *Consider instituting a unit of study on where writers get ideas:* Many primary-grade teachers implement this short unit early in the year. In this unit, teachers read picture books and talk about where the authors got their ideas for the books. The key is to talk about strategies rather than topics. For example, the class might read the author's note for *Roller Coaster* in which Marla Frazee talks about riding roller coasters with her family. On an "If You're Trying to Find a Topic" anchor chart for this unit, the teacher might write, "Think about things you like to do with your family." A strategy like that will be more helpful than recording on the chart the more limited idea, "You could write about roller coasters."

- *Talk with parents about their children's interests:* I'm often amazed when I find out that a student has an interest that I didn't know about, especially when I thought I knew the student well. The problem is that sometimes students don't think their topics are worthwhile or as interesting as the topics of the student sitting next to them who just got back from Disney World. We need to help students see their topics as worthwhile and interesting, even when they might not be our favorites.

Finally, teachers frequently ask about inappropriate topics. The issue, however, often isn't that the topic is inappropriate but how students write about that topic. I know teachers who have banned books about guns or war at school. Yet, the issue with these topics isn't so much the topics but how the student has written about them. For example, I recently worked with a first grader who was writing about the Vietnam War. He must live in front of the History Channel because he knew more about the war than I did. However, the way he was writing about this topic was very appropriate. He wrote about weapons and battles but not in a gross or gory way. It was all very factual, and I learned a lot. He took a topic that could have been written about inappropriately, and wrote about it in an appropriate way. Here's one way that I often explain this to students: "Other students in our class are going to read your book, so you have to write about it in a way that won't make anyone in our class feel uncomfortable." Saying it this way has the dual purpose of setting a guideline while helping young students realize that they are writing for an audience, not just themselves.

Choice of Genre: Sometimes

Teachers are generally more accustomed to thinking about choice of topic than choice of genre, but choice of genre affects energy for writing as much, or more, than choice of topic does. Children, like adults, have favorite, go-to genres.

Imagine that at your next faculty meeting, I asked everyone to write for the next 30 minutes. I know two things about what would happen: First, everyone would not choose the same genre. Someone would write a fictional story, whereas someone else would write a poem. There would be a wide range of genres chosen. The second thing I know is that no one would choose their least favorite genre. No one would say, "I want to write a story, but instead I'm going to write a how-to article." Everyone would choose their favorite, go-to genre.

Your coworkers would also write with more energy if we spent just a couple of minutes brainstorming different genres. They would hear their friends choosing different genres that they might not have considered on their own. In the same way that we can help adults and children find topics, we can also help them find genres.

Different students have different favorite genres, and all students don't have the same level of energy for the same genre. Some students are often more interested in informational writing, whereas others are much more interested in story writing. Even within a broad category like story, some students love fiction stories, while others want to write true stories that really happened to them.

The challenge becomes how to organize units of study so they take choice of genre into account. Each year, there are certain genres that students have to study. The Common Core State Standards detail the types of text that students have to write, but fortunately the Common Core doesn't prescribe what the genre has to be. For example, at each grade level, students are required to engage in some type of narrative writing, but it could be true stories, realistic fiction, or some other form in this category.

Even though there is some choice as to which genres to study, rarely will everyone in a class have the same level of energy for the same one. Because we know that there will already be plenty of genre studies, teachers will also want to consider units of study in writing workshop that allow for choice of genre, or, non-genre-specific units (see, e.g., Ganske's discussion of multigenre projects in Chapter 9 of this volume).

There are numerous non-genre-specific units that primary-grade teachers might engage students in. Before listing a number of possibilities, let's look at one unit and see how it could be non-genre specific.

Most kindergarten classes I know start the year with a unit on launching writing workshop, which can easily allow for choice of genre. The goals for a kindergarten launching unit are often focused on establishing the routines and procedures of writing workshop. Do students not know what to do when their pencil breaks? That's tomorrow's minilesson. Do they not know where to put their folder at the end of writing workshop? That's the next day's minilesson. Do they not know how to not interrupt the teacher when he or she is having a conference with someone else? That's a week's worth of minilessons.

Because the goals for this unit are to establish routines and to build stamina for writing, it will be easier for students to write for long periods of time if they choose their own genre. Because all students don't have the same level of energy for the same genre, we can maximize their energy by allowing them to choose their genre.

Sometimes teachers ask, "Don't students need to know about a genre before they can write in it?" On the first day of book making in kindergarten, I've never had a student ask, "What genre should I write in?" Students will start making books, and then we can see what type of books they're making. Even in upper grades, students often try out genres on their own that they have never been formally taught. I know numerous fifth graders (and live with one) who have notebooks full of their own songs even though they've never had a unit of study on song writing. However, just being familiar with a genre isn't enough to write it well. That's where genre studies come in, where teachers and students engage in deep study of genres and teachers support students in using the features of a genre.

Also, by not making this first unit genre specific, we can focus solely on the unit goal of working independently, or as Leah Mermelstein (2013) emphasizes, being self-directed. Then, later in the year when we're studying a genre, we can focus on the skills needed to write in that genre.

With advances in grade level, the balance of genre-specific and non-genre-specific units will shift to more and more genre studies. But even in fourth and fifth grades, teachers will want to consider having a unit or two that allows for choice of genre.

Table 4.1 shows some additional non-genre-specific studies that would be appropriate for the primary grades. Some are better earlier in the school year so students can use that skill throughout the year (e.g., finding topics on reading like a writer), whereas others might be better later in the year

Table 4.1. A Sample of Non-Genre-Specific Studies

• Where authors get ideas	• Reading like a writer	• Illustration study
• Genre overview	• Punctuation	• Conventions
• Text structure	• Author study	• Having better peer conferences

(Glover, 2009). Some studies are better for certain grades as well. For example, the hope is that by the time students are in third grade, they have been using strategies to find topics for several years and won't need a unit on where writers get ideas. But if they're having a hard time finding topics, they might need this unit.

Each of these studies (and there are others) has the potential to allow students to choose their own genre. Whether these units are genre specific or not is ultimately determined by the books that teachers put in their stack for the unit. For example, if a teacher puts only true stories in the stack for the "Where Writers Get Ideas" unit, then it basically becomes a story unit. But if the teacher includes books from a variety of different genres, then it opens up the possibility for students to choose their genre.

Recently, I was working with a school district to look at and coordinate their writing units of study across the years. On a large piece of chart paper, we listed by grade all of their units of study. We then looked across grades and units for trends and patterns. One of the most striking findings that the teachers saw was that in this district, students would go through seven years of school, kindergarten through sixth grade, without ever choosing their genre. The district's curriculum comprised more than 50 units of study, but they were all genre based. Students would go through seven years of school without ever practicing how to determine which genre would match their chosen audience and purpose.

The teachers and administrators in this district hadn't realized this. They each thought other grades had choice of genre. Once they realized that they inadvertently had only genre-specific units, they decided to act. Working with their district administrators, teachers revised their units to include at least one non-genre-specific unit in each grade, with more than one in the primary grades.

Organizational Choices

I'd also like to mention another choice: the organizational choices a student makes while composing. Think back to our example of students writing informational books about animals. I frequently see informational books in the primary grades, where basically every student book looks the same. For example, each book starts off with a table of contents. The first section introduces the animal. The second section tells what the animal eats, and then the third section tells where the animal lives. Next, there's a diagram of the animal followed by a section on how the animal moves. Everyone's book ends with fun facts about their animal and a glossary.

The question with this type of book is, What organizational decision did the student make while composing this book? One would argue that the student didn't make any decisions. The student didn't have to struggle with what the sections would be or how many sections to have, because those decisions were made for the student.

The struggle here is between product and process. If the teacher organizes the book for the student, the end product will be well organized. It should be; it was organized by the adult. If the student organizes the book, it won't be as well organized. It will look like it was organized by a 7-year-old (which it was). The student will learn much more about organizing by struggling with the book's organization. The teacher will have to decide where this balance between process and product will fall, based on the goals for the unit.

Conclusion

Ultimately, teachers are the ones who make important decisions about how writing instruction will unfold each day. What texts will the teacher put in the stack of texts? How will the teacher use the stack in minilessons and conferences? When will the teacher model noticing an author's crafting decisions, and when will students do the noticing? What choices will students make regarding topic? When during the year will students choose their genre?

The answers to these questions set the tone of writing workshop. Teachers, rather than program writers, are best equipped to make these decisions. The teacher is the only one who knows this particular class of students. The teacher is the only person present to see how students react and to make skillful, "in the moment" adjustments. Teaching embodies the art of noticing, analyzing, and deciding what action to take. Effective teaching requires skillful decision making. When teachers consider these questions in light of the importance of vision and choice, students will become more energized, thoughtful writers, just like Andrew.

REFERENCES

Anderson, C. (2000). *How's it going? A practical guide to conferring with student writers.* Portsmouth, NH: Heinemann.

Fletcher, R. (1993). *What a writer needs.* Portsmouth, NH: Heinemann.

Glover, M. (2009). *Engaging young writers, preschool–grade 1.* Portsmouth, NH: Heinemann.

Glover, M., & Berry, M.A. (2012). *Projecting possibilities for writers: The how, what and why of designing units of study, K–5.* Portsmouth, NH: Heinemann.

Kittle, P. (2008). *Write beside them: Risk, voice, and clarity in high school writing.* Portsmouth, NH: Heinemann.

Mermelstein, L. (2013). *Self-directed writers: The third essential element in the writing workshop.* Portsmouth, NH: Heinemann.

Ray, K.W. (with Cleaveland, L.B.). (2004). *About the authors: Writing workshop with our youngest writers.* Portsmouth, NH: Heinemann.

Ray, K.W. (2006). *Study driven: A framework for planning units of study in the writing workshop.* Portsmouth, NH: Heinemann.

Ray, K.W., & Glover, M. (2008). *Already ready: Nurturing writers in preschool and kindergarten.* Portsmouth, NH: Heinemann.

ABOUT THE AUTHOR

 Matt Glover is the author or coauthor of four books on teaching writing, including *Projecting Possibilities for Writers: The How, What, and Why of Designing Units of Study, K–5* (Heinemann, 2012), which supports teachers in designing units of study based on a stack of mentor texts. His other three books, all published by Heinemann, are *Engaging Young Writers: Preschool–Grade 1* (2009), *Already Ready: Nurturing Writers in Preschool and Kindergarten* (2008), and *Watch Katie and Matt…Sit Down and Teach Up* (2011), a video-enhanced e-book that includes video clips of writing conferences with young children. Matt is a frequent presenter at conferences and in school districts across the country on topics related to nurturing young writers and supporting students' intellectual growth and development. He has been an educator for more than 25 years, including 12 years as the principal and instructional leader of Creekside Early Childhood School in West Chester, Ohio, USA. Matt lives in Cincinnati, Ohio, with his wife and four children.

CHAPTER 5

Growing Writers
Teaching Argumentative Writing Through Evidence-Based Thinking

Carol Jago, *California Reading and Literature Project, University of California, Los Angeles*

Many teachers are wary of mandates requiring argumentative opinion writing in elementary school. Is it even developmentally appropriate? Before you respond, think about an 8-year-old you know who wants a puppy. Is that child not accomplished at compiling powerful evidence and unable to marshal ethos, logos, and pathos to make the case for a pet? It isn't that writing argumentatively is developmentally inappropriate but rather that we don't yet possess the pedagogical prowess to teach opinion writing.

Children have strong opinions. They care about endangered species, developments in bicycle helmet technology, and child labor in Pakistan. They want to learn more about topics that matter to them and are keen to assert their views. It's possible that by only inviting students to write imaginary stories or about their own experiences, we have shortchanged them. This is not to say that writing fictional and personal stories should be banished from the curriculum. But maybe past practices have overlooked a kind of writing that could engage those young writers who don't particularly like making up stories or writing about themselves.

This instructional shift shouldn't require choosing between creative writing and opinion writing. Students need practice in both. The elephant in the room is that students simply aren't doing much writing of any kind. According to survey data from the National Assessment of Educational Progress, 97% of fourth graders report spending three hours a week or less on writing assignments, about 15% of the time they spend playing video games (Rideout, Foehr, & Roberts, 2010). Most students don't write enough to learn to write well. Given the critical importance of writing for success in school and in life, students need to be writing every day for a range of purposes and audiences. As eloquently expressed in *The Neglected "R": The Need for a Writing Revolution*, a report by the National Commission on Writing in America's Schools and Colleges (2003),

> Developing fluency in writing has always been a fundamental aim of education, even if the promise has never been fully realized. In today's complex, high-technology world, the importance of writing as a fundamental organizing objective of education is no less valid or practical. Writing, properly understood, is thought on paper. Increasingly, in the information age, it is also thought on screen, a richly elaborated, logically connected amalgam of ideas, words, themes, images, and multimedia designs. Whether on paper or on screen, writing is an overlooked key to transforming learning in the United States. (p. 13)

If you need further evidence of the scope of the problem that the Common Core State Standards initiative is attempting to remedy, results of the National Assessment of Educational Progress from 1998 indicated that only 23% of students in grade 4 were "able to produce an organized response within the time allowed that shows an understanding of the writing task they have been assigned" (Greenwald, Persky, Campbell, & Mazzeo, 1999, p. 21). Proficient papers had to "include details that support and develop the main idea of the piece, and its form, content, and language should show that these students are aware of the audience they are expected to address" (p. 21). Barely 1% of fourth graders performed at an advanced level. Clearly, we want our students to write better.

Making the Shift to Evidence-Based Writing

For too long, the traditional curriculum has separated the teaching of writing from reading. Instruction began with an engaging prompt accompanied by encouragement of students to brainstorm ideas. Drafting, revising, and editing followed suit. What is missing from the familiar process is research. Without realizing it or consciously meaning to, we have been requiring students to find all the evidence they need for their argument on the hard drive between their ears. A better plan for helping students support their opinions is to require them to learn more about a subject before and as they write.

Unfortunately, the practice of writing off the top of one's head often reflected the kind of task that was being assessed on state writing exams. Persuasive prompts such as, "Should the school year be longer?" or "What is the best season?" became common because test developers felt they could only pose questions that all students possessed enough background knowledge to write about. This is about to change. Both the Smarter Balanced Assessment Consortium and the Partnership for Assessment of Readiness for College and Careers assessment systems, along with other "next generation" texts, include performance assessment tasks. These integrated reading and writing items require students to read a collection of texts, analyze those texts, synthesize the information, and posit a claim of their own that must be supported with evidence from the readings. It's a tall order. It is also dramatically different from the kind of prompt-driven writing that most elementary instructional materials prescribe.

Does this mean that students with poor reading skills will be doubly penalized as writers? Possibly. But it could also be argued that providing students with material to read on the subject that they have been asked to write about levels the playing field. No longer will students be disadvantaged by not having facts at their fingertips. Evidence-based writing tasks also discourage writers from making facts up for the sake of an argument.

For too long, we have offered many elementary students only lockstep, template-driven writing tasks. No wonder the resultant writing has been lackluster. Integrated reading and writing lessons on topics that matter to students have the potential to engage them in genuine inquiry. When there's an authentic purpose for the task, such as a letter to the principal, an article for the school newsletter, a missive to the mayor, or advice to kindergartners, students have a reason to revise.

Preparing the Ground for Argumentative Writing

One way to begin teaching opinion writing is with a bouquet of texts. Modeled after Common Core–aligned performance tasks, this approach assumes that the best test preparation is excellent instruction. Students who read extensively, write often, listen attentively, and speak thoughtfully about their ideas *every day* rarely find performance assessments daunting.

Students who are used to grappling with challenging texts have internalized the process for constructing an argument.

You'll want to gather a collection of readings around a compelling topic, such as the use of robots as helpers and companions, and have students read and discuss their emerging views on the subject. Consider including visual texts, data displays, and short videos along with informational readings in your "bouquet." For example, you could have students read this collection of texts in preparation for writing to the performance task in Figure 5.1.

Have students read and view these texts, stopping after each one to jot down their thoughts, share what they have written and thought with a partner, and bring their ideas about the benefits and potential problems with robot technology to the whole group. During this background knowledge building period, avoid encouraging students to take sides.

Figure 5.1. Sample Performance Task

Write an article for your school newsletter explaining why you think robots will help or hinder humans in the future. Support your claim with details from what you have read, viewed, and discussed with your classmates.

- *Video:* "Fujitsu's Cute Teddy-Bear Robot Shows What It Can Do" (https://www.youtube.com/watch?v=AwWeN1ARy74)
- *Video:* "ASIMO Robot Next-Generation Unveiled!" (https://www.youtube.com/watch?v=ReN2l816L8k)
- *Informational text:* Lee Ann Obringer and Jonathan Strickland's "How ASIMO Works" (science.howstuffworks.com/asimo.htm)
- *Wikipedia entry:* "ASIMO" (en.wikipedia.org/wiki/ASIMO)
- *News article:* Julien Hawthorne's "Touchdown! A Powerful Robot Called Curiosity Lands Safely on Mars and Begins to Explore the Planet" in *Time for Kids* (www.timeforkids.com/news/touchdown/43251)
- *Book review:* Jeffrey Young's "Programmed for Love" about Sherry Turkle's book *Alone Together: Why We Expect More From Technology and Less From Each Other*, which warns of the dangers of social technology (chronicle.com/article/Programmed-for-Love-The/125922/). Although written for an adult audience, Young's ideas are compelling to students. If you're doubtful, check out the opening sentences: "Imagine standing in front of a robot, gazing into its wide, plastic eyes, and falling in love. Your heart revs up, and you hope this Other—this humanoid machine—turns your way again, tilts its head in interest, likes you back." You might choose to read the article aloud to your students.

Although students are ultimately tasked with making a claim regarding the use of robots in the future, it is essential that students explore a topic before attempting to write about it.

Although high-stakes assessments do not allow for conversation among test takers, evidence-based discussion is essential for developing students' ability to construct an argument. Rather than starting out with a firm position and reading to search for evidence that supports their claim, we want students to see that although thoughtful opinion writers may have initial ideas about a topic and a tentative point of view, they are always open to new ideas and information that might cause them to rethink or refine their opinion. Additional excellent, reliable, and free sources of informational texts for students include *Time for Kids* (www.timeforkids.com), *Scholastic News for Your Classroom* (magazines.scholastic.com), and *National Geographic Kids* (kids.nationalgeographic.com/kids).

Another way to initiate a unit on opinion writing is to begin with a question. The best queries resist simple answers and invite research, for example:

- Why is it important to save water?
- What kind of person makes the best president?
- Should the rules of soccer/football/baseball be changed?
- What would your ideal play space look like?
- What time should children be required to go to bed?
- Should parents limit their children's time playing video games?
- What is the best book you've ever read?
- What can be done about bullying?
- What kind of animal makes the best pet?
- Why is it important to eat healthy food?

Although it may seem controlling, I find it more coherent to have the whole class reading, researching, discussing, and writing about the same topic rather than having individual students choose from a menu of questions. It has been my experience that students benefit greatly from one another's findings and, as a result, produce better papers overall. In order to introduce an element of choice into the work, you can have the class brainstorm a collection of possible topics and then help students come to a consensus on the one they'll be focusing on in their essays.

Sound writing instruction begins with reading and research. Too often, we ask students to take a position before they know much about the topic. Instead of decrying the pedestrian nature of your students' claims and evidence, consider designing a persuasive writing lesson around a collection of texts—informational, literary, visual, video—and inviting students to analyze these "readings" before deciding what it is they have to say about an issue.

Everything's an Argument

The next step in teaching argument is to help students understand what effective opinion writing looks like. Asserting one's views (e.g., I like it, I hate it, that's not fair) isn't enough. Writers need to craft a carefully argued position and support that opinion with substantial and persuasive evidence. A common misunderstanding about argumentative writing is that it must focus on an issue that one is either for or against with grounds for dispute. Not at all. As Andrea Lunsford, a professor of English at Stanford University, has been saying for years, everything's an argument. "All language, including the language of visual images, is persuasive, pointing in a direction and asking for a response" (Lunsford, Ruszkiewicz, & Walters, 2012, p. 12).

Persuasion is an attempt to influence the beliefs and behavior of others so they might see the world as we do. To accomplish this end, writers often appeal to emotion as well as logic. Using a historical example, following the Boston Massacre, Samuel Adams went to his good friend Paul Revere and asked the master engraver to create a plate portraying what happened on March 5, 1770 (see Figure 5.2). Sam and his fellow revolutionaries wanted to print and distribute the picture in leaflets and newspapers throughout the colonies. In order to help students understand how visual texts can be argumentative, invite them to do a close reading of the iconic image and to talk with a partner about what they notice, using the following questions:

1. Who are the bad guys in this picture? How can you tell?

2. Who are the victims? What evidence can you find in the picture to support your view? (You might need to remind students that the colonists actually incited the Boston Massacre.)

Figure 5.2. "The Bloody Massacre Perpetrated in King Street Boston on March 5th 1770 by a Party of the 29th Regt." by Paul Revere[a]

[a]Revere, P. (1770). The bloody massacre perpetrated in King Street Boston on March 5th 1770 by a party of the 29th Regt. [Engraving]. Retrieved from www.loc.gov/pictures/item/2008661777

3. What effect does the background architecture have on the engraving's message?

4. Do you think a puppy would really have been standing in the middle of the fight as the British soldiers' guns were going off? Why do you think Paul Revere included a dog in this picture?

The engraving is a piece of propaganda put out by Revolutionary leaders to persuade their compatriots to commit treason. As British citizens, many colonists were understandably reluctant to do so and needed to be persuaded. The image "argues" that British rule must be opposed. It is also longer on persuasion than it is on historical accuracy. A few of the details that Revere chose to manipulate include the dead man at the center of the fight. This was Crispus Attucks, a black man depicted as white, who was the first martyr of the American Revolution. Also, nothing in the picture suggests that the Boston Massacre took place at 9:00 on a cold winter night. Despite these inaccuracies, or possibly as a result of them, Revere's engraving energized anti-British sentiment and, in so doing, accomplished what it set out to do: persuade.

Helping students learn to write effective opinion pieces entails demonstrating for them the moves that writers and artists make when they set out to persuade, appealing to readers' hearts as well as their heads. Writers make conscious decisions about what to include as well as what to exclude. Have students talk about the choices they make as they construct an argument.

Argumentative Mentor Texts

Young readers are often long on experience with narrative text but short on exposure to persuasive texts. Karen Kaufman Orloff's (2004) picture book *I Wanna Iguana* is an ideal argumentative mentor text for young writers. The book includes a series of notes written by a child trying to persuade his mother to let him keep an iguana. Orloff (2010) also wrote *I Wanna New Room* about a boy who's tired of sharing his room. Another persuasive picture book is Lynne Cherry's (2000) *The Great Kapok Tree: A Tale of the Amazon Rain Forest*. With gorgeous illustrations and elegant language, she argues that all living things depend on one another, and therefore they need to be protected. A zanier persuasive mentor text featuring a truly unreliable narrator is *The True Story of the 3 Little Pigs!* by Jon Scieszka (1996). In this retelling of the classic tale, Alexander T. Wolf—in prison for his alleged crimes against little pigs—makes the claim that he has been framed and was simply in the wrong place at the wrong time. Have students identify the wolf's support for his claim and invite them to take a critical stance toward his "evidence."

For fifth- and sixth-grade readers, Jim Murphy and Alison Blank's (2012) *Invincible Microbe: Tuberculosis and the Never-Ending Search for a Cure* argues that despite the best efforts of doctors and scientists, tuberculosis continues to plague and panic the human race. The authors offer fascinating evidence, from tuberculosis scars on Egyptian mummies to the globe's current battle with drug-resistant strains, to support their claim that the mighty microbe has yet to be defeated. Other nonfiction books for upper elementary students that are examples of powerful claims supported by convincing and compelling evidence include the following:

- *Moonbird: A Year on the Wind With the Great Survivor B95* by Phillip Hoose
- *We've Got a Job: The 1963 Birmingham Children's March* by Cynthia Levinson
- *The Dust Bowl Through the Lens: How Photography Revealed and Helped Remedy a National Disaster* by Martin W. Sandler
- *Bomb: The Race to Build—and Steal—the World's Most Dangerous Weapon* by Steve Sheinkin

The shift to include more nonfiction in our classrooms has sometimes been characterized as a death knell for children's literature. But how can students learn to write persuasively without exposure to first-rate argumentative texts? Mentor argumentative texts make excellent vehicles for demonstrating the moves that writers make as they construct a persuasive argument.

Constructing an Argument

Once young writers have explored a topic thoroughly, it's time for them to stake a claim. In the Common Core State Standards (National Governors Association Center for Best Practices & Council of Chief State School Officers, 2010), the term *claim* replaces *thesis*. I am hoping that this more transparent expression will take some of the mystery out of what we need students to do when constructing an argument. One of the most common organizational structures for arranging an argument so it unfolds naturally and persuasively is the Toulmin method (e.g., see Weida & Stolley, 2014). Kids can do this kind of complex thinking. The structure of effective argumentation is the same whether one is making the claim that zoos should be outlawed or crafting a philosophical treatise. The following Toulmin guidelines have been adapted for young writers:

Claim: The overall idea the writer will argue for

- Do you care about your idea enough to want to write about it?
- Is your claim debatable? Might some people feel otherwise about this subject?
- Is your claim clearly stated? Read it aloud to a partner and check that what you have written makes sense. If not, rewrite and check back with your partner.

Data: Evidence gathered to support the claim

- Do you have enough facts to support your claim?
- Are the sources of your evidence trustworthy?
- Are your sources varied? Personal experiences and stories can make strong supporting evidence, along with statistics and data.
- Should you do more research before beginning to write?
- How should you order your evidence? Is it better to cite the strongest piece of evidence first or last? Where would a personal anecdote be most effectively placed?

Warrant: Explanation of why or how the data support the claim; the underlying assumption that connects your data to your claim

- Turn to a partner and explain how the evidence you've gathered supports the claim you want to make. Write down what you just said to your partner. Does what you've written sound persuasive to you? Did it persuade your partner?
- Think of the warrant as a bridge between your claim and your evidence. It's like the glue that makes the evidence stick to the claim.
- Is any of the evidence difficult to connect to your claim? Should this fact be discarded in order to highlight examples that best support your argument? More isn't always better.

Counterclaim: A claim that negates or disagrees with the thesis/claim

- Why might someone disagree with what you claim?
- What evidence could someone arguing against your claim offer?

- Listing counterclaims demonstrates that you have researched and thought through what others have argued, and found their arguments to be shallow compared with your own superior reasoning.
- Don't be afraid of counterclaims. They often give you an opportunity to make your strongest points in rebuttal.

Rebuttal: Evidence that negates or disagrees with the counterclaim

- Answer the arguments posed by those who disagree with you. Explain why your supporting evidence overwhelms the counterclaim.
- Conclude with a restatement of your claim that demonstrates its importance. Ask yourself, Why does this matter?

Clearly, this kind of writing sets the bar extraordinarily high for students. It also has the potential to engage students in writing tasks that actually matter to them. By inviting students to take up an issue in their community, their school, or their lives, we demonstrate respect for students.

It is also time to stop telling kids, "Writing is fun!" Not because it can't be but because when we tell students that writing is fun, we put it in competition with pizza and video games. In that comparison, writing will always lose. Writing well is hard work and always will be. I want to help students experience the satisfaction that can come with having produced a strong piece of writing that contributes to a larger conversation and that maybe in some small way makes a difference in the world.

Citing Evidence (and Avoiding Plagiarism)

Did it surprise you to see a Wikipedia entry on my list of readings in the collection about robots? I believe teachers have erred in steering students away from this site as a source of information. An unintended consequence of our cautioning students regarding the unreliability of Wikipedia—a crowd-sourced, free-content encyclopedia supported by the Wikimedia Foundation—is that students are instead trusting Google, a for-profit search engine that is monetized through advertising. In her fascinating new book *It's Complicated: The Social Lives of Networked Teens*, danah boyd (2014; she spells her name without the caps) makes clear that "analyses have shown that Wikipedia's content is just as credible as, if not more reliable than, more traditional resources like *Encyclopedia Britannica*" (p. 187). She goes on to explain:

> Wikipedia can be a phenomenal educational tool, but few educators I met knew how to use it constructively. Unlike other sources of information, including encyclopedias and books by credible authors, the entire history of how users construct a Wikipedia entry is visible. By looking at the "history" of a page, a viewer can see when someone made edits, who did the editing, and what that user edited. By looking at the discussion, it's possible to read the debates that surround the edits. Wikipedia isn't simply a product of knowledge; it's also a record of the process by which people share and demonstrate knowledge. (pp. 188–189)

Teachers need to help students use resources critically, engaging them in a close reading of the provenance and possible biases in every text.

We also need to help students cite evidence. Kids are good at cutting and pasting quotations from a source into their papers, but that isn't the only way to cite evidence. There are three common ways to incorporate words and ideas from sources: direct quotation, paraphrase, and summary. The critical distinction between paraphrase and summary is that whereas a paraphrase offers all or almost all the information presented in the direct quotation recast in the student writer's own words, a summary focuses only on the main ideas in the passage. I use a short passage about robots by Lee Ann Obringer and Jonathan Strickland (2007) called "How ASIMO Works" to illustrate the distinctions:

- *Direct quotation:* Obringer and Strickland (2007) explain that "rather than building a robot that would be another toy, Honda wanted to create a robot that would be a **helper** for people—a robot to help around the house, help the elderly, or help someone confined to a wheelchair or bed. ASIMO is 4 feet 3 inches (1.3 meters) high, which is just the right height to look eye to eye with someone seated in a chair. This allows ASIMO to do the jobs it was created to do without being too big and menacing. Often referred to as looking like a 'kid wearing a spacesuit,' ASIMO's friendly appearance and nonthreatening size work well for the purposes Honda had in mind when creating it" (p. 1).
- *Paraphrase:* In "How ASIMO Works," Lee Ann Obringer and Jonathan Strickland (2007) describe how Honda set out to design

not a toy but a machine that could help people around the house or with tasks that became difficult for anyone whose movement was confined or constrained. The designers didn't want ASIMO to seem threatening, so they made it a height that would be right for looking at a sitting person in the eye. Engineers designed the robot to seem friendly. This design matched what Honda envisioned as the robot's potential use.

- *Summary:* In "How ASIMO Works," Lee Ann Obringer and Jonathan Strickland (2007) describe Honda's vision for the design of their robot ASIMO. Honda wanted to create a friendly machine that can help with tasks that humans need doing.

As students become increasingly comfortable with online environments for writing and discover the ease with which charts, graphs, and other data displays can be dropped into their papers, teachers will need to remind them of the critical importance of commentary. Writers cannot assume that readers automatically understand how the evidence offered supports the claim. Writers need to explain how the information presented contributes to their argument. Sometimes it's helpful to have students highlight their evidence in one colored marker and their commentary in another. Students often have an aha moment when they notice that they're missing the warrant or bridge between the evidence and the claim.

Conclusion

Although instructional materials for teaching writing typically make distinctions among the various types of writing—narrative, informative, and argumentative—in fact, most of the nonfiction we read conjures all three types at once. Artful essayists orchestrate narration, evidence, and appeals to emotion to lure readers in and to persuade them to think as the writer does. Often, a piece opens with an engaging anecdote. Then, the writer presents information about the subject: data, interviews, facts, and figures. All of this is preamble to the argument that, when finally presented, seems self-evident. The best opinion writers perform this dance with uncanny skill. I want students to possess this same skill.

The Common Core makes clear where students are going. It describes what today's students need to know and be able to do in order to thrive in postsecondary education and the workplace. By focusing on results (the destination) rather than the how (the means of transportation), the Common Core allows for a variety of teaching methods and many different classroom approaches. The challenge for teachers is to turn the daily journey toward this destination into an intellectual adventure. One way to think about the Common Core is as a kind of GPS device to situate curriculum. Although some students may choose the road less traveled, the objective is fixed. When students become lost through a wrong turning, teachers recalculate the route, providing a calm and confident voice that guides all students to academic achievement and deep literacy.

REFERENCES

boyd, d. (2014). *It's complicated: The social lives of networked teens.* New Haven, CT: Yale University Press.

Greenwald, E.A., Persky, H.R., Campbell, J.R., & Mazzeo, J. (with Jenkins, F., & Kaplan, B.). (1999). *NAEP 1998 writing report card for the nation and the states* (NCES 1999-462). Washington, DC: National Center for Education Statistics, Office of Educational Research and Improvement, U.S. Department of Education. Retrieved from nces.ed.gov/nationsreportcard/pdf/main1998/1999462.pdf

Lunsford, A.A., Ruszkiewicz, J.J., & Walters, K. (2012). *Everything's an argument with readings* (6th ed.). New York, NY: Bedford/St. Martin's.

National Commission on Writing in America's Schools and Colleges. (2003). *The neglected "R": The need for a writing revolution.* New York, NY: College Board.

National Governors Association Center for Best Practices & Council of Chief State School Officers. (2010). *Common Core State Standards for English language arts and literacy in history/social studies, science, and technical subjects.* Washington, DC: Authors.

Obringer, L.A., & Strickland, J. (2007, April 11). *How ASIMO works.* Retrieved from science.howstuffworks.com/asimo.htm

Rideout, V.J., Foehr, U.G., & Roberts, D.F. (2010). *Generation M²: Media in the lives of 8- to 18-year-olds.* Menlo Park, CA: Kaiser Family Foundation. Retrieved from kff.org/other/event/generation-m2-media-in-the-lives-of/

Weida, S., & Stolley, K. (2014). *Organizing your argument.* Retrieved from https://owl.english.purdue.edu/owl/resource/588/03/

Young, J.R. (2011, January 14). Programmed for love [Review of the book *Alone together: Why we expect more from technology and less from each other*, by S. Turkle]. *The Chronicle of Higher Education.* Retrieved from chronicle.com/article/Programmed-for-Love-The/125922/

CHILDREN'S AND YOUNG ADULT LITERATURE CITED

Cherry, L. (2000). *The great kapok tree: A tale of the Amazon rain forest.* New York, NY: Voyager.

Hawthorne, J. (2012, August 6). Touchdown! A powerful robot called Curiosity lands safely on Mars and begins to explore the planet. *Time for Kids*. Retrieved from www.timeforkids.com/news/touchdown/43251

Murphy, J., & Blank, A. (2012). *Invincible microbe: Tuberculosis and the never-ending search for a cure*. New York, NY: Clarion.

Orloff, K.K. (2004). *I wanna iguana*. New York, NY: G.P. Putnam's Sons.

Orloff, K.K. (2010). *I wanna new room*. New York, NY: G.P. Putnam's Sons.

Scieszka, J. (1996). *The true story of the 3 little pigs!* New York, NY: Puffin.

ART CITED

Revere, P. (1770). The bloody massacre perpetrated in King Street Boston on March 5th 1770 by a party of the 29th Regt. [Engraving]. Retrieved from www.loc.gov/pictures/item/2008661777

ABOUT THE AUTHOR

Carol Jago has taught for 32 years and is the associate director of the California Reading and Literature Project at the University of California, Los Angeles, USA. She served as the president of the National Council of Teachers of English (NCTE) and currently chairs the College Board's English Academic Advisory Committee. She has published six books with Heinemann, including *With Rigor for All: Meeting Common Core Standards for Reading Literature* (2nd ed., 2011). She has also published books on contemporary multicultural authors for the NCTE. Carol wrote an education column for the *Los Angeles Times*, and her essays have appeared in newspapers across the nation. She edits *California English*, the journal of the California Association of Teachers of English, and served on the National Assessment of Educational Progress's planning committees for the 2009 reading framework and the 2011 writing framework.

CHAPTER 6

Turning Broccoli Into Ice Cream Sundaes

Self-Regulated Strategy Development for Persuasive Writing Using Informational Text

Karen R. Harris, Steve Graham, Amber B. Chambers,
& Julia D. Houston, *Arizona State University*

Recently, a second grader excitedly told her mom (an English language arts coordinator for the district where her daughter attends school) that she now loves writing and is really good at it! The mother contacted her daughter's teacher and asked, "How did you turn writing, which used to be like broccoli in our home, into ice cream sundaes?" The teacher, delighted with the question, launched into a brief description of the writing "tricks" that she had taught her students after recent, intensive professional development in the self-regulated strategy development (SRSD) approach to teaching strategies for writing and self-regulation of the writing process (L. Laud, personal communication, February 4, 2014).

In this chapter, we share with you the SRSD approach to teaching writing, which has been used effectively in grades 2–12, as well as with adults. Although the strategies taught become progressively more sophisticated and complex across grades and development, the basic instructional methods remain the same. Here, we describe instruction with struggling fourth- and fifth-grade students who learned to write strong persuasive essays using informational text as a source.

Why We Need to Focus on Writing Instruction

Poor writing abilities make it difficult for students to effectively use writing as a tool for learning, communication, and self-expression. Writing about

Write Now! Empowering Writers in Today's K–6 Classroom, edited by Kathy Ganske.
© 2014 by the International Reading Association.

material read or presented in class enhances students' learning (Bangert-Drowns, Hurley, & Wilkinson, 2004; Graham & Hebert, 2010). Beyond the school years, good writing is also critical, as over 90% of white-collar workers and 80% of blue-collar workers report that writing is important to job success (National Commission on Writing for America's Families, Schools, and Colleges, 2006).

A major problem facing schools today is that the majority of students are not capable writers. On the National Assessment of Educational Progress in the United States (Salahu-Din, Persky, & Miller, 2008), only 33% of grade 8 and 24% of grade 12 students performed at or above the proficient level (defined as solid academic performance) in writing. Further, 55% of grade 8 and 58% of grade 12 students scored at or below the basic level, denoting only partial mastery of the writing skills needed at these grade levels. Other countries report similar challenges (Festas et al., in press).

Why are students facing such difficulties in learning to write? First, writing is challenging and typically must be developed across grades K–12 and into postsecondary employment or education. Skilled writing is complex, requiring extensive self-regulation of a flexible, goal-directed, problem-solving activity. In addition to basic skills, students must also develop knowledge and understandings about the writing process, genre knowledge, and strategies for writing and self-regulating the writing process (Bereiter & Scardamalia, 1987; Fitzgerald, 2013; Harris & Graham, 2009). The National Commission on Writing for America's Families, Schools, and Colleges (2006), however, reported that of the three Rs, writing has become the most neglected in classrooms; reading, math, and science have also received priority over writing in funding for research (Harris, Graham, Brindle, & Sandmel, 2009). Further, research indicates that the majority of teachers report inadequate pre- and inservice preparation in writing instruction and infrequently using evidence-based approaches to teaching writing. Finally, many of the major approaches to teaching writing used in schools today have been developed based on theoretical or paradigmatic stances and general research on learning and writing and lack a sound evidence base.

In the United States, concern about writing development is reflected in the new grade-level expectations for writing to meet the Common Core State Standards (National Governors Association Center for Best

Practices & Council of Chief State School Officers, 2010). The Standards focus on the acquisition of foundational writing skills, such as handwriting and spelling, as well as the following: (1) writing for multiple purposes (narrative, opinion/persuasive, informational/explanatory); (2) producing and publishing well-organized text that is appropriate to the task and the purpose by increasingly applying processes involving planning, revising, editing, and collaborating with others; (3) using writing to build knowledge about specific topics or materials read; and (4) applying writing to extend and facilitate learning in a range of discipline-specific subjects as well as across purposes and audiences.

A prominent emphasis in the Common Core is learning how to write logical, coherent, and compelling arguments. Opinion essays (based on one's own ideas and experiences) are emphasized in the early grades, with persuasive essays (using your own ideas and reading source material that can provide facts, details, and so forth) emphasized beginning in grade 4 (Graham, Harris, & Santangelo, in press). The Common Core specifies that fourth and fifth graders need to be able to use texts they've read to write persuasive essays that support a clearly presented position with logically ordered and linked reasons. These reasons should be backed by facts and details, and the essay should end with an effective conclusion. Further, Common Core requirements, such as reading text to assist in writing persuasive essays, underscore the need to develop reading and writing strategies that work together, because learning to write and writing to learn are critical across the school years and beyond (Harris & Graham, 2014). In this chapter, after providing the evidence base for SRSD, we share how to use SRSD instruction to teach students to do a close reading of informational text and then use what they have learned in writing a persuasive essay. Figure 6.1 includes an overview of the strategies that our fourth and fifth graders have learned to succeed at this task.

Developing Writers Who Meet Common Core Expectations: The Role of Evidence-Based Practices

Although the Common Core is far from perfect in the area of writing and changes will undoubtedly be needed (Graham et al., in press), it offers an orderly progression and road map for writing development across the grade

Figure 6.1. POW + TREE + TWA Mnemonic Chart

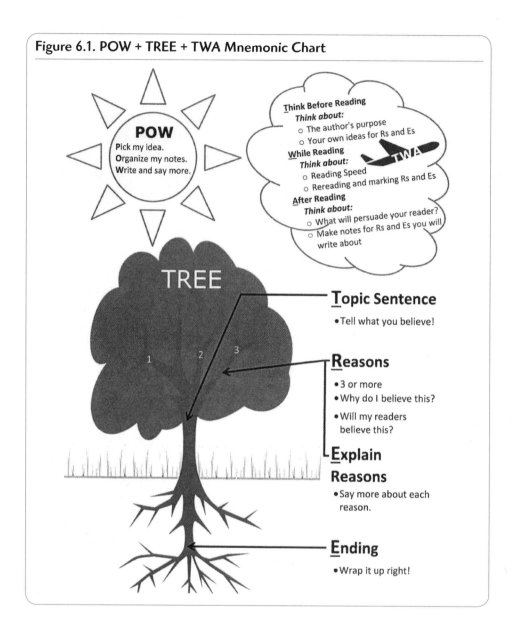

POW
Pick my idea.
Organize my notes.
Write and say more.

Think Before Reading
Think about:
o The author's purpose
o Your own ideas for Rs and Es
While Reading
Think about:
o Reading Speed
o Rereading and marking Rs and Es
After Reading
Think about:
o What will persuade your reader?
o Make notes for Rs and Es you will write about

TWA

TREE

Topic Sentence
• Tell what you believe!

Reasons
• 3 or more
• Why do I believe this?
• Will my readers believe this?

Explain Reasons
• Say more about each reason.

Ending
• Wrap it up right!

levels. This is a major advance and one we hope will contribute to better writing development. The Common Core is purposefully silent, however, about how these writing benchmarks are to be achieved. No guidance regarding how to teach writing is provided. We believe that using evidence-based approaches in teaching writing will make a critical difference, as will increasing the time and attention given to writing development (Graham et al., in press).

A large body of evidence-based practices for teaching writing now exists (as can be seen in Chapter 2 of this book), although more work is clearly needed. We focus in this chapter on one powerful evidence-based approach making a difference in students' writing development: SRSD. More than 100 studies of SRSD (including true experiments, quasi-experiments, and single-subject design studies) have been conducted across grades 2–12 and with adults (cf. Graham, Harris, & McKeown, 2013). These studies provide convincing evidence that SRSD is an effective method for teaching writing strategies to students who represent the full range of writing ability in a typical class, as well as struggling writers and students with writing and other disabilities. As Harris, Graham, and Adkins (2014) explain, SRSD has been used effectively with whole classes (Tier 1), small groups (Tier 2), and individual students (Tier 3).

SRSD for writing has been deemed an evidence-based practice in the Institute for Education Sciences' practice guide *Teaching Elementary School Students to Be Effective Writers* (Graham et al., 2012) and by a panel of independent researchers (Baker et al., 2009). SRSD received strong ratings from the National Center on Intensive Intervention and was identified as having the strongest impact of any strategies instruction approach in writing in *Writing Next: Effective Strategies to Improve Writing of Adolescents in Middle and High Schools*, commissioned by the Carnegie Corporation of New York (Graham & Perin, 2007). SRSD research has resulted in the development of writing strategies (with the assistance of teachers and their students) for multiple genres, including personal narratives, opinion and persuasive essays, report writing, expository essays, story writing, and state writing tests. SRSD research has also been conducted on the integration of reading and writing strategies to improve both reading and writing (Mason, Reid, & Hagaman, 2012).

SRSD in Writing: What and How

In this section, we provide an overview of the SRSD instructional model and process. First, we describe key characteristics critical to success with SRSD. Next, we outline the six stages in the SRSD instructional framework. Finally, we illustrate how SRSD was used to teach fourth- and fifth-grade students how to plan and write persuasive essays using informational text as required in the Common Core. Although we did this work with small groups of struggling writers in grades 4 and 5, the strategies taught have been validated with whole classes (see Harris et al., 2012, for further discussion of whole-class instruction and effective professional development for teachers). Our description of SRSD here must be brief. Interested readers, however, can find more detailed information about the instructional stages and process, a wide range of strategies, lesson plans, recommendations for evaluation, and other SRSD-related materials in the resources listed in Table 6.1.

Extensive research and practice indicate that six characteristics are essential to optimizing outcomes with SRSD; ignoring these critical

---

Table 6.1. Resources for Self-Regulated Strategy Development (SRSD)

Publications for Teachers

- Graham, S., & Harris, K.R. (2005). *Writing better: Effective strategies for teaching students with learning difficulties.* Baltimore, MD: Paul H. Brookes.
- Harris, K.R., & Graham, S. (1996). *Making the writing process work: Strategies for composition and self-regulation* (2nd ed.). Cambridge, MA: Brookline.
- Harris, K.R., Graham, S., Mason, L.H., & Friedlander, B. (2008). *Powerful writing strategies for all students.* Baltimore, MD: Paul H. Brookes.
- Mason, L.H., Reid, R., & Hagaman, J.L. (2012). *Building comprehension in adolescents: Powerful strategies for improving reading and writing in content areas.* Baltimore, MD: Paul H. Brookes.
- Sandmel, K.N., Brindle, M., Harris, K.R., Lane, K.L., Graham, S., Nackel, J., Mathias, R., & Little, A. (2009). Making it work: Differentiating Tier two self-regulated strategies development in writing in tandem with schoolwide positive behavioral support. *Teaching Exceptional Children, 42*(2), 22–33.

Web-Based and Other Resources

- A website devoted to teachers implementing SRSD will be launched in the fall of 2014 and hosted by Arizona State University.
- IRIS Center modules on SRSD and writing: iris.peabody.vanderbilt.edu
- Selected lesson plans and teaching materials from Project Write: kc.vanderbilt.edu/projectwrite
- This video shows SRSD being implemented in an elementary and a middle school classroom: Harris, K.R., Graham, S., & Deshler, D. (2002). *Teaching students with learning disabilities in the regular classroom* [DVD]. Alexandria, VA: Association for Supervision and Curriculum Development.
- Two nonprofit organizations are using a research-based approach to professional development in SRSD for teachers that has produced meaningful improvements in students' writing performance: Hill for Literacy (www.hillforliteracy.org) and thinkSRSD (www.thinksrsd.com).

characteristics can undermine SRSD instruction (cf. Harris et al., 2009). First, with SRSD, students are provided with supported, explicit instruction targeting (1) writing strategies for specific genres (e.g., persuasive essays); (2) general writing strategies (e.g., using powerful vocabulary, crafting engaging opening and closing sections); (3) self-regulation procedures that help manage the writing process and use of writing strategies (i.e., goal setting, self-monitoring, self-instructions, self-reinforcement); and (4) relevant declarative, conditional, and procedural knowledge (i.e., knowing what to do; how to do it; and when, where, and why to do it). The intensive and direct focus on developing writing processes and knowledge is a cornerstone of SRSD.

Second, many developing writers, especially those who experience difficulty with learning to write, also face affective and behavioral challenges in writing. Each of these is, therefore, addressed with SRSD. As part of this approach, teachers deliberately and repeatedly support students in their development of self-regulation, motivation, positive attitudes toward writing, and belief in themselves as capable writers. Numerous strategies are used to accomplish these goals. For instance, learning to write is an interactive, engaging, and collaborative process among teachers and students. Teachers initially provide the necessary level of scaffolding and support to ensure that students learn the targeted knowledge and strategies, but then gradually and purposefully release control for applying what is learned to the students. To help them overcome negative perceptions and attitudes toward writing, SRSD is embedded in an affirming and supportive instructional environment where writing is valued and prioritized. Examples of how teachers achieve this goal include the following:

- Projecting contagious enthusiasm during SRSD instruction
- Designing interesting, meaningful, and appropriately challenging writing projects
- Establishing a low-risk environment during writing time
- Making it clear to students how their effort and strategy use contribute to their writing development
- Providing frequent, constructive feedback
- Creating multiple opportunities for positive peer interactions and support

Third, SRSD instruction is individualized to optimize each student's writing development. Teachers use their knowledge of students' strengths and needs to differentiate both what and how they teach (see, e.g., Sandmel et al., 2009). For example, a teacher might modify a strategy to make it more complex for some students while initially simplifying it for others. Instruction is further individualized by having students establish personalized goals. The nature and frequency of support and feedback provided to students are also adjusted in response to their individual needs. When SRSD is used with an entire class, there are times when it is appropriate and beneficial for students to work together as a large group. At other times, teachers employ flexible grouping and have students work independently or with them in small groups, pairs, or individually (Harris et al., 2012, 2014).

Fourth, students move through SRSD instruction at their own pace. In other words, there is no preestablished, standardized timetable for moving through the SRSD instructional stages; rather, each student advances from one stage to the next when ready. Students are also provided with opportunities to revisit an earlier stage of instruction as needed. With this criterion-based approach, SRSD instruction ends for each student when he or she can independently apply and manage the targeted writing and self-regulation strategies successfully.

Fifth, multiple procedures that promote long-term maintenance (the desire and ability to continue using strategies after instruction ends) and generalization (appropriately and effectively applying strategies to other writing tasks and settings) are integrated throughout the stages of instruction. Here are some examples of how teachers facilitate maintenance and generalization:

- Helping students understand the purpose and benefits of using a strategy
- Providing booster sessions to review, discuss, and support strategy use as needed
- Facilitating students' critical consideration of when and how they should use a newly learned strategy and then evaluating these experiences
- Exploring how to adapt a strategy for different writing tasks and settings

- Creating a variety of peer support opportunities that target generalization and maintenance
- Bolstering strategy use through collaboration with other school professionals (e.g., other teachers, specialists) and family members

Finally, SRSD instruction should occur across genres and grade levels, allowing students to continue developing their use of writing and self-regulation strategies. Teachers lay the foundation for this developmental growth by helping students understand and appreciate the meaning and benefits of a particular strategy, along with its inherent limitations or weaknesses. Then, as students improve, they are provided with opportunities to refine and expand previously learned strategies, as well as learn new strategies that are aligned with evolving writing goals and tasks.

The SRSD Instructional Process

The framework for SRSD instruction consists of six instructional stages: (1) develop background knowledge, (2) discuss it (the strategies and writing process), (3) model it, (4) memorize it, (5) support it (gradual release of control), and (6) independent performance. A detailed outline is provided in Table 6.2. The six stages of SRSD instruction are a flexible set of guidelines intended to be thoughtfully combined, modified, and revisited in response to students' and teachers' needs. For example, stages 1 and 2 typically are integrated together in the early lessons rather than being taught as distinctly different lessons. Advanced writers at any grade level may need individualized instruction and more challenging goals and strategies, whereas we have learned that struggling writers need to be able to write a complete sentence (even if it is simple, e.g., "The dog ran.") in order for SRSD to be appropriate for them.

SRSD lessons typically last 20–45 minutes and occur three to five days a week, depending on the students and time available for instruction. The total time required for students to learn and independently use targeted writing and self-regulation strategies will, of course, vary; however, it often takes less time than teachers anticipate. With elementary-age students, 8–15 lessons conducted over four to eight weeks is often sufficient to reach independent performance when addressing a writing genre.

Table 6.2. Self-Regulated Strategy Development Stages of Instruction

Stages 1 and 2 are often combined in instruction; a stage or combination of stages may take several lessons to complete; Stages 3 and 5 typically take the most time in instruction; instruction is often recursive across stages, and students should progress across stages as they meet criteria for doing so.

1. Develop and Activate Knowledge Needed for Writing and Self-Regulation

- Read and discuss works in the genre being addressed (persuasive essays, reports, etc.) to develop declarative, procedural, and conditional knowledge (e.g., "What is an opinion?" "What are the parts of a persuasive essay, and are they all here?" "How do you think the author came up with this idea, and what would you do?" "What might the author have done to organize the ideas?" "What might the author do when he/she gets frustrated?"); appreciation of characteristics of effective writing (e.g., "How did the writer grab your interest?"); and other knowledge and understandings targeted for instruction. Continue development through stage 3 as needed until all key knowledge and understandings are clear.

- Discuss and explore both writing and self-regulation strategies to be learned; typically, begin development of self-regulation, introducing goal setting and age-appropriate means of self-monitoring (e.g., rocket graphs for elementary students, bar graphs for older students).

2. Discuss It (Discourse is critical!)

- Discuss students' current writing and self-regulation abilities, their attitudes and beliefs about writing, what they are saying to themselves as they write, and how these factors might help or hinder them as writers; emphasize the roles of both effort and learning powerful strategies in becoming a better writer.

- Graphing the number of genre-specific essay elements and other targeted goals included in pretest or prior essays may be done; this will assist with goal setting (graphing prior writing can be skipped or done during a later stage if students are likely to react negatively).

- Further discuss writing and self-regulation strategies to be learned: purposes, benefits, and how and when they can be used or might be inappropriate (begin generalization support).

- Introduce a graphic organizer for the writing genre and task being addressed.

- Analyze good, grade-appropriate model papers, taking notes from these papers on the graphic organizer to assist students in learning to make notes.

- Analyze poor essay models, take notes on a graphic organizer for a better essay, and write this essay collaboratively.

- Establish students' commitment to learning strategies and acting as collaborative partners; establish the roles of student effort and strategy use in becoming an effective writer.

(continued)

Table 6.2. Self-Regulated Strategy Development Stages of Instruction (*Continued*)

3. Model It

- Use interactive teacher modeling and/or collaborative modeling of writing and self-regulation strategies (including self-statements).
- Analyze and discuss strategies and the model's performance; make changes as needed.
- Students develop and record personal self-statements to assist them when writing.
- Model self-assessment and self-recording through graphing of modeled, collaboratively written compositions.
- Promote student development of self-regulation strategies across other tasks and situations; discuss use in other settings (generalization support).

4. Memorize It

- Although begun in earlier stages, require and confirm memorization of strategies, the meaning and importance of each step in each strategy, any mnemonics, and self-instructions as appropriate.
- Continue to confirm and support memorization in following stages, making sure students have memorized the mnemonics, what they mean, and the importance of each step before stage 6.

5. Support It

- Teachers and students use writing and self-regulation strategies collaboratively to achieve success in composing, using prompts such as strategy charts, personal self-statements sheets, word lists (e.g., linking words, "million dollar words"/effective vocabulary), and graphic organizers.
- Challenging initial goals for genre elements and characteristics of writing are established collaboratively with students and individualized as needed; criterion levels are increased gradually until final goals are met.
- Prompts, guidance, and collaboration are faded individually (e.g., graphic organizer replaced with student creating mnemonic on scratch paper) until the student can compose successfully alone.
- Self-regulation components (goal setting, self-instructions, self-monitoring, and self-reinforcement) are all being used by this stage; additional forms of self-regulation, such as managing the writing environment and using imagery, may be introduced.
- Discuss plans for maintenance; continue support of generalization.

6. Independent Performance

- Students are able to use writing and self-regulation strategies independently; teachers monitor and support/enhance as needed.
- Fading of overt self-regulation may begin (e.g., graphing may be discontinued, self-statements sheets may not be out during writing).
- Plans for maintenance and generalization continue to be discussed and implemented.

SRSD for POW + TREE + TWA

Here, we present a brief description of how Chambers and Houston (the third and fourth authors of this chapter) recently taught small groups of fourth- and fifth-grade students to write persuasive essays using informational source text, as required by the Common Core. Each group consisted of three students; each student scored below the 25th percentile on a normed writing test but was able to write complete sentences when given a pretest. These students wrote strongly improved persuasive essays using source text after SRSD instruction, as we will illustrate.

It is unusual to ask fourth and fifth graders to write persuasive essays using source text. Typically, students in grades 2–5 have worked on writing opinion essays in which they take a stand on a topic, provide reasons and elaborations of these reasons in support of their opinion, and finish with a strong ending. They write these essays without source text, using their own ideas and experiences. A large body of research indicates that using SRSD to teach strategies referred to as POW + TREE has been very successful for teaching second through fifth graders to write opinion essays. POW (pick an idea, organize notes, and write and say more) guides students through the writing process and makes them a "POWerful" writer. TREE (topic sentence [Tell what I believe.], reasons [three or more; Why do I believe this? Will my readers believe this?], explain reasons [Say more about each reason to help convince your reader.], and ending [Wrap it up right!]) assists students in making and organizing notes for persuasive writing.

SRSD with other, more complex strategies for persuasive writing has been successful with middle and high school students (Harris et al., 2008; Mason, Davison, Hammer, Miller, & Glutting, 2013). These strategies for middle and high school students require both close reading of text and refuting opposing positions. We believed these strategies to be too difficult for struggling fourth- and fifth-grade writers. Because POW + TREE does not incorporate use of source text, we turned to another validated strategy for close reading of text referred to as TWA (think before reading, while reading, and after reading; Mason et al., 2013) and modified it to work for fourth and fifth graders in conjunction with POW + TREE. The resulting SRSD instruction for POW + TREE + TWA (see Figure 6.1) is described next. (Sample lesson plans and additional materials will be posted on the SRSD website mentioned in Table 6.1 when it launches.)

Prior to instruction, we read an informational text on being fit aloud with the students and then asked them to write a pretest essay responding to the following prompt: "Write an essay to your classmates persuading them to be fit kids." This pretest essay was written by a 9-year-old fourth grader named Avery and was typical of these students' essays (spelling is corrected):

> You should get fit because you will be fat unless you eat healthy foods. If you are not fit you might not be able to play sports. If you don't like sports, it is OK, you don't have to play sports. People play sports to get fit. It helps them lose weight faster. You should work out for 1 hour because you will be in shape. If you don't have money to go the gym, it is OK just run around the block or walk your dog. When you're done doing all of that go outside and just sit in the front of your house for now. If you have any questions for me, just ask me. Thank you for reading my story. Hope you enjoyed. Go outside. Don't play games all the time. Get outside. Play football, any sports. Have fun being a fit kid. Hope you like being fit.

Stages 1 and 2: Develop Background Knowledge and Discuss It, POW + TREE

After the pretest, the first lessons combined developing background knowledge and discussing it (see Table 6.2). The initial focus was on POW + TREE for opinion essays on topics such as, "Should children your age get an allowance?" Persuasive essay writing (with informational text) using TWA was not introduced until later in instruction, as we believed it was important for these students to first understand and write opinion essays, providing a foundation for moving to persuasive writing using source text. Instruction included discussion of what students knew about opinion essay writing and foundational knowledge and concepts such as, What is an opinion? What does it mean to persuade someone? and What are the differences between facts and opinions? Students learned about a trick that all good writers use whenever they write (POW) and a trick for remembering the critical parts of a good persuasive essay (TREE; see Figure 6.1). Students discussed that good persuasive essays are fun to write and fun for others to read; make sense; and can convince your reader to agree with you. With their teacher, students found the parts of TREE in model opinion essays (one or two paragraphs in length and with three or more reasons included) and discovered the linking words that told the reader another reason was coming. A record of good linking words was started and added to throughout instruction. A graphic organizer for TREE was introduced (see Figure 6.2) and used to take notes from the sample essays with teacher guidance; this activity was critical because these students needed to develop the ability to take notes rather than write out full sentences when they planned. Students also read poor essays, discussed

---

Figure 6.2. Blank POW + TREE Graphic Organizer

T	Topic Sentence: Tell what you believe.
R **E**	Reasons – 3 or more. Explain each reason further. __ Reason: Explanation:
	__ Reason: Explanation:
	__ Reason: Explanation:
E	Ending: Wrap it up right.

Note. POW = pick an idea, organize notes, and write and say more.

what was wrong with them, and made notes on a graphic organizer for better parts. Together with their teacher, they wrote new essays that had all the necessary parts and were persuasive.

Throughout these lessons and stage 3, memorization of the strategy mnemonics POW + TREE and the meaning and importance of each step was emphasized. Students can also learn to evaluate and graph their performance on a pretest at this time (see Table 6.2); we delayed this until later, however, just before we introduced TWA.

Stage 3: Model It, POW + TREE

Next, the teacher modeled using POW + TREE to write a good opinion essay, with the students helping her as she decided on each element, made notes on the graphic organizer, and then wrote the essay, adding more ideas as she wrote. She began by setting her goals: to include all the parts of a good opinion essay, to write an essay that is fun to read and fun to write, and to try hard to persuade the reader. While modeling, she offered a running think-aloud to help students understand the internal thoughts, dialogue, and actions that good writers use when they compose. For example, she used self-statements to help focus her attention and use the strategy steps ("What is the first thing I need to do?"), stay on task ("Don't think about other stuff. Stay focused!"), monitor performance ("Will this introduction catch my reader's attention?"), cope with frustration ("I can do this. Take a deep breath and try again."), and reinforce effort ("I knew I could think of a better explanation for that reason.").

Self-monitoring of writing performance was introduced by having students evaluate each essay written together, count the number of parts included, and record this number on a rocket graph. Each student received their own sheets of rocket graphs on which to record first the group performance on essays written together and later their independent performance each time they wrote alone (see Figure 6.3). A basic essay should have eight parts: the topic sentence, three reasons with an explanation for each (six total parts), and an ending. When essays included more than one explanation for a reason or more than three reasons (and corresponding explanations), students "busted the rocket" and wrote the total number of parts at the top. Finally, a star by the rocket was colored in for each linking word used in the essay.

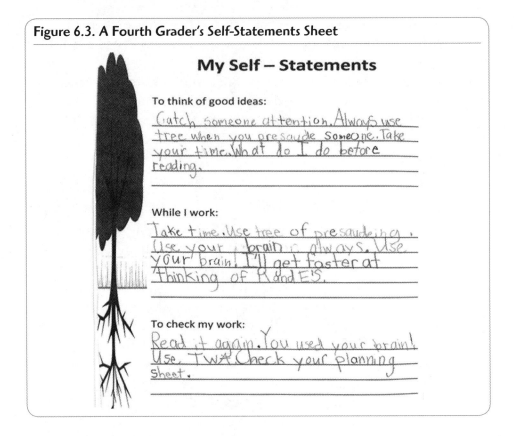

Figure 6.3. A Fourth Grader's Self-Statements Sheet

My Self – Statements

To think of good ideas:

Catch someone attention. Always use tree when you presaude someone. Take your time. What do I do before reading.

While I work:

Take time. Use tree of presaudeing. Use your brain always. Use your brain! I'll get faster at thinking of R and E's.

To check my work:

Read it again. You used your brain! Use TWA Check your planning sheet.

Stage 4: Memorize It, POW + TREE

Students had worked to memorize the strategy steps and their importance, along with the corresponding mnemonics POW + TREE, throughout the previous lessons, using peer practice, rapid fire games, and so forth. At this point, the teacher simply made sure that each student had these down, or provided further practice if needed.

Stages 5 and 6: Support It and Independent Performance, POW + TREE

Following the stages described in Table 6.2, the teacher initially wrote collaboratively with students, providing as much guidance and support as needed. As students became more confident and capable, the teacher gradually released control to them until they were able to write opinion essays with eight parts or more on their own. Instead of using a graphic organizer, students used scratch paper to note the parts of TREE and make notes. In addition, students now evaluated and graphed their performance on the pretest that they had taken. As noted previously, we had delayed this until students learned TWA. They were given the pretests that they had written with the use of source text, and each student scored and graphed their pretest essay using the rockets and guidelines that they had learned. This activity was done in a positive, supportive manner to emphasize how much students had learned and how much their writing was improving. Such visual representations of progress promote motivation.

At this point, it was time to move on to persuasive writing using source text. We began the six stages of SRSD instruction again, but this time we moved into incorporating TWA for use with POW + TREE as described next.

Stages 1 and 2: Develop Background Knowledge and Discuss It; Add TWA and Making Notes Using Source Text

Students were introduced to the TWA strategy for close reading (see Figure 6.1). We developed the texts used with these struggling writers to control for length, reading level, and complexity, as recommended by Mason et al. (2013) for initial development of the TWA strategy with students. The teacher guided discussion of the characteristics and purpose of informational text; helped students understand that informational text includes main ideas, details, and facts; and discussed how the TWA strategy would help them identify information from text that can be used in writing to persuade. The teacher and students discussed how main ideas, details, and facts can help us think about how to persuade our readers. The big/main ideas can help us with reasons, and the details can help us with explanations or even reasons. Facts can help persuade a reader, too.

The importance of also using your own ideas for reasons and explanations was emphasized strongly, as good writers do both. The teacher and students read several informational texts together until students were comfortable marking texts for potential reasons and explanations. Students were offered highlighters to mark the source text for potential reasons and explanations but preferred to underline selected parts of text and mark them with *R*s and *E*s instead.

Stage 3: Model It; Add TWA

As described previously and further detailed in Table 6.2, the teacher now modeled again with collaboration from the small group of students, using TWA in conjunction with POW + TREE. Two or more essays were written together, the teacher and students evaluated each essay for the number of elements included, and students graphed the scores on rockets as described previously. In addition, students now also colored a star for each linking word used and for each element developed from the source text. Finally, students generated personal self-statements to use with the steps of TWA and wrote these on their self-statements sheets.

Stages 4 and 5: Memorize It and Support It; Add TWA and Evaluate Pretest Performance

These stages again mirrored the earlier descriptions.

Stage 6: Independent Performance; POW + TREE + TWA

As the teachers gradually released control to the students (see Table 6.2), each student reached independent performance and was ready for posttesting. These students reached independent performance in approximately twenty 35-minute lessons. Although this is longer than typical for elementary-age students and SRSD, these students learned more strategies than is typical as well. Avery's posttest, which follows, provides an illustration of the gains made in this relatively short period of instruction. Informational text was provided and the prompt was, "Write an essay to your classmates persuading them that teamwork is a good idea." Avery read, planned, and then wrote the following:

> Listen up! You should have teamwork. Teamwork is fun. One of my major reasons is teams are good for people. A team can help you meet new kids. Next, you can split chores at home or school. Each kid can do a chore. The strong kid can lift heavy trash bags. The smaller kid can clean under the beds. My third reason is you can make new friends on teams. That makes teamwork fun. Finally, people are working together. People can work together in sports, home, and school. That is why you should have team work so you can split up chores, work together, and make new friends. That is good for people.

In addition to this pretest and posttest example, we provide further illustrations using the work of another student, Taurean. Figure 6.3 includes the self-statements that Taurean developed during the POW + TREE phase of SRSD instruction. Figure 6.4 captures his marking of possible reasons and explanations on source text, and Figure 6.5 illustrates the notes he made for this essay in a graphic organizer created on scratch paper. Figure 6.6 is the essay that Taurean wrote independently after completing his notes on

Figure 6.4. "Rainforests" Text Marked by Taurean

Rainforests

Rainforests are forests that get lots of sun and lots of rain. Many kinds of tall trees and many kinds of plants live in the rainforests. Millions of animals and insects live in rainforests. Scientists say there may be more than a million plants and animals in the rainforest we have not discovered yet. Some people live in the rainforests too.

Rainforests are very important. They help people and the Earth in many ways. Rainforests help make rain clouds and the Earth needs rain. Rain also helps the rainforest to stay healthy. People need rain so that they have water to drink and use. Rainforests also make lots of the oxygen we have on Earth. People and animals need oxygen to live. Rainforests also help keep our air clean and healthy.

Many plants only grow in rainforests. Scientists study these plants and learn how to make new medicines people need. Over 70% of the medicines we have to fight cancer come from rainforest plants. Many more medicines people need come from rainforest plants. Scientists believe we will discover thousands of new medicines by studying rainforest plants. Many foods come from rainforest plants too, like chocolate and bananas.

Rainforests are being cut down. They use to cover 14% of the Earth's surface. Rainforests now cover only 6% of the Earth's surface. Soon we may have no rainforest at all! People cut down and sell the trees. People dig up and sell minerals from the ground. They make roads to get to the trees and minerals. Roads help people take away more and more trees. Plants and animals die. Some people lose their homes.

What will happen if we keep cutting down rainforests? When the plants are gone, we cannot find new medicines. Will we have enough rain? Will we have enough oxygen and clean air? Will foods we like be hard to get? What else can you think of that will be a problem if we keep cutting down rainforests?

Figure 6.5. Taurean's Completed Notes in a Scratch Paper Graphic Organizer

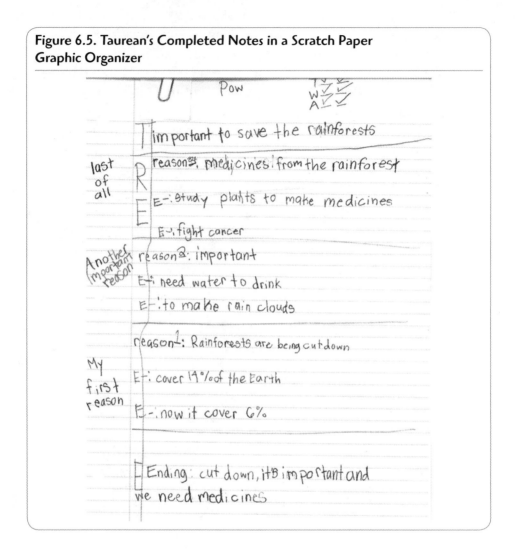

his graphic organizer. Finally, Figure 6.7 is his sheet of completed rockets, beginning with his pretest and showing the number of parts (see the number above each rocket) in essays written in stages 5 and 6.

Conclusion

In approximately 10 hours of instructional time, spread over 35-minute lessons held four times a week, these struggling 9–10-year-old writers made

Figure 6.6. Taurean's Essay Written Independently From His Graphic Organizer

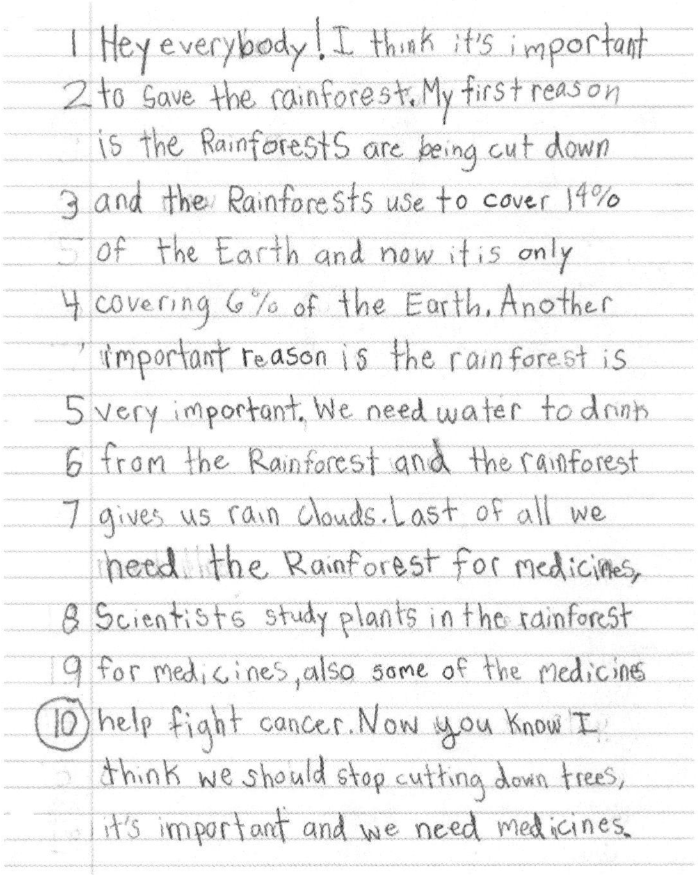

1 Hey everybody! I think it's important
2 to save the rainforest. My first reason
is the Rainforests are being cut down
3 and the Rainforests use to cover 14%
5 of the Earth and now it is only
4 covering 6% of the Earth. Another
important reason is the rainforest is
5 very important. We need water to drink
6 from the Rainforest and the rainforest
7 gives us rain clouds. Last of all we
need the Rainforest for medicines,
8 Scientists study plants in the rainforest
9 for medicines, also some of the medicine
⑩ help fight cancer. Now you know I
think we should stop cutting down trees,
it's important and we need medicines.

remarkable gains. Are they done learning and developing as persuasive writers? Of course not. SRSD provides a beginning, as we have long argued. These students now have a strong foundation on which they can build as they learn to set new goals, write longer and more persuasive essays using revising strategies and more sophisticated persuasive writing strategies, read and analyze more complex text, use more than one source text, and rebut opposing viewpoints (see Harris et al., 2008; Mason et al., 2012). All of this takes time and development, and we hope the time and

Figure 6.7. Taurean's Completed Rockets Sheet: Pretest and After POW + TREE + TWA

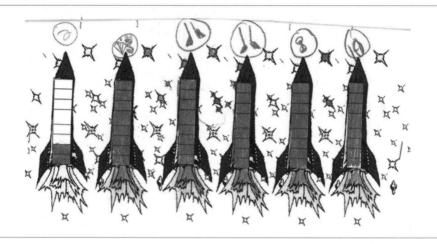

instruction that these students need to become competent writers will be provided as they progress through the grades to come.

Further, SRSD for writing is neither a complete writing program nor a silver bullet. Many more components of evidence-based instruction in writing are important in building strong writers, and each student and class will have differing needs (see Chapter 2 in this book). Much more research is needed on SRSD; additional strategies for differing genres at different grade levels need to be developed. More research on effective professional development for SRSD (cf. Harris et al., 2012, 2014) is also needed. For now, the evidence base allows us to encourage you to learn more and use the validated SRSD instructional approach and validated writing strategies with your students.

REFERENCES

Baker, S.K., Chard, D.J., Ketterlin-Geller, L.R., Apichatabutra, C., & Doabler, C. (2009). Teaching writing to at-risk students: The quality of evidence for self-regulated strategy development. *Exceptional Children, 75*(3), 303–318.

Bangert-Drowns, R.L., Hurley, M.M., & Wilkinson, B. (2004). The effects of school-based writing-to-learn interventions on academic achievement: A meta-analysis. *Review of Educational Research, 74*(1), 29–58. doi:10.3102/00346543074001029

Bereiter, C., & Scardamalia, M. (1987). *The psychology of written composition*. Hillsdale, NJ: Erlbaum.

Festas, I., Oliveira, A., Rebelo, J., Damião, M., Harris, K.R., & Graham, S. (in press). The effects of self-regulated strategy development (SRSD) on the writing performance of eighth-grade Portuguese students. *Contemporary Educational Psychology*.

Fitzgerald, J. (2013). Constructing instruction for struggling writers: What and how. *Annals of Dyslexia, 63*(1), 80–95. doi:10.1007/s11881-011-0063-z

Graham, S., Bollinger, A., Olson, C.B., D'Aoust, C., MacArthur, C., McCutchen, D., & Olinghouse, N. (2012). *Teaching elementary school students to be effective writers: Educator's practice guide* (NCEE 2012-4058). Washington, DC: National Center for Education Evaluation and Regional Assistance, Institute of Education Sciences, U.S. Department of Education.

Graham, S., & Harris, K.R. (2005). *Writing better: Effective strategies for teaching students with learning difficulties*. Baltimore, MD: Paul H. Brookes.

Graham, S., Harris, K.R., & McKeown, D. (2013). The writing of students with learning disabilities, meta-analysis of self-regulated strategy development writing intervention studies, and future directions: Redux. In H.L. Swanson, K.R. Harris, & S. Graham (Eds.), *Handbook of learning disabilities* (2nd ed., pp. 405–438). New York, NY: Guilford.

Graham, S., Harris, K.R., & Santangelo, T. (in press). Research-based writing practices and the Common Core: Meta-analysis and meta-synthesis. *The Elementary School Journal*.

Graham, S., & Hebert, M. (2010). *Writing to read: Evidence for how writing can improve reading*. Washington, DC: Alliance for Excellent Education.

Graham, S., & Perin, D. (2007). *Writing next: Effective strategies to improve writing of adolescents in middle and high schools*. Washington, DC: Alliance for Excellent Education.

Harris, K.R., & Graham, S. (1996). *Making the writing process work: Strategies for composition and self-regulation* (2nd ed.). Cambridge, MA: Brookline.

Harris, K.R., & Graham, S. (2009). Self-regulated strategy development in writing: Premises, evolution, and the future [Monograph]. *British Journal of Educational Psychology, Series 2*(6), 113–135. doi:10.1348/978185409X422542

Harris, K.R., & Graham, S. (2014). Integrating reading and writing instruction. In B. Miller, P. McCardle, & R. Long (Eds.), *Teaching reading and writing: Improving instruction and student achievement* (pp. 35–44). Baltimore, MD: Paul H. Brookes.

Harris, K.R., Graham, S., & Adkins, M. (2014). Practice-based professional development and self-regulated strategy development for Tier 2, at-risk writers in second grade. *Contemporary Educational Psychology*. Advance online publication. doi:10.1016/j.cedpsych.2014.02.003

Harris, K.R., Graham, S., Brindle, M., & Sandmel, K. (2009). Metacognition and children's writing. In D.J. Hacker, J. Dunlosky, & A.C. Graesser (Eds.), *Handbook of metacognition in education* (pp. 131–153). New York, NY: Routledge.

Harris, K.R., Graham, S., & Deshler, D. (2002). *Teaching students with learning disabilities in the regular classroom* [DVD]. Alexandria, VA: Association for Supervision and Curriculum Development.

Harris, K.R., Graham, S., Mason, L.H., & Friedlander, B. (2008). *Powerful writing strategies for all students*. Baltimore, MD: Paul H. Brookes.

Harris, K.R., Lane, K.L., Graham, S., Driscoll, S.A., Sandmel, K., Brindle, M., & Schatschneider, C. (2012). Practice-based professional development for self-regulated strategies development in writing: A randomized controlled study. *Journal of Teacher Education, 63*(2), 103–119. doi:10.1177/0022487111429005

Mason, L.H., Davison, M.D., Hammer, C.S., Miller, C.A., & Glutting, J.J. (2013). Knowledge, writing, and language outcomes for a reading comprehension and writing intervention. *Reading and Writing, 26*(7), 1133–1158. doi:10.1007/s11145-012-9409-0

Mason, L.H., Reid, R., & Hagaman, J.L. (2012). *Building comprehension in adolescents: Powerful strategies for improving reading and writing in content areas.* Baltimore, MD: Paul H. Brookes.

National Commission on Writing for America's Families, Schools, and Colleges. (2006). *Writing and school reform.* New York, NY: College Board.

National Governors Association Center for Best Practices & Council of Chief State School Officers. (2010). *Common Core State Standards for English language arts and literacy in history/social studies, science, and technical subjects.* Washington, DC: Authors.

Salahu-Din, D., Persky, H., & Miller, J. (2008). *The Nation's Report Card: Writing 2007* (NCES 2008-468). Washington, DC: National Center for Education Statistics, Institute of Education Sciences, U. S. Department of Education.

Sandmel, K.N., Brindle, M., Harris, K.R., Lane, K.L., Graham, S., Nackel, J., Mathias, R., & Little, A. (2009). Making it work: Differentiating Tier two self-regulated strategies development in writing in tandem with schoolwide positive behavioral support. *Teaching Exceptional Children, 42*(2), 22–33.

ABOUT THE AUTHORS

 Karen R. Harris is the Warner Professor in the Division of Educational Leadership and Innovation at the Mary Lou Fulton Teachers College, Arizona State University, Phoenix, Arizona, USA. Before earning her doctoral degree, she taught kindergarten and fourth-grade students and then elementary and secondary students in special education. Her research focuses on children's writing. She developed the SRSD model of strategies instruction, and her current research focuses on professional development for SRSD for teachers working in general and special education. A former editor of the *Journal of Educational Psychology*, she also served as lead editor of the *APA Educational Psychology Handbook* (American Psychological Association, 2012) and has authored more than 200 peer-reviewed publications. She is the president of the Division for Educational Psychology of the American Psychological Association and has served as the president of the Division for Research of the Council for Exceptional Children and as an officer for the American Educational Research Association.

Steve Graham is the Warner Professor of Education at Arizona State University in Phoenix, Arizona, USA. He is the former editor of *Exceptional Children, Contemporary Educational Psychology,* and the *Journal of Writing Research* and the incoming editor of the *Journal of Educational Psychology.* Graham served as a coeditor of the *Handbook of Learning Disabilities* (2nd ed., Guilford, 2013), *Handbook of Writing Research* (Guilford, 2008), and *APA Educational Psychology Handbook* (American Psychological Association, 2012). He also coauthored three Carnegie Corporation reports, all published by the Alliance for Excellent Education: *Writing Next: Effective Strategies to Improve Writing of Adolescents in Middle and High Schools* (2007), *Writing to Read: Evidence for How Writing Can Improve Reading* (2010), and *Informing Writing: The Benefits of Formative Assessment* (2011).

Amber B. Chambers is a doctoral student in the College of Education at Arizona State University, Tempe, USA. She is working toward her PhD in learning, literacy, and technology, with a specialization in special education. Amber's passion for working with individuals with disabilities began when she was a camp counselor and a director for youths and teens with disabilities. She has experience in teaching students with learning disabilities, autism, intellectual disabilities, and emotional and behavioral disorders. Amber was also the director of a high school special education program. Her research interests focus on reading and writing interventions to help students with disabilities succeed in school. She is interested in strategy and self-regulation approaches to instruction for students who struggle with learning. Amber aims to use her knowledge, gained through research, to help current teachers and prepare future teachers to use effective instructional techniques when teaching struggling learners and students with disabilities.

Julia D. Houston is working toward her PhD in learning, literacy, and technology at the Mary Lou Fulton Teachers College at Arizona State University, Tempe, USA. She spent nearly 15 years as a general education classroom teacher, teaching all the content areas and all grades, K–12, while teaching in district and charter schools, in online and on-site settings. Julia's master's degree in curriculum and instruction with an emphasis in early childhood education provides a strong foundation for her research interests, which include using instructional strategies to develop effective classrooms. Her research will enhance schools by helping educators and students understand themselves as learners and optimally utilize available technology.

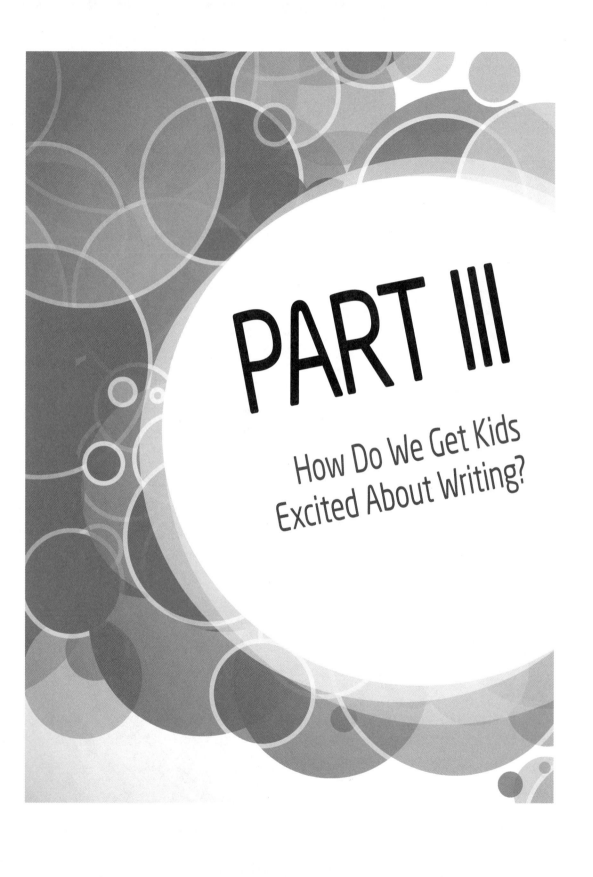

PART III

How Do We Get Kids Excited About Writing?

CHAPTER 7

Boys and Multiplicity

Expanding the Writing and Writers
That Count in School

Michael W. Smith & Jon-Philip Imbrenda, *Temple University*

Jeffrey D. Wilhelm, *Boise State University*

Recently, we heard a mother express concerns about her 11-year-old son because he was struggling in his language arts class. When advised to find ways to use his existing interests as a way to foster more engagement in his schoolwork, she responded, "I don't know how to do that. The only thing he cares about is this video game called Minecraft." Her frustration is easy to sympathize with. After all, each of us has looked at a struggling boy writer in our classroom and thought, If only he spent as much time on writing as he did on video games, he'd be doing just fine. We suspect that most of you have had some very similar thoughts.

When we have had those thoughts, we've reminded ourselves of the growing line of research that argues for bringing in-school and out-of school into closer connection. Dyson (1999), for example, has called for schools to develop curricula that are permeable—that is, allowing free movement between what students do inside and outside of school. More recently, Alvermann proposed a sieve metaphor "for noticing relationships between in-school and out-of-school literacy learning that have been obscured previously" (Alvermann & Moore, 2011, p. 158).

Michael and Jeff (first and third authors) have been noticing those relationships for years (see, e.g., Smith & Wilhelm, 2002, 2006) and have argued for using young men's out-of school literacies as resources to help them develop more conventional academic literacies, especially the understanding and appreciation of literature. Jon-Philip (second author), however, has been pushing Michael and Jeff to see those literacies not only as resources but also as important ends in themselves, especially with regard to boys and writing. This chapter is the result of that pushing. We take a hard look at one feature of "texts" such as Minecraft that make them so appealing to young men, a feature that we, following Calvino (1988), call multiplicity. We'll consider not only how allowing multiplicity to permeate the classroom can help young men become better writers in a conventional sense but also how doing so can help them navigate the multimodal, media-rich, and robustly interconnected milieu that they experience in their day-to-day lives.

What Is Multiplicity, and Why Is It Important?

Let's begin with a consideration of Minecraft. It's a tough game to describe. The game drops players into a three-dimensional world that, initially, resembles our own: There are beaches and forests, flowers and trees, and domestic animals lolling around the countryside. The blocky and pixelated graphic style looks like it belongs to a past generation of games, and the simple controls and spare interface suggest that there isn't much depth to it—that is, until your character walks up to a tree and starts punching it. Only then is the ingenious dynamic of the game revealed: The entire world is composed of LEGO-like blocks that can be removed and replaced to rebuild the world however the player sees fit. Mining the world in this manner also nets raw materials that can then be used to craft tools, many of which can then be further recombined into even more complex things.

Spend a little time exploring the world, and the strangeness of it starts to show itself. The overland is vast and varied, with mountains, deserts, glaciers, lakes, and rivers. When night falls—something that occurs about every 20–30 minutes of game time—the once peaceful landscape comes alive with wolves, zombies, skeletons, and other nasty creatures whose only desire is to kill the player on sight. Start digging into the ground, and you soon discover a sprawling subterranean world of caverns and stone corridors. Even more monsters lurk down there, as well as dungeons with treasure chests, and rare ores that can be mined to craft better equipment. Dig down deep enough, and you'll find pools of lava, precious gems, and even magic gizmos. Many of these things have multiple uses, and over time you find yourself crafting enchanted swords and potions, planting crops to keep yourself fed, taming wild animals to adopt as pets, and collecting lava in buckets to build a fully functional obsidian generator.

It sounds pretty complicated, doesn't it? What makes it even more complicated is the complete lack of direction that the game provides. There is no overarching story, no scoring system, and no specific ending. It's up to you as the player to set your own goals and, in doing so, to define your own story. At first, you focus on basic survival: building a shelter, crafting rudimentary tools, and foraging for food. As time passes, the possibilities gradually multiply. Do you want to build a majestic castle for yourself? Do you want to develop a wheat farm to bake a never-ending supply of bread? Do you want to dig deeper into the ground to secure the rarest and most precious materials? Maybe you want to do some combination of all of these things. Maybe you just want to build a cozy log cabin and bake cookies. And when that's all over, players can, as our friend's son has done, create their own server, invite friends to join, and redefine the rules of the game to their liking. Whatever you choose, what connects these seemingly random and disparate elements into a cohesive whole isn't found in the formal structure of the game; rather, it is the intricate web of connections that you build through the activity of playing.

OK, that was something of an extended detour, but we think it's a detour well worth taking. Minecraft, with its web of seemingly unconnected associations, is emblematic of many texts that appeal to boys. Think of plot-driven stories characterized by the "'flippant, slapstick, almost bathroom humor'" that teachers in Peterson's (1998, p. 194) study said were characteristic of adolescent boys. Think of the parody of Arlene Mosel's *Tikki Tikki Tembo* written by two fourth-grade boys that Newkirk (2002) documents, a parody that ultimately includes Rumpelstiltskin, Superman, Dumbo, and the Nightmare on Elm Street movies.

This web of associations is what Calvino (1988) calls multiplicity. He praises novels that demonstrate "a network of connections between the events, the people, and the things of the world" (p. 105), that are built not on any kind of formal logic but rather that bring together "a multiplicity of subjects, voices, and views of the world" (p. 117). The world, as Calvino and the writers he most admires see it, is not an orderly place. Instead, it resembles "a tangled skein of yarn" (p. 106). The writer's job, then, is "to represent it without in the least diminishing the inextricable complexity or, to put it better, the simultaneous presence of the most disparate elements that converge to determine every event" (p. 106). Sherlock Holmes provides an excellent example of the power of multiplicity. He always sees multiple, complex causes, whereas Dr. John Watson plods along, bound by conventional deduction. Take a look at just the first page of Sir Arthur Conan Doyle's (1902) *The Hound of the Baskervilles* for an example. Watson and Holmes try to puzzle out the identity of a visitor whose call they missed on the basis of the walking stick the visitor left behind. Watson's method yields only an obvious and incomplete conclusion, whereas Holmes makes a series of brilliantly associative inferences that capture the essence of the individual down to the size of his dog.

Calvino (1988) was thinking about the work of some of the most celebrated writers in our history, from Miguel de Cervantes to Donald Barthelme. How would multiplicity look in the work of a student? The case of Max, one of Jon-Philip's students, comes to mind. Max's early passion for fantasy novels led him into the literary arts magnet program where Jon-Philip was the instructional leader. However, such passion quickly waned when Max was immediately thrust into a world where creative writing meant producing formally cohesive realistic fiction and stylized poetry characterized by sophisticated diction. Confronted with these demands, Max had all but selected himself out of the program, maintaining a cursory level of interest and merely going through the motions to receive an average grade. But for his culminating project—a portfolio of revised works reflecting his efforts to write in a number of narrative, expository, and poetic forms—he turned in what was perhaps the most bizarre goulash of work an educator has ever seen. His portfolio was part sci-fi screenplay, part video game design document, part philosophical manifesto, and part lampooning satire. Fetishistic superheroes clashed with aliens and FBI agents. Villains found comeuppance by being buried under mounds of excrement. Every woman was a femme fatale, every child an urchin. It incorporated writing, comics, diagrams, charts, and even an accompanying soundtrack on CD. Taken individually, none of the sections seemed fully realized; yet, as a whole, the portfolio offered an encyclopedic glimpse into Max's world that was at once both exotic and incisive—and, quite frankly, exciting. It validated his unique style and vision.

At the time he taught Max, Jon-Philip was ill-equipped to respond to Max's efforts. He gave Max the gentlest feedback he could muster and a passing grade, and a month later, he was signing forms so Max could transfer out of the program. Had Jon-Philip better understood the value of multiplicity at that time, he might not have failed Max the way he did. Jon-Philip might have known how to name what Max was doing, why it was valuable, and how to connect it to other literacies to extend this kind of work into his future.

Reconsidering Max's portfolio in light of what we've learned from Calvino (1988) has helped us articulate why we believe it's important to assert that value in the context of boy writers. We now see that multiplicitous texts have value for at least three reasons: (1) They're driven by an inner logic that reflects the contemporary world; (2) they're inherently creative and original; and (3) they generate opportunities for students to be mindful about the choices they make in their writing, while at the same time thinking abstractly about how things are connected.

Despite these important qualities, prevailing trends in language arts education over the past few decades have made it increasingly difficult to utilize such texts in the classroom. For example, recent reform movements such as the Common Core State Standards (National Governors Association Center for Best Practices & Council of Chief State School Officers [NGA Center & CCSSO], 2010), with its emphasis on instrumental uses of writing as a means toward college and career readiness, inevitably conjure up a view of texts as unitary, formal, and inert. We don't discredit the value of such a view, but it can be especially dangerous to our boy writers when it overshadows other possibilities, especially those that afford us opportunities to capitalize on things we know about boys and their writing.

So, What to Do?

Respect Boys' Literacies

Our first suggestion may seem obvious, but we think it's crucially important. Too often, we think, boys' literacy is contrasted unfavorably with girls'. We understand the reason for such contrast given the wealth of evidence that boys underperform girls on reading and especially writing tasks, although the evidence is more complicated than it might initially appear (Smith & Wilhelm, 2009).

Boys' lives, as it turns out, are richly literate (Newkirk, 2002; Smith & Wilhelm, 2002, 2006). Boys are often enamored by the critical relationships they hold with texts of all varieties, especially popular cultural texts, such as magazines, comics, video games, rap songs, and box scores. Their social worlds often hinge on these interests. Unfortunately, their academic lives often do not. Rarely are the kinds of texts that boys enjoy valued or reinforced in their classrooms. Every boy in Michael and Jeff's study (Smith & Wilhelm, 2002), even the at-risk kids, had intense interests around things they felt they were good at that involved literate behavior. Their rejection of school literacy, therefore, has to be seen not as a function of their attitude toward literacy in general but rather as a comment on the particular kinds of literate activity they typically encounter in school.

We have reason to believe that what goes on in many classrooms does not capitalize on the things that boys are good at and the reasons why they're good at them. Among the diverse population of boys that Michael and Jeff worked with for *"Reading Don't Fix No Chevys": Literacy in the Lives of Young Men* (Smith & Wilhelm, 2002), one common theme that stood out among them was their clear divide between texts they had to read and produce in class and the ones they read and produced elsewhere. They didn't see a purpose in much of their schoolwork, nor did they experience a personal connection to it. Newkirk's (2002) research testifies to the value of many texts often preferred by boys and relegated to the status of pop culture, low culture, junk culture, or any of a number of designations used to maintain a divide between what is and isn't useful, valuable, or appropriate for schooling. Furthermore, he illuminates the functional power of many of these types of "subliterature," from graphic novels to tables displaying the standings of NBA teams, to foster sophisticated thinking and engaged writing.

In the wake of this divide between what kinds of texts do and don't belong in school, teachers can sometimes lose sight of the unique vision that boys bring to their literate habits. It's important to reconsider the nature of the "literacy gap" between boys and girls as a symptom of the kinds of things that are implicitly valued in school, and not necessarily as predetermined differences in their interests and abilities.

Expectancy–value theory (Eccles & Wigfield, 2002) provides an elegant explanation of the importance of this advice. In brief, the theory holds that one's willingness to engage in an activity is a function of one's expectation for success multiplied by how much one values the activity. Respecting boys' literacies increases both how much they value their English language arts classrooms and the extent to which they see themselves as being successful in them.

Give Choice

Fletcher (2006) distills much of the insight on boys' literacy habits into practical advice for teaching writing. Topic choice is one of his most urgent suggestions. Many conventional writing tasks carry with them a kind of fine print that excludes opportunities for boy writers to capitalize on their interests and passions. They are given restricted access to some of the tools that are most natural to them: cartoonish violence, irreverent humor, and subversive criticism, to name a few. Such limitations can inadvertently set a clear mandate in the mind of the boy writer that this whole writing thing is simply not for him.

If we think about the reasons why we value multiplicity, we can see how choice is integral to the creativity, excitement, and ingenuity it can nurture. First, the world that boys inhabit outside of school is full of choices: what sports to follow, what websites to visit, what bands to listen to, what video games to play, and what action heroes to admire. The freedom afforded to them in this interconnected world fosters literate habits. Jon-Philip once had a student who helped develop on online guide for a video game just because he was so passionate about it. He intricately detailed the locations of over a dozen secret artifacts and even used Photoshop to create an interactive map to help guide players to these locations. All of this was done on his own time and for the simple pleasure of doing it. Had he been given more choice in school, he might have found ways to bridge that passion into an assignment for class or even as a way to collaborate with his peers.

Second, choice is inherently creative. This may seem like a statement of the obvious until we think about how little freedom to choose boys often have in the classroom and how powerful a tool choice can be in connecting their inner worlds to the outer worlds they're learning to navigate. In Jeff and Michael's most recent work (Wilhelm & Smith, 2014), they found that passionate readers of texts that are marginalized in school (e.g., romance, dystopia, horror, vampire, fantasy) used those texts not only to develop new literate behaviors and engage in social and intellectual pleasure but also as a form of work, applying what was learned to the world and using it to do the inner work of rehearsing for the future and for considering what kind of person they wanted to become. For one seventh-grade boy, his connection to a video game wasn't about a desire to be like the hard-boiled detective protagonist but rather to mirror the game's clever system for interpreting people's facial cues and gestures to tell if they were lying. Through the literate habits he chose for himself, he crafted a set of deeply personal, and immensely practical, goals.

Third, giving boys the opportunity to make choices means you're creating opportunities for them to reflect on those choices. Think about a general scenario: You give an assignment in which boys have to read a short text and then write a brief response to it. Now, think about that same assignment as a series of choices. First, the boys must choose their texts, then they must choose a style of responding to it, and then they must share and evaluate the choices of their peers. See how the onus shifts away from responding to the texts themselves and instead into the interconnected web of relationships that underlines their creation? This kind of mindfulness about how texts reflect the authors and contexts in which they are produced supports the transfer of writing skills across disciplines, a skill that is highly valued and useful, especially once boys reach the upper grades. However, remove the choices from the equation, and you're encouraging something fundamentally different and, in our opinion, less useful.

Although we realize that many teachers view it as the bane of their existence, Wikipedia stands as a testament to the power of choice and the pervasiveness of multiplicity in the texts of the world around our boy writers. It is a work of tremendous ambition—a true equalizer of what is and isn't valued in the world. See for yourself how the popular 1980s sitcom *Cheers* is given as lengthy and exhaustive an entry as the scientific concept of DNA. What's more is that Wikipedia is the result of the literate efforts of many people—and according to a 2008 study reported in *Slate* magazine, many of them young boys—who did it just because they took pleasure in both the immediate experience of researching and writing entries, as well as the ongoing joy of having been part of something bigger (Wilson, 2008). Had they not been given the freedom to choose, none of this would have happened.

Modify Evaluation to Support Multiplicity

Let's take a look at the grades 3–5 scoring guidelines for informational and opinion writing provided by the Pennsylvania System of School

Assessment (www.portal.state.pa.us/portal/server.pt/community/state_
assessment_system/20965/pennsylvania_system_of_school_assessment_
(pssa)/1190526). Here's what a successful piece of writing looks like
according to these guidelines: (1) It has a sharp, distinct point or topic; (2) it
is thoroughly elaborated; (3) it has an effective order and organizational
structure; (4) it has a consistently maintained formal style; and (5) it
adheres to conventions of grammar, spelling, and mechanics. This sounds
reasonable, right? We chose these because Michael and Jon-Philip work in
Pennsylvania, but we imagine that many assessments from the state to the
classroom level across the United States carry a comparable set of criteria.

Now, let's think about some of the most visible and commonplace
texts of today that do not follow any of these rules, such as Facebook;
Amazon.com; IGN's online game guide for Minecraft; "Happy" by Pharrell
Williams, the first song to ever top as many as six of Billboard's radio
format charts; Discussion Board posts by Michael's doctoral students;
a monthly newsletter that Jon-Philip receives from the landlord of his
building; and the Lotsa Helping Hands community website that Jeff created
to support his wife, Peggy Jo, in her battle against traumatic brain injury.
The list could go on and on.

In fact, sometimes we wonder where in the world outside school one
does find texts that reflect the standards set forth by so many rubrics for
writing assessment. We're not saying that such standards are completely
devoid of merit. They demonstrate a very specific kind of competency, one
that schools and high-stakes assessments value. The point is that we don't
always think critically enough about the extent to which our evaluation
suggests what and who we value.

For example, a second claim made emphatically by Fletcher (2006) is
that on the sentence level, boy writers tend to rely on slangy constructions,
stark or graphic details, and abrupt shifts in tone throughout a single text.
Although these things are causes for alarm in the mind of the writing
teacher who may view such choices as mistakes attributed to laziness or
a lack of responsible deference to conventions, mixing competing voices
within a single text is actually a defining quality of multiplicity, and it can be
really valuable.

Let's go back to Max's portfolio for a second. Throughout the entire
work, he frequently used the word *pwn* (pronounced "pawn"). Unfamiliar
with the term (and unsure of whether it was simply some kind of spelling

mistake), Jon-Philip asked Max to explain what it meant, and he eagerly did so. It's a term commonly used in online video games, and it can actually mean different things in different contexts. If a player defeats a powerful enemy, he can say he "pwn'ed" it. However, the same term can be used to describe tactics that can avoid conflict altogether. In different situations, a group of players working together toward a common goal are "pwn'ing" it. Or, in games that utilize a chat function, cleverly punning another player's chat text is also considering a "pwn." In light of this, Jon-Philip asked Max to add a glossary to his portfolio. Surely, this so-called mistake in his writing had now been leveraged into a new opportunity to think deliberately about words and their meanings in different contexts.

When dealing with texts, especially multiplicitous texts, evaluation can and sometimes should look quite different from the standards described previously. A peer review session might be guided by questions such as, What made you laugh? What surprised you the most? Did the writing make you think of things that weren't part of it? Is there any outside knowledge that would have made you think differently about it? Through what other medium could you see the same ideas being demonstrated? and Why? This kind of feedback invites kids to become mindful about the choices a writer makes, and such mindfulness is yet another way to facilitate the transfer of writing skills across different contexts. Instead of turning evaluation into a fault-finding mechanism, it becomes a catalyst for new thinking. Individual texts become potentialities, not inert products.

Assign Multiplicitous Writing

Let's bring this all together by thinking about some possible writing assignments that could generate multiplicitous texts in the classroom, and then we'll test them against our three beliefs in the value of multiplicity.

Nowadays, with access to programs like Microsoft Word becoming more widely available to students and schools, the comment function affords some great opportunities for students to create multivoiced texts. Imagine giving students an assignment in which they were to draft a conventional text such as a five-paragraph essay and then use the comment function to provide a commentary on their own writing and writing process. Jon-Philip tried this, and the results were richly varied, constructive, and, at times, hilarious. Boy writers were especially eager to make jokes about their own awkward phrasing, to admit that they had just written about a book they didn't even read, to invent comical narrators who made counterpoints to their own claims, and to question and suggest other possibilities for their own choices in diction. If you can't get computer access for all of your students, they could do something similar simply by writing in the margins of their papers. All of us have had boys who would, unbidden, provide cartoon commentary on their work. Or, if computers are available but Microsoft Word is not, Google Docs could work, too. Students could provide commentary using a different colored font or use the highlight tool to indicate the comments.

The texts generated through this assignment certainly would contain an inner logic that reflects the logic of a world where Netflix users post reviews that range from thoughtful and erudite to irreverent and obscene, where YouTube videos are supplemented by user comments that express personal tastes and provoke meaningful critiques, and where Instagram users combine words and images in strange and artful ways. The assignment fosters creativity as students are tasked with engaging with their own writing through different personas and perspectives. They are able to defer to the demands of the assignment while also resisting and rejecting them. Perhaps most importantly, they are engaging with the interaction between the text and its creation and, in doing so, becoming keenly aware of how their writing often serves as a negotiation between their personal interests and the expectations of the classroom.

Moreover, such texts help achieve conventional academic ends as well. Common Core Reading Anchor Standard 4 for grades K–5 includes the following: "analyze how specific word choices shape meaning or tone" (NGA Center & CCSSO, 2010, p. 10). Why not have students practice with their own work? Moreover, such an assignment fosters transfer. We've long argued that transfer is crucially important for teachers to keep at the forefront of their attention (see Smith, Appleman, & Wilhelm, 2014, for our most recent example). Transfer of knowledge means applying what you learn in one situation to what you do in another. As Byrnes (2008) points out, transfer doesn't automatically occur. It's more likely to happen if students "approach their learning in a mindful way" (p. 79). The commentary assignment forces students to distance themselves from their writing and, in so doing, cultivates that mindfulness. To illustrate, one student commented that the first sentence of his persuasive essay, one that offered a generalization about "problems in today's society," was so broad that he might as well have just written "night is darker than day." Another invented a persona who mocked his oversophisticated diction and poor use of participial phrases.

Conversational texts such as texting are inherently multiplicitous. Turner (2010) makes a compelling argument that "digitalk" is a teacher's ally and not his or her enemy, for having students think about their texting practices provides much the same benefits as does our essay with comments assignment. She argues instead that "rather than seeing it as a deficiency, a lazy representation of Standard English, we should recognize its power in the digital, adolescent community" (p. 46) and that we should use students' understanding of texting as a way to help them become conscious of the language choices they make.

Having students write long jokes is another way to include multiplicity in your classroom. Long jokes can range anywhere from four or five sentences to several paragraphs. They're generally thought of as the kinds of jokes that comedians tell to other comedians because the artistry of their invention is more important than the fast laughs they can evoke. While it dates back to the vaudevillian tradition, some more recent examples of long jokes are Andy Kaufman's trademark style of antihumor, and the deadpan anecdotal humor of Steven Wright. What separates the long joke from more conventional, shorter jokes that often rely on explicit gags and wordplay is in both its form and the effect it is trying to achieve.

To explain, the long joke has three parts: a setup or premise, an act, and a discordant punch line. The setup is usually something very simple: "A guy walks into a place...." The beauty of the long joke comes afterward, in the second part, the act. It is here that the storyteller can elaborate that setup in an almost infinite variety of ways. The more bizarre and outrageous it gets, the better. The purpose of the act is to distract the reader through a combination of narrative momentum, surprise, and absurdity. By the time the punch line is reached, the joke has already been told, and it's for this reason that the punch line is usually highly discordant with the joke leading up to it.

To illustrate briefly, a student could set up a long joke with something like this: "Four guys are fishing together, and each one explains all the things he had to do for his mother to get her to let him go." Then, each of the first three guys can give a more and more elaborate account of the zany things his mom made him do, such as brush the dog's teeth, paint the cat blue, or take the goldfish swimming. Each story should be more bizarre than the previous one, and each one could have a theme (e.g., the pet theme in our example). Then, when they ask the fourth guy what he had to do, his reply might be something like, "Nothing, my mom is a tackle box." The punch line here is more of a whimper because the purpose of the joke was in the process of getting there.

Mentor texts for this assignment can be found in many places, from stand-up comics to parody shows such as *Saturday Night Live*. Our example joke was adapted from one we found on the Vague but True website (www.vaguebuttrue.com). Another website, Good Clean Jokes Sites (www.goodcleanjokes.com), has similar examples that could work on their own or offer up starting points that could work with just a bit of modification.

Assigning long jokes may seem frivolous, but it's not. Kotthoff (2007) explains how long jokes, what she calls "absurd meta-jokes which violate the well-known expectation of a punch-line" (p. 263), are a superb vehicle for helping people see how genres constrain composing and what effects can be realized by transgressing generic boundaries. In addition, the Common Core's section on narrative writing for fifth graders calls on them to

> orient the reader by establishing a situation and introducing a narrator and/or characters; organize an event sequence that unfolds naturally [and] use narrative techniques, such as dialogue, description, and pacing, to develop experiences and events or show the responses of characters to situations. (NGA Center & CCSSO, 2010, p. 20)

No genre puts more emphasis on the initial orientation or on pacing than the long joke does.

To put this assignment to the test again, the inner logic here is much more process oriented than product oriented. Does this reflect the inner logic of the world? We'll let Minecraft serve as an answer to that question. As of February 2014, the game had more than 100 million registered users. And the forums for Lil' Crafters, a Minecraft clan with more than 20,000 members, indicate that the clan is only open to players ages 8–13, which gives plenty of reason to believe that young people make up a big chunk of those users. Process-oriented tasks engage the players, and long jokes are clearly process oriented. Is the long joke inherently creative? We think so. It demands attention to details even if the details themselves lack cohesiveness or a connecting logic. Finally, peer responses to long jokes could easily capitalize on the advice for evaluation that we discussed in the previous section.

A final example of a writing assignment that would introduce multiplicity into the classroom is the creation of group wikis. For those who may be unfamiliar with the term, a wiki is simply a Web-based space where users can collaborate on content and structure. Usually, it's organized around a single topic. Apart from those loose guidelines, wikis can be just about anything, and they can be *about* just about anything. Assigning small-group wikis to your class is a great way to invite students to engage their interests while also learning to work collaboratively, make mindful choices about their writing, and explore the relationships among many different aspects of a common topic or theme.

One way to begin could be to poll your entire class on their hobbies and interests and then group them accordingly. Maybe a group of boys might have a shared interest in video games, whereas another group might be invested in football, and a third might be passionate about anime. This third group, for instance, could work together to plan the layout for their wiki. Maybe they would decide that separate pages should be created to explain each of the most notable elements of anime: manga, television shows, and Japanese-style video games. A separate section could be dedicated to explaining the ways that Japanese-style animation differs from the aesthetic of U.S. animation. Another section could be more personal, in which all the students in the group listed their favorite examples of anime and gave accounts of how they came to enjoy them and why. Finally, another section could give reviews and critiques of recent manga, shows, or games, and students could continue to update this page throughout the marking period.

A wiki may be the best reflection of how information is categorized, organized, and presented in the contemporary world. Whereas the generation of card catalogs and *Encyclopedia Britannica* used subject headings, tables of contents, and indexes to track a line of inquiry, the digital world instead relies on a much more multiplicitous web of connections. Perhaps the greatest contribution of the masterminds behind Google is their success in providing a language that can communicate with the endless grid of virtual space and its infinite possibilities. The wiki as a genre of informational text is both a precursor to and a product of such efforts. Wikis closely resemble the inner logic of the digital world.

Wikis are inherently creative throughout every step of their creation: from the drawing board stages when students must develop and initiate an overall vision for the work, right down to the minute detail that goes into each individual section. More importantly, the form is self-defining, so, like the long joke, rather than fencing students into the constraints of discrete genres, they are tasked with thinking about genre as a flexible tool for organizing and presenting ideas. Of course, they're also writing about things they care about and deepening those interests along the way.

As tools for evaluation, these wikis invite critical responses on many dimensions, from the overall layout, to the choices made in deciding what kinds of sections to include, to the content of those sections. Furthermore, creating them fosters a sense of community among students in the classroom, who are now invited to explore and share in one another's interests. Because most wikis also feature a comment function for individual pages, the process of evaluating, responding, and editing can be a lively, ongoing activity in the classroom.

By no means do we intend these suggestions to be an exhaustive list. Like multiplicity itself, our goal is to inspire new ways of thinking, not to prescribe a rigid set of guidelines for how teachers should teach. Think of them as blueprints, as works in process themselves, and use them to frame your own unique vision for your classroom. The purpose of this chapter is to urge you to think of the texts in your classroom as living, socially situated creations rather than autonomous objects guided by strict, formal rules.

Looking Forward

We'd like to conclude this chapter with an anecdote from one of Jon-Philip's most memorable experiences with Minecraft. A few hours into one of his first times playing, he found himself in a precarious situation. He was mining into the ground not far from the base camp that he'd built for himself, but he dug himself a little too deep, fell into a cavern, and was dangerously short on food and supplies. His pickaxes and swords were worn down to nubs. Monsters were everywhere. Wood, which is needed to craft the ladder that would have got him back to the tunnel he'd carved, was not available underground. Worst of all, he was loaded up with precious gems and ores, all of which would have been lost if hunger or worse fates would have befallen him.

He gathered his wits and starting mining into the side of the cavern, carefully building a stairwell to the surface so as to be sure to not waste a single, precious swing of his degrading pickaxe. When it broke, he switched to his axe and then finally his shovel, desperately digging and digging until he finally hit dirt—a good sign that the surface was nearby—and then digging with his hands until the final block was removed and the light of the world above shone down on him. He had no idea where he was, and doubted he would be able to find his way back to the base he'd built, but at least he was out of the dark and ready to start building up a new base. Of course, he learned valuable lessons along the way about being better prepared for long excavations and never, ever digging into the ground directly underneath him. More importantly, though, his journey into the world below the surface proved to be nothing like he'd expected it to be.

We see this story as an allegory for what many of our young writers experience in their encounters with both the texts they read and the texts they produce. Each experience begins with some expectation and becomes its own kind of journey. The rewards rarely match the expectations, and at the end of the texts, the most compelling hope is to begin anew with fresh perspectives and newfound values. Multiplicity is a lens through which we think about just how closely the encounters with texts we create in our classrooms model those that students experience every day in the world outside of school. Moreover, we think of it as a means though which we can enliven our classrooms with a sense of surprise, spontaneity, and excitement, while also promoting mindfulness and community. Minecraft is not a world without rules, but it is a place where the rules determine the means, not the ends. The texts we ask our students to write, at least from time to time, should do the same thing.

REFERENCES

Alvermann, D.E., & Moore, D.W. (2011). Questioning the separation of in-school from out-of-school contexts for literacy learning: An interview with Donna E. Alvermann. *Journal of Adolescent & Adult Literacy, 55*(2), 156–158. doi:10.1002/JAAL.00019

Byrnes, J.P. (2008). *Cognitive development and learning in instructional contexts* (3rd ed.). Boston, MA: Allyn & Bacon.

Calvino, I. (1988). *Six memos for the next millennium.* Cambridge, MA: Harvard University Press.

Dyson, A.H. (1999). Coach Bombay's kids learn to write: Children's appropriation of media materials for school literacy. *Research in the Teaching of English, 33*(4), 367–402.

Eccles, J.S., & Wigfield, A. (2002). Motivational beliefs, values, and goals. In S.T. Fiske, D.L. Schacter, & C. Zahn-Waxler (Eds.), *Annual review of psychology* (Vol. 53, pp. 109–132). Palo Alto, CA: Annual Reviews. doi:10.1146/annurev.psych.53.100901 .135153

Fletcher, R. (2006). *Boy writers: Reclaiming their voices*. Portland, ME: Stenhouse.

Kotthoff, H. (2007). Oral genres of humor: On the dialectic of genre knowledge and creative authoring. *Pragmatics, 17*(2), 263–296.

National Governors Association Center for Best Practices & Council of Chief State School Officers. (2010). *Common Core State Standards for English language arts and literacy in history/social studies, science, and technical subjects*. Washington, DC: Authors.

Newkirk, T. (2002). *Misreading masculinity: Boys, literacy, and popular culture*. Portsmouth, NH: Heinemann.

Peterson, S. (1998). Evaluation and teachers' perceptions of gender in sixth-grade student writing. *Research in the Teaching of English, 33*(2), 181–208.

Smith, M.W., Appleman, D., & Wilhelm, J.D. (2014). *Uncommon core: Where the authors of the standards go wrong about instruction—and how you can get it right*. Thousand Oaks, CA: Corwin.

Smith, M.W., & Wilhelm, J.D. (2002). *"Reading don't fix no Chevys": Literacy in the lives of young men*. Portsmouth, NH: Heinemann.

Smith, M.W., & Wilhelm, J.D. (2006). *Going with the flow: How to engage boys (and girls) in their literacy learning*. Portsmouth, NH: Heinemann.

Smith, M.W., Wilhelm, J.D., & Fredricksen, J. (2013). The Common Core: New standards, new teaching. *Phi Delta Kappan, 94*(8), 45–48.

Smith, M.W., & Wilhelm, J.D. (2009). Boys and literacy: Complexity and multiplicity. In. L. Christenbury, R. Bomer, & P. Smagorinsky (Eds.), *Handbook of adolescent literacy research* (pp. 360–371). New York, NY: Guilford.

Turner, K.H. (2010). Digitalk: A new literacy for a digital generation. *Phi Delta Kappan, 92*(1), 41–46.

Wilhelm, J.D., & Smith, M.W. (with Fransen, S.). (2014). *Reading unbound: Why kids need to read what they want—and why we should let them*. New York, NY: Scholastic.

Wilson, C. (2008, February 22). The wisdom of the chaperones: Digg, Wikipedia, and the myth of Web 2.0 democracy. *Slate*. Retrieved from www.slate.com/articles/technology/technology/2008/02/the_wisdom_of_the_chaperones.html

LITERATURE CITED

Doyle, A.C. (1902). *The hound of the Baskervilles*. Retrieved from www.literature.org/authors/doyle-arthur-conan/hound

ABOUT THE AUTHORS

Michael W. Smith is a professor in Temple University's College of Education in Philadelphia, Pennsylvania, USA, who joined the ranks of college teachers after 11 years of teaching high school English. He has won awards for his teaching at both the high school and college levels. His research focuses both on understanding how adolescents and adults engage with texts outside school and on how teachers can use those understandings to devise more motivating and effective instruction inside schools. Michael served as the chair of the Literature Special Interest Group of the American Educational Research Association, cochair of the National Council of Teachers of English's Assembly for Research, and coeditor of *Research in the Teaching of English* and is a fellow of the National Conference on Research in Language and Literacy. He has written, cowritten, or edited 14 books and monographs, including *"Reading Don't Fix No Chevys": Literacy in the Lives of Young Men* (Heinemann, 2002), for which he and his coauthor, Jeff Wilhelm, received the 2003 David H. Russell Award for Distinguished Research in the Teaching of English. Michael's writing has appeared in such journals as *Communication Education, English Journal, Journal of Adolescent & Adult Literacy, The Journal of Educational Research, Journal of Literacy Research,* and *Research in the Teaching of English.* He is also an author of National Geographic School Publishing's Inside and Edge, two anthology series designed for struggling readers and English learners.

 Jon-Philip Imbrenda is a doctoral student in the Literacies & Learners program at Temple University in Philadelphia, Pennsylvania, USA. He served as the instructional leader of a literary arts magnet program in Towson, Maryland, where he received ISTE's SIGOL Online Learning Award for his work on the VORSH (Virtual One-Room Schoolhouse), a mentoring project utilizing Web 2.0 tools to facilitate peer-to-peer interaction. His research interests involve developing analytical tools to reveal insights into classroom texts, particularly in understanding how students' engagement is reflected in the texts they produce.

 Jeffrey D. Wilhelm is a professor of English education at Boise State University in Boise, Idaho, USA, and the founding director of the Boise State Writing Project and the Maine Writing Project. A classroom teacher for 15 years, he works in local schools as part of a virtual professional development site network sponsored by the Boise State Writing Project and regularly teaches middle and high school students. Jeff has authored or coauthored 31 books about literacy teaching and learning. He won the two of the top research awards in English education: the National Council of Teachers of English's Promising Research Award for *"You Gotta BE the Book": Teaching Engaged and Reflective Reading With Adolescents* (Teachers College Press & National Council of Teachers of English, 1997) and the David H. Russell Award for Distinguished Research in the Teaching of English for *"Reading Don't Fix No Chevys": Literacy in the Lives of Young Men* (with Michael W. Smith; Heinemann, 2002). Jeff has also written more than 200 chapters, articles, and commentaries about the teaching of reading and writing. He has created numerous materials for students, including Scholastic's e21 and Issues 21, a set of books about social action topics, and has edited a series of 100 books for reluctant readers entitled The Ten. Jeff enjoys speaking, presenting, and working with students and schools. His latest book, *Reading Unbound: Why Kids Need to Read What They Want—and Why We Should Let Them* (again with Michael W. Smith; Scholastic, 2014) reports on an extended study into the reading lives and responses of students who read and engage with nontraditional texts such as video game narratives, manga, horror, fantasy, vampire, and dystopia novels. He is currently researching the effects of inquiry teaching on teachers, students, and learning.

CHAPTER 8

Teaching Digital Writing in K–3

Karen A. Pelekis & Carole C. Phillips,
Greenacres Elementary School, Scarsdale Public Schools

I n the fall, first graders are examining the pumpkins growing in their school garden to learn about plants. Because their teacher wants them to understand that a plant produces seeds so new plants can grow, these students will create pumpkin life cycle slide shows that repeat to help them learn the concept of continuity. They are excited about composing digital drawings with accompanying text on the computer using Pixie software. This tool will also make it easier for them to organize, add to, and edit multiple pages than if they used paper. A page from one student's slide show can be seen in Figure 8.1, and the entire example can be viewed online at www.reading.org/writenow_pumpkinvideo.

Figure 8.1. A Page of a First Grader's Plant Life Cycle Slide Show Created in Pixie

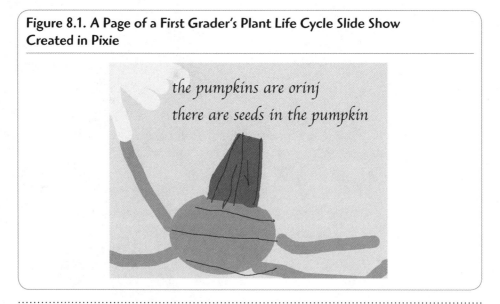

the pumpkins are orinj
there are seeds in the pumpkin

To manage this project with first graders, though, the teacher needs to assist students in small groups while the rest of the class works independently. She also has backup plans to handle technical difficulties, including using the library computers at another time if the wireless network does not work in the classroom with the mobile lab. Because the students are already comfortable with the software, she sets aside three 50-minute sessions over a two-week period to complete this project.

In the end, students' slide shows are stored in their science folders in their computer accounts. The slide shows will be used again in April, when the class hatches chicks, to compare and contrast a plant's life cycle with an animal's life cycle. These slide shows will also be revisited when the pumpkin seeds, previously taken from the fall harvest, are planted in late spring.

Teaching Digital Writing in K–3: The What, Why, and How

As the preceding vignette shows, meaningfully integrating digital tools in a manageable way opens up exciting writing possibilities for even the youngest students. The purpose of this chapter is to begin to explain the what, why, and how of incorporating this technology in the early elementary grades. The first section describes a variety of tools that can be used effectively in grades K–3. The second segment explores reasons why teachers use this technology with early elementary school students. The third shows how digital tools can be employed in classrooms when teachers, students, and the learning environment are properly prepared. Throughout, a number of illustrative examples of successful projects from kindergarten to third grade are highlighted. As a first-grade teacher and an elementary school library media specialist, we hope to provide a practical guide for other primary-grade educators. We aim to show how the teaching of writing can be enriched and young writers empowered through the meaningful use of digital tools.

What Ways Can Digital Tools Be Used for Writing in K–3?

Digital tools are very versatile. They can enhance learning at any stage of the writing process, such as prewriting, organizing ideas, composing, editing, revising, or sharing. They are compatible with all types of writing, including narrative, informational, and opinion. They are helpful tools for young writers, whether the words are composed on paper or on the computer. This technology makes it possible for students to add other creative components to their writing, such as audio, photographs, graphics, and slide shows, as well as to learn from a variety of online, multimedia resources. It also expands opportunities for collaborating and sharing work with others.

The range of benefits for using technology in K–3 writing is shown through the examples that follow. All are from the Greenacres Elementary School in Scarsdale, New York, under the leadership of Principal Gerry Young. The digital tools we describe have worked successfully with students in our school and may include adaptations created to have them meet the needs of younger students. There are certainly many more tools available that we have yet to explore. Because this is a practical guide, we briefly introduce the tools, show some ways they can be used, and include student examples. Links to additional information are provided.

Practicing Skills. With pictures, sounds, and gamelike formats, learning writing skills through apps and games can make this work more engaging. For handwriting, a captivating iPad app called LetterSchool (https://itunes.apple.com/us/app/letterschool/id435476174?mt=8) allows students to use the touch pad to learn to form letters correctly. There are also numerous tools to aid students in learning phonics. Games like Puzzle Me Words from ReadWriteThink (www.readwritethink.org/classroom-resources/student-interactives/puzzle-words-30819.html) help students hear short vowel sounds in words and spell C–V–C words with different levels of play. Programs such as Lexia (lexialearning.com/product) strengthen phonics skills by analyzing student performance through built-in, ongoing assessment. Students can also learn to illustrate and practice storytelling with author/illustrator Mo Willems using the iPad app Don't Let the Pigeon Run This App! (https://itunes.apple.com/us/app/dont-let-pigeon-run-this-app!/id459749670?mt=8).

Organizing Writing. Kidspiration 3 (www.inspiration.com/Kidspiration) helps students sort research and map ideas with graphic organizers that can be crafted in picture view or writing view. As seen in Figure 8.2,

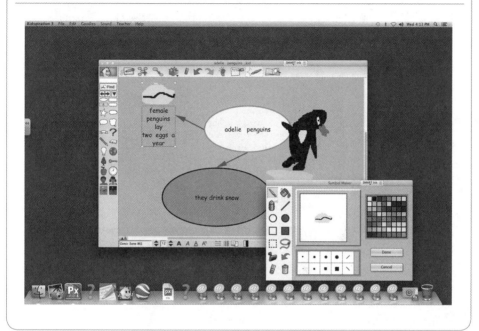

digital illustrations can be created within Kidspiration 3 to accompany text. This figure depicts a work in progress of a student organizing research on penguins for a geography project.

Creating Stories and Much More. Stationery Studio (shop.fablevision learning.com/stationery-studio-writing-collection-deluxe/fa/shop.detail/ productID/2563/#.UtL_SI1VTDk) is easy-to-use stationery for the computer, featuring art by author/illustrator Peter H. Reynolds. It offers a variety of themes and printing options. Students enjoy Stationery Studio so much that they often use it to write notes to family, classmates, and school personnel during their free time. The graphics also inspire students to create stories on a variety of topics. An example of this writing is shown in Figure 8.3, in which a first-grade student uses the stationery to express her opinion about why cats are her favorite pets.

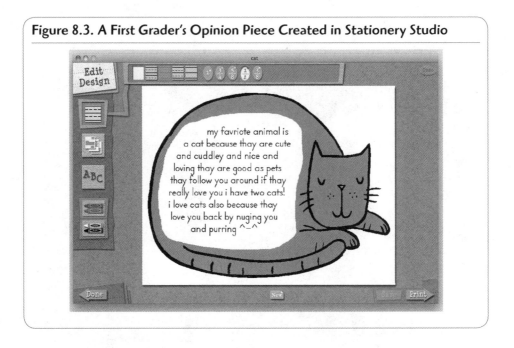

Figure 8.3. A First Grader's Opinion Piece Created in Stationery Studio

With Pixie (tech4learning.com/pixie), the tool used to make slide shows in the opening vignette, students can compose with a number of creative options, including paintbrushes, textured prints, colors, special effects, pictures, audio, music choices, and fonts. It also expands writing possibilities with the use of a built-in camera. The software is easy to learn and fun to explore. Pixie makes it simpler when students write together because the work they produce can be duplicated. It also motivates students because their work can be exported and shared effortlessly with others. Overall, students become very engaged and excited about writing with the use of this software.

More importantly, Pixie features can assist students throughout the writing process. With the audio component, students can record lengthier stories, making it easier for them to remember their ideas when they return to write the text at a later time. This feature also captures how they naturally speak, which helps students hear differences in word choices and vocabulary. Additionally, this software makes it possible for students to more efficiently organize, revise, and revisit their work than crossing out sentences or undoing stapled papers. This is especially useful for certain

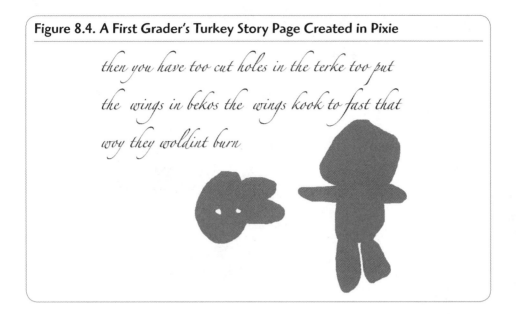

Figure 8.4. A First Grader's Turkey Story Page Created in Pixie

then you have too cut holes in the terke too put the wings in bekos the wings kook to fast that woy they woldint burn

types of assignments, such as adding on to a how-to book. In the example in Figure 8.4, a first grader writing about the steps needed to make a turkey later remembered about how to cook the wings. Because including this information was uncomplicated, he was more eager to add these details. The figure shows this page from his slide show, and the entire movie is available online at www.reading.org/writenow_turkeyvideo.

Microsoft Word allows students to create documents, but it can also serve to strengthen their understanding of words and writing. For instance, third-grade teacher Paula Bautista has her students practice using features of Microsoft Word while learning about parts of speech. The students in her class paint pictures and find adjectives to describe their art. Then, they discover the font collections, styles, colors, sizes, and effects that best express the meanings of the adjectives using a variety of options to create visual impact. The student who created Figure 8.5 chose adjectives to describe his painting of a jack-o'-lantern and expressed his understanding of the words via Microsoft Word.

Comic Life 3 (www.plasq.com/products/comiclife3) makes it possible for students to create their own comic books. Older students can import their drawings or photos to use. Younger students can manage this tool if

---

Figure 8.5. A Third Grader's Adjective List Created in Microsoft Word

Jack o' Lantern

Pumpkiny
Bumpy
SCARY
Bright
Heavy
Orange
Fun
Round
Emerald green
Inky Black
Light Brown
Creepy
Scary
Yummy
Slimy
Giant
Dark
Smelly
C h u b b y
CIRCULAR
lumpy
ROttiNG
Decorated
Fancy

---

the teacher provides set background templates so students only need to add the speech bubbles and text. With this tool, students can produce their own comics based on studies of books that are written in a similar format, using photos from the book for the templates. This is also an effective way to teach dialogue and punctuation.

With iMovie (www.apple.com/mac/imovie/Windows) or Movie Maker (windows.microsoft.com/en-us/windows-live/movie-maker#t1=overview), teachers can produce professional-looking movies, complete with titles, graphics, and transitions. (It is easier to use than it sounds, and it makes end-of-year slide shows memorable.) These movies can be used in numerous ways, such as having a class make shared writing pieces and as teaching tools. For example, in Melissa Genovese's second-grade class, students create illustrations in Pixie depicting words with long and short vowel sounds, which are then exported to create an iMovie for them to study and review.

iBooks Author (www.apple.com/ibooks-author) makes it possible for students to write digital stories using a combination of tools, and then the work can be published to an iPad library. For example, Ms. Genovese collaborated with technology teacher William Yang to have her students create digital stories as part of a yearlong unit on animals. The class worked on the project in the computer lab twice a week over a period of two months. Each student chose a bird to study and researched about it using a variety of resources, including live bird cams. Mr. Yang also customized templates in iBooks Author to make it easier for students to manage their writing via a page for each category, such as diet, eggs and young, cool facts, and sources. Organization and planning time were key factors in making this assignment work.

The project was taught in steps. Students used graphic organizers to record and organize information they learned. They categorized and typed information into sentences using Microsoft Word and then copied and pasted their completed work into the templates. Students recorded themselves reading their digital stories using GarageBand (www.apple. com/mac/garageband) and added illustrations from Pixie to go along with the categories. These books were published in iTunes U (www.apple.com/ education/ipad/itunes-u), to be viewed and heard on any iPad given access to the work, making it possible for students to share their stories with others who lived far away. A page from one of these stories is shown in Figure 8.6.

Researching With Online Resources. Students can conduct research using developmentally appropriate digital resources. Using the text-to-speech function, in which the computer reads the writing aloud, students can learn from sources that are just right to understand but too difficult to read independently. This function is built into some resources or can be added through system preferences on the computer. This gives students greater access to resources so they have more to write about and can take in this

Figure 8.6. A Page of a Second Grader's Bird Research Book Created in iBooks Author

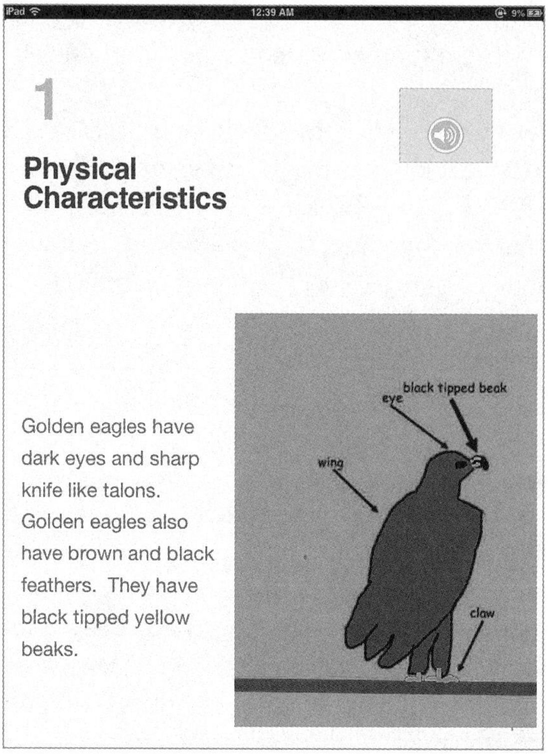

information at their own pace. Our library homepage has links to a variety of resources to make them easier for students to access. They are taught to use the homepage as well as look up resources using the library codes. We have found these sites to be particularly useful with younger students:

- PebbleGo (www.pebblego.com/public/login.php)
- National Geographic Kids (kids.nationalgeographic.com/kids)
- World Book Online for Kids (www.worldbook.com/all/item/ 430-world-book-online-for-kids?wbredirect=1&Itemid=112)
- Google Earth (www.google.com/earth)

Students can also conduct research from teacher-created resources through Web-based sites such as wikis. Wikispaces Classroom (www .wikispaces.com) is an Internet space that can be used for posting resources such as videos, pictures, links, student work, and stories. Videos can be embedded in the wiki using KeepVid (keepvid.com) to avoid young students gaining access to inappropriate material on YouTube. Students use the computer's text-to-speech function to listen to information that is too difficult to read.

Online tutorials are available with step-by-step instructions to set up a wiki, and the time it takes to create one is worth the effort if the wiki can be used over the course of a year or for the same unit in following years. Wikis are versatile and simple enough to employ with any grade, depending on the content and usage. The format for using a wiki is easy for even young students to follow. Students learn to how to log into the wiki independently and navigate choices from the sidebar. They also can access it from home.

Collaborating With Others and Sharing Work. Wikis are designed to be collaborative so certain users can be given access to posting and contributing to them. Younger students can use wikis as a resource, but by third grade, they can learn to add to a wiki on their own to create a class resource. Wikis can be set as private so only people who are invited into them can see them. A class can create a private wiki containing videos, pictures, and stories about themselves. Students can create shared writing pieces to post on the wiki. Using the text-to-speech function on the computer, students can highlight text and have it read aloud to them. As illustrated in Figure 8.7, a kindergarten class wrote about a Thanksgiving activity with their fifth-grade buddies, and the teacher added photos and posted it on the wiki. Throughout the year, students enjoyed reading the stories that they had created.

Blogs (e.g., Edublogs: edublogs.org) are another way for students to use the Internet to post research and collaborate with others. Blogs have a different format than wikis, which are sometimes more difficult for younger students to follow. Blogs can be set up so students can correspond with one another within and across classes. Students can share information through the blog, including research, projects, and website reviews.

Alphabet Organizer from ReadWriteThink (www.readwritethink.org/ classroom-resources/student-interactives/alphabet-organizer-30035.html) makes it easier to create ABC books by providing a template with artistic

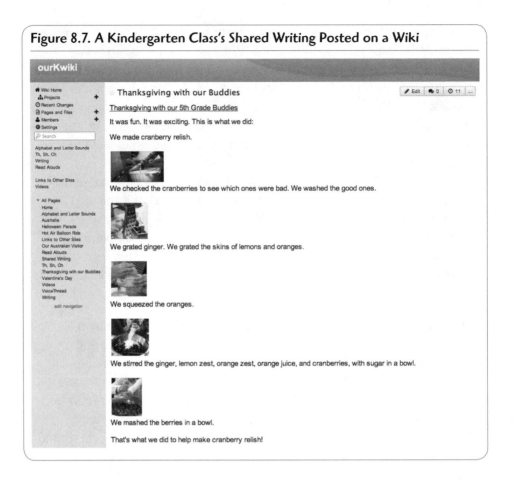

Figure 8.7. A Kindergarten Class's Shared Writing Posted on a Wiki

choices and save features. Each letter of the alphabet cleverly has its own file drawer to store material; clicking on a letter pulls the file drawer out, revealing previous work so users can keep track of it. The save features mean users can return to their projects over time and break them down into manageable pieces. This student interactive is also available as a mobile app with a camera feature (www.readwritethink.org/classroom-resources/mobile-apps/alphabet-organizer-b-30995.html). Figure 8.8 shows a picture overview of a pumpkin alphabet book created by a first-grade class (see the full book at www.reading.org/writenow_abcbook; we split our book into three separate PDFs so it will download quickly for you).

Another online tool, Google Docs (www.docs.google.com), makes it possible for students to work simultaneously on a document. Each student

Figure 8.8. A First-Grade Class's ABC Book Pictures

has a personal account but logs into shared work from their own computer. With this tool, teachers see the progress that students are making from start to finish. Teachers can track changes and write messages to their students. The use of digital tools like Google Docs can make demanding research, writing, and collaborative work more manageable for both students and teachers.

As an example, third-grade teacher Debbie Leitner and technology teacher Mr. Yang incorporated Google Docs into the culminating activity for a two-month unit about space. In the past, students had created a class A-to-Z shape book using texts for research. Each pair of students investigated the resources to carefully select just one word about space for every letter of the alphabet, such as *sun* for *S*. During times set aside for science and writing, students worked in pairs to research space, this time with Internet resources as well as books and using Google Docs to collaborate. Students also worked in the computer lab with Mr. Yang to learn how to use Google Docs.

With this tool, the teacher could easily give feedback to her students. As a result, they did not have to wait to meet with her. As all the students worked together on the computers and made changes, she could quickly conference with them through Google Docs, which provided a clear record of what feedback had been given and followed. Because the teacher could look at the history of what a student had done, it improved assessment and made it possible to learn more about each student. Use of this tool motivated students by improving how they worked together. Google Docs also made it easier to share the completed "Space A to Z" book with parents.

Why Use Digital Writing in K–3?

As the Google Docs and other examples show, there are some clear advantages to using digital tools for writing with early elementary school students. The meaningful integration of these tools can help them learn skills, organize their thoughts, express themselves, remember ideas, and create different genres of writing. Students are better able to understand concepts, visualize information, conduct research, comprehend language, access resources, collaborate with others, edit writing, publish work, reach a wider audience, and assess their progress. The use of digital tools deepens and enriches students' writing experiences when it is thoughtfully incorporated into instruction.

Because these new tools are changing what it means to write, students need to be able to use them effectively. As Hicks (2013) argues in *Crafting Digital Writing: Composing Texts Across Media and Genres,*

> as writing continues to shape and be shaped by digital tools and networked spaces, and as standards for teaching and learning how to write broaden to encompass new genres and media, writers are presented with more and more options. The question is no longer whether we *should* use technology to teach writing; instead we must focus on the many ways that we *must* use technology to teach writing. (p. 2)

The use of digital tools in grades K–3 is specifically required in Common Core Writing Anchor Standard 6: "Use technology, including the Internet, to produce and publish writing and to interact and collaborate with others" (National Governors Association Center for Best Practices & Council of Chief State School Officers [NGA Center & CCSSO], 2010a, p. 18). The Standards also address why these tools need to be used with young authors: "Just as media and technology are integrated in school and life in the twenty-first century, skills related to media use (both critical analysis and production of media) are integrated throughout the standards" (NGA Center & CCSSO, 2010b, p. 2).

The main reason we use digital tools with our students is that it makes a difference in our teaching and the way our students learn. This realization evolved over several years, and we learned it in stages. We began as educators, lacking computer skills, who were just intrigued with the idea of how technology might help our students. Because we were able to get a great deal of professional support at our school and through the New Literacies Research Team at the University of Connecticut for an extended period of time, we began to integrate digital tools in our teaching. About a year after we started using them, an observer who came to our classroom asked us whether we really needed technology to do the work we were doing. It made us stop and reflect. Did we *have* to use digital tools to be able to teach our students as effectively? We wanted to ascertain what the digital piece was truly bringing to the learning and whether it could be accomplished as well without it.

At the time, we were conducting an Internet workshop, in which students were studying the continents, doing research from a wiki loaded with videos, websites, and other sources. Although we used many books to study this topic, technology played a vital role in student learning. Digital tools took students to places in a manner that traditional resources could not; the videos they loved watching made them feel like they had traveled around the world. Plus, the Internet research was designed and organized in a way that made it possible for first graders to understand the material and study it at their own pace, as most of the books on this subject were beyond their reading level. Finally, technology meant they could share their experiences via Skype (www.skype.com) and blogs with a third-grade class in another state who were also studying the continents. As a result, we had to answer yes; we were only able to teach this more fully and deeply because of the meaningful use of digital tools.

Although we had acknowledged the importance of technology for enriching students' content area understanding, it took us longer to realize the positive impact it was having on their literacy learning. Internet inquiry made our students more curious—eager to ask questions and search for answers. We discovered that many students even continued to research topics at home. Because they were so engaged in reading and investigating, they had more reasons to write and became interested in recording what they were finding. In addition, because students were gathering information in multimodal ways, they wanted to share their knowledge with their classmates and teachers in the same manner. Students enthusiastically took computer snapshots of pictures and videos, and included audio for slide shows, to enhance their writing. Informational writing was the natural result of their Internet inquiry work (see the one-page sample in Figure 8.9 and the entire letter at www.reading.org/writenow_firefighterletter).

Despite these experiences, it was yet another leap for us to acknowledge that digital tools could also make a meaningful contribution to narrative writing. After years of conducting an Internet workshop for a 90-minute reading period in each six-day cycle, and believing in the way it helped our students learn, we were finally ready to explore what digital tools might bring to story writing. Just as we had found the right balance

---

Figure 8.9. A Page of a First-Grade Class's Letter to Antarctica Firefighters

Dear Firefighters,
    We are Ms. Pelekis's first grade class. We have been studying about Antarctica. We watched a video from YouTube about your Mc Murdo Fire Department. It was very good. We found out more information about you on a website called Mc Murdo Fire Department. The website was cool because it tells you more about the trucks.
    We have a lot of questions about your fire department and more. We were hoping that you could answer them. Can you please tell us the answers? Here are our questions:

© FableVision, Inc.

of Internet inquiry work in our reading workshop, we had to do the same for writing. As a result, one day in a six-day cycle, we began an hour-long digital writing workshop for the whole class in place of the regularly scheduled writing workshop for that period. During the regular writing workshop periods, students also take turns using the three computers in the classroom.

We found, as in our prior experience, that the thoughtful use of technology makes teaching and learning more effective. Digital storytelling opens up new ways for students to express themselves. They love using the built-in camera to capture what inspires them, such as a special object brought in for sharing or a smile showing that they lost a tooth. Students take care in selecting just the right background music for their work and spontaneously discuss how music choices fit the mood of the writing. Students take pride in recording their stories and adding sound effects to go along with the text. Students thoughtfully incorporate a range of tools, such as speech bubbles or pictures sequenced to produce an animation effect. Students eagerly teach their peers how to use newly found features, and discoveries quickly spread through the room. Sharing their digital stories on the SMART Board becomes a significant highlight of our day. Students continue to enjoy using digital tools to write at home as well (see one student's poem entitled "Wheaters" [i.e., "Weather"] in Figure 8.10). These new tools help students reveal and share who they are, what they sound like, what is important to them, and how they think. (Figure 8.11 shows one page from a first grader's slide show, and the entire movie can be viewed at www.reading.org/writenow_horsevideo.)

How Can Digital Writing Be Manageable in K–3?

Although the use of digital tools can make writing more meaningful for elementary school students, it will only work if it is also manageable for teachers and students and has a valuable place in the learning environment. This can be a challenge because the students are young, but it is worth the time and effort. Preparation is essential for the incorporation of digital tools to be effective. In some instances, like the examples with Pixie and Google Docs, technology can actually make management easier.

Manageable for Teachers. Use of this technology only works if it is manageable for educators. Research shows that the barriers to using digital

Figure 8.10. A First Grader's Poem About the Weather, Written at Home

```
                      wheaters.txt
It is snowing. Mommy, Can I play in the snow?
It is winter.

It is raining. Mommy, Can I jump in the
puddles? It is spring.

Let the leaves fall off the trees. it is fall.

let the sun come out mommy can i eat
watermelon?  it is summer

it is halloween can i go trikertreating?
mommy.its halloween.

its christmas can i get a present mommy? its
christmas. santa is coming.
```

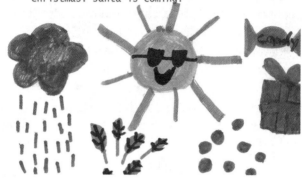

Figure 8.11. A Page of a First Grader's Story About Creating a Horse Mosaic

tools by teachers include lack of confidence, lack of time, and difficulties with equipment (British Educational Communications and Technology Agency, 2004). These factors directly influence whether teachers will try or continue to use digital tools with their students. After spending years of being afraid that we would wreck the computers and feeling helpless when things would inevitably go wrong, we understand why teachers are hesitant to try digital tools. They can be very intimidating. Teachers require time and support to learn the necessary skills. In "Every Teacher a Miss Rumphius: Empowering Teachers With Effective Professional Development," Coiro (2005) writes about her work with teachers who are learning to incorporate digital tools in their classrooms. She provides seven excellent lessons for these educators:

1. Start out small and move through stages.
2. Take a few risks along the way.
3. Take a proactive approach to learning.
4. Encourage your students to share their expertise.
5. Never underestimate the power of collaboration.
6. Seek authentic learning opportunities.
7. Be prepared for change. (p. 212)

When teachers become comfortable with using technology in their classrooms, it is imperative that they have time to plan, work with colleagues, get support from technology teachers, and receive assistance with equipment that is not working properly. The ways to use digital tools are vast and varied. It involves searching for appropriate apps, keeping up with changing tools, learning new programs, and figuring out how to incorporate them into the grade-level curriculum. Teachers need to find resources that can help them, such as those available on the International Reading Association's Technology in Literacy Education Special Interest Group's webpage (www.reading.org/General/AdvocacyandOutreach/SIGS/TechnologySIG.aspx). It takes years for teachers to successfully integrate digital tools in their classrooms (Coiro, 2005). Professional development, collaboration, and support from colleagues and administrators continue to be necessary.

Manageable for Students. Young students require direct instruction, guidance, and support to successfully use technology. Just as students need to learn how to properly use and care for items in their classroom, this is true of computers as well. Students may have used technology outside of school, but they need to learn how to use it in an educational setting. Particularly with younger students, special attention must be given to the pacing of instruction, students' comfort with technology, the setup of equipment, and the introduction of digital tools.

Teachers can make the use of technology easier for students by giving them tools to become self-sufficient and successful. Logging onto the computer is simpler for some students when the headphones are labeled with their username. Student computer docks need to be streamlined, loaded with programs and links to appropriate educational resources and interactives. Students then need to be taught how to use what is on their docks. They have to be clearly instructed on how the programs work and understand what the teacher expects of them.

Manageable in the Learning Environment. A teacher who is prepared to integrate technologies needs to find the most effective ways to do so, especially for younger students. Meshing technology in a classroom setting means dealing with the complexities of orchestrating new and old routines. After a great deal of trial and error, we eventually discovered the key to making it workable for our students and for us: The principles behind good classroom management practices do not change in a digital classroom. The addition of technology needs to be a natural extension of what and how we already teach. When we finally realized this simple idea and kept what already worked in our routine, incorporating technology fell into place.

We began structuring our Internet workshop the same way we ran our reading workshop. The students already knew the routine, and we knew how to make it run smoothly. Other management techniques worked with digital tools as well. We allowed students time to explore some programs before giving them an assignment. Because difficulties occurred most often when the lesson was too ambitious and we expected that the students could do more than they really could, we worked with small groups and broke down tasks. When projects required one-on-one help, we had older buddy classes assist the younger students. For example, when the kindergartners used the mobile lab for the first time, the fifth graders worked with them to explain how to properly use the laptops. The older students modeled and taught the younger students how to carry the computers, understand the desktop features, and save information in folders.

The classroom also needed to be arranged so students could work together more easily. We began using the mobile lab in the classroom to have more flexibility so students could function better in pairs or small groups. We found that when students were researching with a partner, it worked best when they sat with their computers side by side. It is very difficult for young students to split one computer screen to look at both the resources and write about their research. It is easier for the pair to use one of the computers to show the research and the other computer for writing about their findings. In Figure 8.12, one student has a photograph on her computer of a pumpkin from the school garden, and the other student is drawing it with the partner on the other computer.

Teachers need to also manage how best to include technology in their schedules. For several of the projects described in this chapter, teachers used time set aside for writing or content area study for technology work. Some teachers found it easier to incorporate this learning by creating a regularly scheduled Internet workshop or digital writing workshop. For all of these educators, the use of technology enhanced traditional instruction, strengthened curricular goals, and thus deserved a place in the schedule.

Figure 8.12. Partner Research Using Two Computers

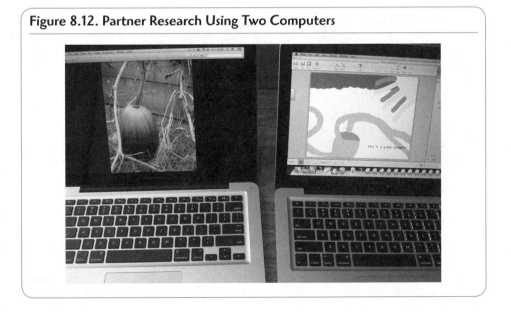

Conclusions

Technology can be incorporated into the writing curriculum in innovative ways to improve both teaching and student learning. Successful integration of digital tools requires a great deal of time and thought, but it is worth the effort. Digital tools offer teachers an opportunity to make writing a more enriching experience for their students. Thoughtfully integrating technology into the curriculum enhances learning for young authors. Students develop a better understanding of the writing process, have additional opportunities for creative expression, better organize their thinking, and can access a variety of resources. Digital tools encourage collaboration by expanding possibilities for sharing work and reaching a broader audience.

When educators understand how learning can be enriched by technology, why it is important, and how to manage the incorporation of digital tools in writing, students benefit. When the use of these tools in grades K–3 is both meaningful and manageable, it significantly enhances the teaching and students' learning of writing. For even for the youngest students, technology opens up exciting possibilities for writing. Students become more motivated writers, and it empowers them as authors. The purposeful integration of digital tools enhances writing experiences for young students and is an opportunity for dramatic, worthwhile change.

REFERENCES

British Educational Communications and Technology Agency. (2004). *A review of the research literature on barriers to the uptake of ICT by teachers.* Coventry, UK: Author. Retrieved from dera.ioe.ac.uk/1603/1/becta_2004_barrierstouptake_litrev.pdf

Coiro, J. (2005). Every teacher a Miss Rumphius: Empowering teachers with effective professional development. In R.A. Karchmer, M.H. Mallette, J. Kara-Soteriou, & D.J. Leu, Jr. (Eds.), *Innovative approaches to literacy education: Using the Internet to support new literacies* (pp. 199–219). Newark, DE: International Reading Association.

Hicks, T. (2013). *Crafting digital writing: Composing texts across media and genres.* Portsmouth, NH: Heinemann.

National Governors Association Center for Best Practices & Council of Chief State School Officers. (2010a). *Common Core State Standards for English language arts and literacy in history/social studies, science, and technical subjects.* Washington, DC: Authors.

National Governors Association Center for Best Practices & Council of Chief State School Officers. (2010b). *The Common Core State Standards Initiative: A state-led effort to create shared high standards to make sure all American students are ready for college and work.* Retrieved from www.corestandards.org/assets/KeyPointsELA.pdf

Karen A. Pelekis is an elementary school teacher at Greenacres School in Scarsdale, New York, USA, and has been an early childhood educator for more than 15 years. She collaborated for several years with the New Literacies Research Team at the University of Connecticut to enrich literacy learning through the use of technology. Her first-grade students utilize a variety of Internet resources and digital tools to conduct research. Karen has presented at workshops, the International Reading Association's Technology in Literacy Education Special Interest Group's sessions, and conferences. She has written about her work for publications such as *Reading Today Online* and is also on the ReadWriteThink Advisory Board. Karen can be reached at kpelekis@scarsdaleschools.org.

Carole C. Phillips is the library media specialist at the Greenacres Elementary School in Scarsdale, New York, USA. She has a New York State reading specialist certificate and has collaborated with the New Literacies Research Team at the University of Connecticut for the past five years on online reading comprehension projects spanning the K–5 spectrum. Recently, she has been working with elementary classes on Internet workshop and inquiry research projects, mostly with classroom teacher Karen Pelekis and technology teacher William Yang on developing research projects for elementary students. Carole can be reached at cphillips@scarsdaleschools.org.

CHAPTER 9

Multigenre Projects

Building Knowledge, Motivation, Collaboration, and Writing Expertise in Grades 4–6

Kathy Ganske, *Vanderbilt University*

At the end of a fifth-grade writing workshop in a challenging urban classroom, two students, who are often not engaged with writing, excitedly talked with the teacher:

Student 1: [holding up a paper] Are we gonna work on this Friday? I'm hoping to finish my newspaper article about the Battle of Gettysburg.

Student 2: Yeah, and you should see the script we're writin' about Harriet Tubman. It's cool!

Teacher: Whoa! Wow! You're really into our Civil War multigenre project! That's great! You'll have about half an hour Friday and the whole workshop time on Monday to work on your writing.

Does this exchange sound like your classroom? Sadly, in most classrooms, writing is limited, and worksheets and prompts still predominate, although we know that the latter do not lead to the kind of writing needed to meet current standards (Culham, 2014). The Common Core State Standards (National Governors Association Center for Best Practices & Council of Chief State School Officers [NGA Center & CCSSO], 2010) call for writing to be integrated with science and social studies. It requires that learners be able to write informational/explanatory, opinion, and narrative pieces "for a range of tasks, purposes, and audiences" (p. 18) and that they engage in research and use technology to produce and publish writing.

Write Now! Empowering Writers in Today's K–6 Classroom, edited by Kathy Ganske.
© 2014 by the International Reading Association.

The type of multigenre project referred to in the opening vignette aligns well with these demands. Multigenre projects provide avenues for students to apply what they've learned about writing in various modes and for specific purposes through process writing and a workshop approach. These projects also afford a platform for enhancing student comprehension and deepening understandings from social studies and/ or science through genre writing (Graham & Hebert, 2010; Youngs & Barone, 2007). Furthermore, they can develop students' abilities to take on different historical perspectives (D'Adamo & Fallace, 2011). Although there are clearly potential advantages for both writing and content area performance, another important possibility, as evidenced in the vignette, is the fostering of student motivation for writing: Students often love the work of multigenre projects and become totally immersed in learning and writing.

There are many aspects of multigenre projects that contribute to students' engagement. For instance, intermediate- and middle-grade learners are motivated by collaboration, choice, and the opportunity to make decisions (Miller & Meece, 1997, 1999), and these can play major roles in multigenre projects. This was the case with the project highlighted at the start of the chapter, and these opportunities led the students to be highly motivated. Hard work, on-task behavior, excitement for learning, pride in accomplishment, and teamwork were the results. After the final celebration session, the young scholars could be seen flashing the product of their labors—a collaborative zine (rhymes with *lean*)—to others in the hallway. The turnaround that characterized the students' behaviors led others in the building to marvel at their engagement. Painter (2009) noted similar engagement and limited need to redirect behaviors in her project work with an academically diverse group of sixth graders.

Considering the curricular and motivational benefits of multigenre projects—whether published as zines; displayed as posters; shared as recordings; or compiled in other formats, such as a digital PechaKucha, a form that consists of 20 slides with 20 seconds devoted to each slide—they should be part of teachers' instructional repertoires. The remainder of this chapter explores how teachers can build this type of writing project into their English language arts and content area studies in the intermediate and middle grades.

Getting Started

There are many things to consider when planning a multigenre project. For example, it's important to think about such questions as these:

- What are my goals for the project, and what genres will support them?
- What will be the design of the project?
  - Will the project be completed by individuals, with a partner, or as a group effort?
  - Will the focus connect to a content area theme or an essential question, or will the topic be individually chosen by students?
  - What time frame will be used to complete the projects?
  - What form will the final product take?
- What types of support or scaffolding will students need?
  - What texts will support students' efforts to gain knowledge about the topic?
  - Which students will need to have additional assistance, and what kind?

Determining the Goals and Genres

Goals for the project will vary. Given the significance of standards, whether the Common Core or other state standards, it's important that project goals connect to the writing standards, but they may connect to other areas as well, such as reading, speaking and listening, language, literature, science, or social studies. My goals generally address learning in three areas: writing; social studies or science content; and one or more dispositional areas, such as engagement or collaboration. Because the aims for the project will directly connect to the writing modes, genres, and forms you choose, it's important to consider them at the same time.

The terms *modes*, *genres*, and *forms* can be confusing; however, understanding their meanings can be helpful in thinking about which to use and when. *Mode* refers to the purpose for writing: narrative (tell a story), expository (explain or inform), persuasive (present an argument), or technical (perform an on-the-job task that draws on a specialized vocabulary). *Genre* is more commonly associated with reading. But with the recognized relationship between reading and writing and the growing use of mentor texts to guide writers, the term also has come to be widely associated with writing, where it sometimes refers to categories of writing. In the narrative mode, these might be realistic fiction, biography, fantasy, or historical fiction; in the nonfiction mode, the term might refer to a content area, such as geography, history, or environmental science (Culham, 2011). At times, *genre* may denote one of the many forms that writing can take. For instance, when writing an expository piece on immigration, students might create a survey, brochure or pamphlet, speech, newspaper article, or blog. Similarly, in the narrative mode, historical fiction is often conveyed through a story, but other genres might include a poem, song, script, diary, letter, memoir, or even a graphic novel. Some forms or genres can be used with multiple modes. For example, comics could be used to tell a story; describe an event; or persuade someone, as is often the case with political cartoons. Several extensive listings of forms or genres are available on the Internet; to take a look, search for the phrase "modes, forms, and genres of writing." Here are a few that students have particularly enjoyed in the process of making the self-published magazines known as zines: informational texts, how-to works, poetry, ABC books, Q and As, interviews, essays and arguments, diary entries, obituaries, scripts, memoirs, maps, comics, timelines, charts and graphs, diagrams, autobiographies, brochures, newspapers, letters, and flyers.

Students need to know the characteristics and processes for writing in the forms or genres that they will be using. Mentor texts, such as those described in Chapters 3 and 4 of this volume, can play a key role in making the traits of a genre transparent to students. It's important to select exemplary illustrations of the genres and explicitly highlight the features.

The Design

The goals and standards will influence the design, as will the time frame (days and length of each session) available for completing the project. Collaborative projects typically take less time to complete than individual projects, as do projects with fewer genres included. Multigenre projects can span nine weeks, especially if different genres are being taught and practiced as part of the project. Lengthy projects are often closely intertwined with the study of particular content, such as a historical period.

By contrast, a weeklong collaborative project might be used to culminate a particular study, with individuals or groups of learners each writing a different genre to contribute to the project.

I've designed different types of multigenre projects, including some that engage preservice teachers in creating personal zines around interests of passion as preparation for planning and implementing lessons for a multigenre project of their own with groups of learners. Although these college students had no difficulty in choosing topics (e.g., Civil Rights, extreme weather, amphibians, 1950s pop culture) or researching information to deepen their understanding of the topic, I find that most students in grades 4–6 benefit from a more limited palette of topics, as when teachers select a theme connected to a content study and then offer students limited choice in the genres or in a focus topic. For instance, a teacher might select historical figures related to the Civil War as the theme and then expect students to choose a historical figure related to that theme to explore further by capturing the figure's character from different perspectives, such as through a letter to a friend, a newspaper article or flyer with factual information about an event, or a script that explores a conversation with another historical figure. Sometimes teachers limit choice of topic to different aspects of the big idea for a unit. For instance, with the big idea that weather affects our world in significant ways, students might choose to write about one of the following through various genres: floods, hurricanes, droughts, tornadoes, or blizzards. Or they might consider a particular event through the eyes of various persons. A Civil War focus might give rise to students exploring an aspect of the war or a particular event through the eyes of several different people: a slave, a soldier, a shop owner, a farmer, a general, or even a prominent historical figure, such as President Abraham Lincoln, Clara Barton, Frederick Douglass, Mary Lincoln, General Robert E. Lee, or Dr. Mary Edwards Walker. With learners in the intermediate and middle grades, I like to incorporate lots of collaboration: Students may write one genre independently but another with a partner or small group. Or the collaboration may come from peer conferencing and topic investigations. Students in these grades tend to be social, and integrating collaborative elements allows teachers to turn what can be a negative characteristic into a positive learning tool.

Students will need access to numerous resources. For the content work, these may include textbooks, fictional texts, picture books, informational books, and magazines. The resources should encompass primary sources as well, such as those available through the Library of Congress (www.loc.gov/teachers), including the American Memory collection (memory.loc.gov/ammem/index.html), which provides access to a wide range of newspaper articles, cartoons, letters, songs, photographs, and so forth on many social studies–related topics. Table 9.1 lists other online resources for finding primary source material for science and social studies. In addition to content resources, students will need mentor texts for the genres they

---

Table 9.1. Online Resources for Primary and Secondary Sources for Science and Social Studies

Science

- The Society for Science & the Public (www.societyforscience.org) offers a wealth of information in various forms and provides links to other websites as well.
- The National Geographic Kids website (kids.nationalgeographic.com/kids) includes photos, videos, and other materials.
- Science Buddies (www.sciencebuddies.org) provides an option to e-mail questions to a science expert.
- Enchanted Learning (www.enchantedlearning.com) offers a wealth of resources on a variety of science and social studies topics, such as explorers, inventors, geography, U.S. history, biomes, astronomy, human anatomy, and rain forests; there's also a newspaper link that takes navigators to an assortment of templates for creating front pages.
- The Project WILD website (www.projectwild.org) offers lots of resources on topics such as habitats and birds.
- InsectIdentification.org (www.insectidentification.org) is a website where learners can discover information about insects, from butterflies to cockroaches, as well as noninsects, such as spiders; students will love the amazing photographs.
- The Urban Programs Resource Network website (urbanext.illinois.edu) includes a special Just for Kids section that addresses topics like earthquakes and volcanoes, insects, and plants; a beneficial feature for some students is the availability of audio access to the information.
- The Wisconsin Fast Plants Program's website (www.fastplants.org) has, among other resources, numerous video options that display time-lapse photography of plants' lives.
- All About Birds (www.allaboutbirds.org), maintained by the Cornell Lab of Ornithology, is a website where you can learn about birds' characteristics, habitats, and songs.

(continued)

Table 9.1. Online Resources for Primary and Secondary Sources for Science and Social Studies (*Continued*)

Social Studies

- The Library of Congress American Memory (memory.loc.gov/ammem/index.html) website provides primary source documents, videos, interviews, music, maps, and a wealth of other information.
- The National Archives webpage "Finding Primary Sources" (www.archives.gov/education/research/primary-sources.html) includes primary source documents, as well as videos and audios related to the history, government, and politics of the United States.
- The Museum of the Moving Image's The Living Room Candidate (www.livingroom candidate.org) is a wonderful resource for studying past presidential candidates from 1952 to the present day through videos of commercials aired at the time.
- The Constitute website (https://www.constituteproject.org) includes a collection of constitutions from around the world for examining and comparing.
- The Miller Center's website (millercenter.org) is affiliated with the University of Virginia and makes accessible nearly 5,000 hours of secret recordings of telephone conversations and meetings by U.S. presidents, from Franklin Roosevelt to Richard Nixon.
- The United States Census Bureau's website (www.census.gov) offers population statistics as well as other information.
- Historic Map Works' webpage "Historic Maps" (www.historicmapworks.com/Articles/historic_maps.php) allows investigators to examine changes across time by examining historical maps from around the globe.

are using. These may be garnered from primary sources, but they may also be found in children's literature, including picture books, as well as newspapers and other texts. For example, if students are writing obituaries for a Civil War figure, they should have access to several different obituaries so they can discuss the shared and unique qualities. Access to examples from the historical period being studied, as well as contemporary examples, will enable students to look for differences in language as well as what is included.

When a zine is the final product, the structure typically includes lots of artwork and graphic elements interspersed with the several genres of writing, as well as a letter to the reader that introduces the content, short biographies of the writers, and a table of contents. Although zines are usually written by individuals, they can be authored by groups of students. Zines focus on themes or topics that are of particular interest to the writers.

The word *zine* stems from the fanzines (*fan* + *magazines*) of the 1930s that were self-published responses to fantasy and other writings. Zines come in various sizes and shapes, tend to have a cut-and-paste look, and are often left in libraries and other public places for people to take and read; some are published electronically. You can learn more about them through resources such as Todd and Watson's (2006) *Whatcha Mean, What's a Zine?*, which is written like a zine, as well as websites such as the one for *The Book of Zines: Readings From the Fringe* (Rowe, 2012; see, e.g., Koyen, 1995).

Scaffolding

When considering support for diverse student needs, be sure to think about the necessity of texts on a wide range of reading levels, as well as audiotaped materials, to ensure that all students have access to information. Another form of support comes from knowing your learners and being conscious of the fact that too much choice can sometimes restrict a learner's ability to move forward with decision making. This knowledge will enable you to plan appropriately for the topic selection part of the project. Being told you can write about anything you want can be overwhelming. Another form of support relates to the genres. Here, too, it's possible to have too much choice, as there are many, many forms in which a student might write. Some may be better suited to the topic than others, others may not have been explicitly taught and need to be, and still others may better match your goals than others. Students will need various writing supports as well, such as dictionaries; thesauruses; computers, notebooks, or e-readers; sticky notes; and colored pencils. The students themselves can also be a form of support and should not be overlooked. They can provide assistance and encouragement to other students through response-group sharing of works in progress, peer editing groups, and so forth. I like to use triads for response groups. This format takes its name not only from the fact that groups consist of three writers but also from the physical structure of the group: Writers form a triangle, facing one another, when they provide feedback. I've used triads for both formal and informal feedback sessions. For the former, everyone in the class shares and responds at the same time, and I have predetermined the makeup of each group. For the

Figure 9.1. A Fifth-Grade Triad Providing Feedback to One Another

latter, a group of three writers initiates a feedback session to talk about the writing of one or more group members (see Figure 9.1).

Students will be able to be more independent if the structure for the process of sharing is predictable and known by all group members. The structure described in Figure 9.2 relies on general guidelines I received years ago through the National Writing Project. It also works well for whole-class sharing. I model the process early on in the year during writing workshop and then follow up periodically by showcasing the work of an effective group via a fishbowl. The time spent preparing students to give peers valuable feedback (critical as well as positive) is well worth it; instead of a single teacher acting as the feedback provider, with lines of students waiting for questions to be answered, the classroom has a wealth of response givers.

Implementing a Multigenre Zine Project

Working with the big idea from a social studies unit—people choose to immigrate to the United States and begin new lives for many reasons—

> **Figure 9.2. Feedback Sharing With Small Groups or the Whole Class**
>
> **Guidelines for Response Groups**
>
> *Writer*
> - Make no apologies about your writing.
> - Read your piece aloud, pause, and then read it aloud again (or pass it to partners for a silent reading).
> - Listen and take notes while the group responds; commenting, discussing, or arguing is not appropriate.
>
> *Listeners/Readers*
> - While the writer reads aloud, listen; during the second reading, take notes for your response.
> - Respond in the assigned order.
> - Address the writer, making eye contact.
> - Respond with constructive comments only, as practiced.
> - Follow this sequence in responding:
>   - Briefly summarize the piece; relate it to a personal experience.
>   - Point out what you like; be specific.
>   - Ask questions or pose wonderings that show what you want to know more about.

I once decided to initiate a collaborative zine project with a group of fifth-grade students to be worked on in connection with a nine-week immigration unit in social studies. I created groups with three writers on each team and then identified the following forms/genres as options: fictional story, informational text, essay, timeline, how-to, ABC text, script, poem, newspaper, letter, and comic. Each team was expected to complete four forms/genres. In addition, they needed to include a "Dear Reader" letter to open the zine, a table of contents, and an "About the Authors" page, as well as artwork. I gathered numerous resources, besides the social studies text, for them to read and explore, including picture books, newspapers, magazines, and primary source materials from the Library of Congress. A sampling is shown in Table 9.2.

I wanted the students to use perspective as a means for bringing coherence to the various writings in their zines. From grade 1 onward, the Common Core (NGA Center & CCSSO, 2010) requires learners to demonstrate understandings about point of view for interpreting literature, and perspective is key to various aspects of the Standards for fifth grade. For example, the Writing Standards require students to "write opinion

Table 9.2. A Selected List of Resources on Immigration, for Grades 4–6

Literature

- Ada, A.F. (1997). *Gathering the sun: An alphabet in Spanish and English* (R. Zubizarreta, Trans.). New York, NY: Rayo. (PB, in Spanish and English)
- Alexander, K., & Witthöft, V. M. (2009). *Davy Brown discovers his roots.* Savannah, GA: Big Tent. (YA)
- Bode, J. (1999). *The colors of freedom: Immigrant stories.* New York, NY: Franklin Watts. (YA)
- Bunting, E. (2006). *One green apple.* New York, NY: Clarion. (PB)
- De Capua, S. (2004). *How people immigrate.* New York, NY: Children's. (in the A True Book series)
- Freedman, R. (2009). *Immigrant kids.* Paradise, CA: Paw Prints. (also available on CD)
- Hopkinson, D. (2003). *Shutting out the sky: Life in the tenements of New York 1880–1924.* New York, NY: Orchard.
- Karapetkova, H. (2010). *Landing at Ellis Island.* Vero Beach, FL: Rourke. (PB)
- Lai, H.M., Lim, G., & Yung, J. (1999). *Island: Poetry and history of Chinese immigrants on Angel Island, 1910–1940.* Seattle: University of Washington Press. (YA, poems in Chinese and English)
- Lawlor, V. (1997). *I was dreaming to come to America: Memories from the Ellis Island Oral History Project.* New York, NY: Puffin. (PB)
- Maestro, B. (1996). *Coming to America: The story of immigration.* New York, NY: Scholastic. (PB younger)
- Mazer, A. (Ed.). (2009). *America Street: A multicultural anthology of stories.* Paradise, CA: Paw Prints. (YA)
- Peacock, L. (2007). *At Ellis Island: A history in many voices.* New York, NY: Atheneum Books for Young Readers. (PB)
- Pérez, A.I. (2009). *My diary from here to there/Mi diario de aquí hasta allá.* San Francisco, CA: Children's. (PB)
- Say, A. (1993). *Grandfather's journey.* New York, NY: Houghton Mifflin. (PB)
- Streissguth, T. (2009). *Welcome to America? A pro/con debate over immigration.* Berkeley Heights, NJ: Enslow.
- Tan, S. (2006). *The arrival.* New York, NY: Arthur A. Levine. (PB)
- Woodruff, E. (1999). *The memory coat.* New York, NY: Scholastic. (PB younger)
- Woodruff, E. (2000). *The orphan of Ellis Island: A time-travel adventure.* New York, NY: Scholastic.
- Yep, L. (with Yep, K.S.). (2008). *The dragon's child: A story of Angel Island.* New York, NY: HarperCollins.

(continued)

pieces...supporting a point of view," "orient the reader by establishing a situation and introducing a narrator and/or characters," and "develop experiences and events or show the responses of characters to situations" (p. 20), as well as apply the Reading Standards to literature to "compare and contrast two or more characters, settings, or events in a story or a drama, drawing on specific details in the text" (p. 21). To help my students grasp what it means to take a perspective and to understand how different people can have different perspectives, learners discussed situation examples, examined photos of an event taken at different locations, and acted out different perspectives of an event. Next, we reviewed the genres on my list, and I introduced a few forms that we had not used in writing workshop: interviews, comics, scripts, and ABC books. We used the zine project itself to review the how-to genre. I explained the process of creating a zine and then asked students to help boil down the steps into a "recipe,"

> **Figure 9.3. Steps for Making a Zine**
>
> 1. Plan
>   - Read and explore resource materials.
>   - Identify a perspective to unify the zine parts.
>   - Choose four forms in which to write.
> 2. Research
>   - Read and investigate to learn more about the theme.
>   - Study examples of the chosen forms closely.
> 3. Writing process: Prewriting, drafting, conferring and feedback, revising, editing, and polishing
>   - Remember: Conferring and feedback can occur at multiple points in the process.
>   - Consider the best way to polish your zine: careful handwriting, typed, or mixed.
> 4. Continue step 3 with the other chosen forms.
>   - If needed, revise your choice of form.
>   - Remember the perspective you're using to tie the zine all together.
> 5. Compose and polish a "Dear Reader" letter in which you describe highlights of the zine.
> 6. Compose and polish an "About the Author" letter and decide whether you want to include a photo.
> 7. Put the works in order and create a table of contents.
> 8. Add additional artwork and relevant glitz to the zine.
> 9. Fasten the works together and check the page order.
> 10. Prepare to celebrate your hard work and to share your zines!

which we wrote on chart paper for later reference during our zine-making work. Their final steps are shown in Figure 9.3. Last, across a series of days, we explored the four new genres.

Interviewing

Although most of the students had observed interviews before, virtually no one had written and conducted an interview, so we discussed specifics and practiced the process of carrying out and writing up an interview. Key points included the following:

1. Interviews are based on real conversations.
2. Interviews range from simple questions and answers to elaborate descriptions that include commentary related to the context, the individual, and so forth.

3. Interviews are facilitated or hindered by the questions asked (yes/no questions end talk rather than encourage it).

4. Interviews depend on the preparedness of the interviewer.

It's important to research the topic, plan the questions and keep them short, put the interviewee at ease, be a good listener, and take notes. To prepare, students reviewed interview protocols and published products by examining books, newspapers, online author interviews, and primary sources, such as those available on the Library of Congress's webpage "Interviews With Today's Immigrants" (www.loc.gov/teachers/classroommaterials/presentationsandactivities/presentations/immigration/interv/toc.php). Then, the class dove into the process of drafting a set of interview questions. After discussing and refining them, those who planned to write interviews for the immigration zine brainstormed possible interviewees, such as an immigration officer, an immigrant, a family member in the country of origin, or a citizen in this country.

Comics

Because comics belong to a genre that many students have enjoyed but haven't been formally introduced to during writing workshop, I decided to research the merits of comics, which tend to relate to reading. Here are some of the key findings: The Canadian Council on Learning (2010) notes that comics are often missing from the curriculum, although the genre is one of boys' favorites and has the potential to benefit student comprehension, as well as helping English learners and struggling readers. Krashen (2005) also mentions the popularity of comics with boys and highlights the finding that comics can scaffold students toward more difficult reading. Likewise, Cary (2004) points out that comics are a good way to bridge students to more challenging reading, and he informs us of their value in working with English learners, where their popularity crosses gender lines. Maliszewski (2013) suggests that there has been limited research on writing comics because of the limited attention to writing in recent years. Among the benefits she notes are motivation for writing and developing voice.

I shared the results of my research with students and then engaged them in analyzing enlarged panels of comics to better understand just how they work. McCloud's (1994, 2006) *Understanding Comics: The*

Invisible Art and *Making Comics: Storytelling Secrets of Comics, Manga and Graphic Novels* are wonderful resources for teachers to increase their knowledge about the way comics are constructed and what is considered in creating them. Whether cartoon, comic, or graphic novel, meaning is conveyed through pictures, lines, and words. The illusions of motion and time result from our inferring what happens between panels, within panels, and through the way the comic or graphic novel ends. Following our scrutiny and discussion of the comics, I presented my own rough draft of a four-panel cartoon strip (see Figure 9.4). We talked through the elements and about what I might do to make it better, especially in terms of the use of words, which in my draft are more like captions; there are no speech bubbles. "I'm wondering, Do the captions take away the need to infer and read between the panels?" I asked, and we discussed. After this, I encouraged students to try a quick sketch on a similar layout and provided them just a few minutes to sketch in something before asking them to turn to a shoulder partner and discuss their start.

Figure 9.4. My Four-Panel Comic Strip on Immigration

Script Writing

We also explored script writing (see Strickland, Ganske, & Monroe, 2002). An effective way to introduce this genre is to read aloud with a partner Phillip and Hannah Hoose's (1998) delightful book *Hey, Little Ant*, which is written as a dialogue between an ant and a boy who is contemplating stepping on the ant. A Spanish version is also available (Hoose & Hoose, 2003). A plus about the book is that it works as a natural segue into persuasive writing. At the end, the reader is left to decide what should happen to the ant. After reading and discussing the book, you can introduce students to the concept of a dilemma. Invite them to brainstorm pairs of characters who might find themselves in a dilemma, both real (e.g., policeman and motorist) and fantasy related (e.g., toothbrush and tooth). Then, model the process for paired script writing: "Write down two characters, circle the one for whom you are going to write the first speech, and then write the speech." Next, ask for a volunteer to dictate the other character's first speech. Once this is recorded, describe the use of stage directions and continue with the back-and-forth script. After a number of exchanges, strive to resolve the dilemma. Debrief to answer any questions the students may have, and then provide an opportunity for them to engage in the process.

Students carry out the process with a partner (much like that modeled by the teacher and volunteer but with slight differences). After each learner records a pair of characters, everyone chooses one of their two characters and writes the first speech for that character. Next, partners exchange papers, write the response of the second character on their partner's paper, and then return it. Swapping papers continues for several turns. Then, students are asked to resolve the dilemma during the next exchange. Without exception, I have found script writing to be highly motivating to students in terms of writing, reading, and oral performance. Once students are comfortable with the process of writing in pairs, it's easy for them to transition to writing their own scripts independently or to writing collaborative scripts with more than two characters. Figure 9.5 shows an example of a script written by a fifth grader as part of a Civil War multigenre project. The writer included a couple of slang phrases from the time period to add authenticity. A longtime favorite resource of mine for examples of scripts with multiple characters is *Play* magazine, now available online as Plays: Scripts for Young Actors (www.playsmagazine.com).

Figure 9.5. A Fifth Grader's Civil War Script

Ammunition War

RIFLE:	(Proudly said) I have tons of ammunition.
JEFFERSON DAVIS:	(Determinedly said) I'm taking all your ammunition.
RIFLE:	(Angrily said) Quit jawing your mouth you bad egg.
JEFFERSON DAVIS:	How dare you say that? Let's settle this like real men.
RIFLE:	(Surprised) Everybody load and get ready.
JEFFERSON DAVIS:	Fire the cannon.
RIFLE:	Hold! How about we share the ammunition?
JEFFERSON DAVIS:	OK.

ABC Texts

ABC texts, also known as alphabet books, vary greatly. They range from very simple texts—typically with a presentation of upper- and lowercase letters on each page, along with a picture that exemplifies the letter, such as "Dd dog"—to complex texts that also include in-depth information related to the picture. A prime example of the latter is a beautifully illustrated fictional text about Queen Elizabeth's travels through the countryside, *The Queen's Progress: An Elizabethan Alphabet* by Celeste Davidson Mannis (2003), which is geared toward learners in the intermediate and middle grades. Some ABC texts, such as the student-created example in Figure 9.6 from an extreme weather zine created by third- and fourth-grade students, include alliterative phrases. Although expecting an individual multigenre project or even some group projects to include A–Z examples may be overly ambitious, it is a valuable genre to consider because students have the ability to demonstrate their knowledge of the content in a truly unique way. If the zine is a class collaboration, each student might contribute just one or two letters.

Celebrating the Accomplishment

After forms/genres that may be used in the multigenre project have been taught or reviewed, students begin to examine resources and determine which forms/genres they will use. Framing ideas, drafting, receiving

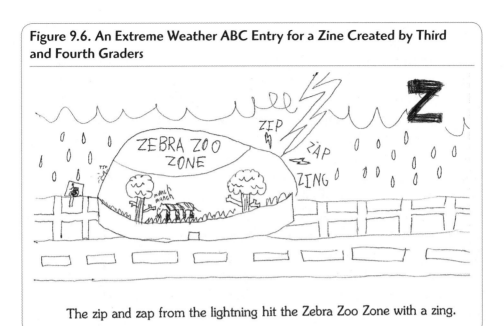

The zip and zap from the lightning hit the Zebra Zoo Zone with a zing.

and providing feedback, revising, and editing require time and effort, as all writing does. Because there is much pride in accomplishment and enthusiasm for the process, writers need opportunity to celebrate their final product(s) when completed. One form that the celebration might take is that of an Authors' Tea or a Hot Chocolate Café, during which a beverage is served to readers and guests (e.g., parents, principal, other classes or teachers) as writings are shared via a microphone. A variation of this is Roundtable Discussions, in which small groups of students share their works with other students and a few invited guests. With this approach, collaborating writing team members are dispersed at different tables. A Gallery Walk might also be used. With this format, the products are displayed, and students circulate and read all or portions of the products as they move from display to display. Some teachers encourage readers to leave positive comments on a card for the writer. Gallery Walks may be combined with Roundtable Discussions to ensure that students get to share their works with the entire class, not just a few students. Making sure that each learner receives a copy of a collaborative product is essential.

Conclusion

Multigenre projects can empower students in multiple ways. They can reinforce students' writing of various genres, provide opportunities for students to hone their research skills with print and digital media, deepen content knowledge, motivate reluctant writers (and readers), and afford opportunities for students to collaborate and make decisions. The projects can empower teachers as well. With increasing curricular pressures, many teachers struggle to fit everything in and devote only limited time to explicit teaching of writing. Much of their instruction is often focused on decontextualized skills (Cutler & Graham, 2008). The multigenre project affords an opportunity to maximize teaching time, and therefore student learning, by integrating writing, reading, social studies or science, and much more. As the Common Core and other state standards push writing to greater prominence, multigenre projects can serve as one more vehicle for teachers to prepare students to be the effective writers they need to be.

REFERENCES

Bauml, M., Field, S.L., & Ledbetter, M. (2013). Immigration, any small goodness, and integrated social studies. *Social Studies and the Young Learner, 26*(1), 17–21.

Canadian Council on Learning. (2010). *More than just funny books: Comics and prose literacy for boys.* Retrieved from www.ccl-cca.ca/CCL/Reports/LessonsInLearning/ LinL20100721Comics.html

Cary, S. (2004). *Going graphic: Comics at work in the multilingual classroom.* Portsmouth, NH: Heinemann.

Ciardiello, V.A. (2009). Echoes of Angel Island: Developing historical empathy for detained immigrants. *Social Studies and the Young Learner, 22*(2), P1–P4.

Culham, R. (2011, August 22). Modes, genres, and formats and the Common Core State Standards [Web log post]. Retrieved from ruthculham.wordpress.com/2011/08/22/ modes-genres-and-formats-and-the-common-core-state-standards

Culham, R. (2014). *What principals need to know about teaching and learning writing.* Bloomington, IN: Solution Tree; Alexandria, VA: National Association of Elementary School Principals; New York, NY: Scholastic.

Cutler, L., & Graham, S. (2008). Primary grade writing instruction: A national survey. *Journal of Educational Psychology, 100*(4), 907–919.

D'Adamo, L., & Fallace, T. (2011). The multigenre research project: An approach to developing historical empathy. *Social Studies Research & Practice, 6*(1), 75–88.

Graham, S., & Hebert, M. (2010). *Writing to read: Evidence for how writing can improve reading.* Washington, DC: Alliance for Excellent Education.

Koyen, J. (1995). *The zine & e-zine resource guide: Adventures in the e-zine trade.* Retrieved from www.zinebook.com/resource/koyen.html

Krashen, S. (2005). *The "decline" of reading in America, poverty and access to books, and the use of comics in encouraging reading.* Retrieved from www.sdkrashen.com/content/articles/decline_of_reading.pdf

Libresco, A.S., Balantic, J., & Kipling, J.C. (2011). Uncovering immigrants' stories: It all begins with picture books. *Social Studies and the Young Learner, 23*(4), P1–P4.

Maguth, B.M., Dustman, J., & Kerr, M. (2013). Re-examining the Statue of Liberty: Different perspectives on history and the promise of America. *Social Studies and the Young Learner, 25*(4), 9–14.

Maliszewski, D. (2013). The benefits of writing comics. In C.K. Syma & R.G. Weiner (Eds.), *Graphic novels and comics in the classroom: Essays on the educational power of sequential art* (pp. 233–244). Jefferson, NC: McFarland.

McCloud, S. (1994). *Understanding comics: The invisible art.* New York, NY: William Morrow.

McCloud, S. (2006). *Making comics: Storytelling secrets of comics, manga and graphic novels.* New York, NY: Harper.

Miller, S.D., & Meece, J.L. (1997). Enhancing elementary students' motivation to read and write: A classroom intervention study. *The Journal of Educational Research, 90*(5), 286–299. doi:10.1080/00220671.1997.10544585

Miller, S.D., & Meece, J.L. (1999). Third graders' motivational preferences for reading and writing tasks. *The Elementary School Journal, 100*(1), 19–35. doi:10.1086/461941

National Governors Association Center for Best Practices & Council of Chief State School Officers. (2010). *Common Core State Standards for English language arts and literacy in history/social studies, science, and technical subjects.* Washington, DC: Authors.

Painter, D.D. (2009). Providing differentiated learning experiences through multigenre projects. *Intervention in School and Clinic, 44*(5), 288–293. doi:10.1177/1053451208330900

Rowe, C. (Ed.). (2012). *The book of zines: Readings from the fringe.* New York, NY: Henry Holt. Retrieved from www.zinebook.com

Strickland, D.S., Ganske, K., & Monroe, J.K. (2002). *Supporting struggling readers and writers: Strategies for classroom intervention 3–6.* Portland, ME: Stenhouse; Newark, DE: International Reading Association.

Todd, M., & Watson, E.P. (2006). *Whatcha mean, what's a zine? The art of making zines and mini-comics.* Boston, MA: Graphia.

Youngs, S., & Barone, D. (2007). *Writing without boundaries: What's possible when students combine genres.* Portsmouth, NH: Heinemann.

CHILDREN'S AND YOUNG ADULT LITERATURE CITED

Ada, A.F. (1997). *Gathering the sun: An alphabet in Spanish and English* (R. Zubizarreta, Trans.). New York, NY: Rayo.

Alexander, K., & Witthöft, V. M. (2009). *Davy Brown discovers his roots.* Savannah, GA: Big Tent.

Bode, J. (1999). *The colors of freedom: Immigrant stories.* New York, NY: Franklin Watts.

Bunting, E. (2006). *One green apple.* New York, NY: Clarion.

De Capua, S. (2004). *How people immigrate.* New York, NY: Children's.

Freedman, R. (2009). *Immigrant kids.* Paradise, CA: Paw Prints.

Hoose, P., & Hoose, H. (1998). *Hey, little ant.* Berkeley, CA: Tricycle.

Hoose, P., & Hoose, H. (2003). *Oye, hormiguita* [Hey, little ant]. Berkeley, CA: Tricycle.

Hopkinson, D. (2003). *Shutting out the sky: Life in the tenements of New York 1880–1924*. New York, NY: Orchard.

Karapetkova, H. (2010). *Landing at Ellis Island*. Vero Beach, FL: Rourke.

Lai, H.M., Lim, G., & Yung, J. (1999). *Island: Poetry and history of Chinese immigrants on Angel Island, 1910–1940*. Seattle: University of Washington Press.

Lawlor, V. (1997). *I was dreaming to come to America: Memories from the Ellis Island Oral History Project*. New York, NY: Puffin.

Maestro, B. (1996). *Coming to America: The story of immigration*. New York, NY: Scholastic.

Mannis, C.D. (2003). *The queen's progress: An Elizabethan alphabet*. New York, NY: Viking.

Mazer, A. (Ed.). (2009). *America Street: A multicultural anthology of stories*. Paradise, CA: Paw Prints.

Peacock, L. (2007). *At Ellis Island: A history in many voices*. New York, NY: Atheneum Books for Young Readers.

Pérez, A.I. (2009). *My diary from here to there/Mi diario de aquí hasta allá*. San Francisco, CA: Children's.

Say, A. (1993). *Grandfather's journey*. New York, NY: Houghton Mifflin.

Streissguth, T. (2009). *Welcome to America? A pro/con debate over immigration*. Berkeley Heights, NJ: Enslow.

Tan, S. (2006). *The arrival*. New York, NY: Arthur A. Levine.

Woodruff, E. (1999). *The memory coat*. New York, NY: Scholastic.

Woodruff, E. (2000). *The orphan of Ellis Island: A time-travel adventure*. New York, NY: Scholastic.

Yep, L. (with Yep, K.S.). (2008). *The dragon's child: A story of Angel Island*. New York, NY: HarperCollins.

ABOUT THE AUTHOR

 Kathy Ganske is a professor of the practice of literacy at Peabody College, Vanderbilt University, in Nashville, Tennessee, USA, where she teaches various literacy-related courses and directs the Graduate Elementary Education Program. She is the author or coauthor of several books, including *Word Journeys: Assessment-Guided Phonics, Spelling, and Vocabulary Instruction* (2nd ed.; Guilford, 2000), *Word Sorts and More: Sound, Pattern, and Meaning Explorations K–3* (Guilford, 2006), *Mindful of Words: Spelling and Vocabulary Explorations 4–8* (Guilford, 2008), and *Supporting Struggling Readers and Writers: Strategies for Classroom Intervention 3–6* (Stenhouse & International Reading Association, 2002). In addition, Kathy is a coeditor with Douglas Fisher of *Comprehension Across the Curriculum: Perspectives and Practices K–12* (Guilford, 2010), as well as the author of numerous articles and book chapters. Her current research interests include meeting literacy needs in high-needs schools, discussion during small-group word study instruction, and literacy teacher preparation. Kathy's work is grounded in more than 20 years of elementary classroom teaching experience. She is a fellow of the National Writing Project.

CHAPTER 10

Supporting Writers in Grades 4–6 With Digital Media and Sources

Thomas DeVere Wolsey, *University of Central Florida*

Dana L. Grisham, *National University*

Linda Smetana, *California State University, East Bay*

In a fifth-grade classroom, a group of four students is engaged in creating a digital dictionary page for a vocabulary word they have chosen. Each group is clustered around two computers, one for composing and the other for researching. The animated conversation among the students centers on the choice of words, text selections, and images to incorporate into their project. Students are accessing the digital thesaurus as they seek to refine their word choice. A series of graphic organizers is being reviewed for the one that best represents their thinking. One student reminds the group that the visual image of the project is as important as the written word.

As the students work together, conversations revolve around clarifying their ideas and sharing them with others. They consider the audience who will be reading their final product—a product in which language and images are skillfully placed to communicate thoughts, information, perspectives, and/or feelings. The students are composing in a multimodal environment using their knowledge of digital spaces (and gaining new knowledge of those spaces), language and language-based texts, and content emphasized in standards adopted by their school and state.

Reflecting on the experience, Anabel (a pseudonym) shared her thoughts:

> I liked looking for really cool pictures on websites. The pictures had to tell what your word was about. I ended up reading about *solution* [her group's word from a

science lesson] on a website and looked for more information on solution on other websites, but we only had space for one. You have to be careful because some websites are not what they say they are. You have to get along with your partners because you need to work together, and not one person can hog everything. The project was like bubble gum: the more you chew it, the more you get from it.

Why Use the Terms *Writing* and *Composing*?

Often, we educators may use the terms *writing* and *composing* somewhat interchangeably. This is a good point to stop and note that we have chosen the terms and used them with some deliberate attention to the context in this chapter. *Writing* tends to call up the idea of words and sentences on a digital or paper page and the act of creating a text using those words and sentences. In contrast, *composing*, as we use the term, serves two purposes in this chapter: encompassing the act of creating text with words and sentences and connoting the cognitive work associated with language production. In our posttypographic world (cf. Reinking, McKenna, Labbo, & Kieffer, 1998), composing tasks may result in creative work that blends words, images, video, or audio components. An example of multimodal work that blends many types of media and information is provided in our description of a vocabulary self-collection activity (see the What Do Digital Environments Change About Composing? section).

Readers of this chapter will explore ideas to help their intermediate-grade students work nimbly and accurately with sources found in digital and traditional environments when composing texts, including those with multimodal elements. Because digital environments also tend to include many images, videos, and other graphic displays, particular attention will be paid to how readers and writers work with multimodal texts.

What Do Digital Environments Add to Writing?

Digital environments—virtual places that make use of any number of digital devices—bring to composing tasks a variety of possibilities that were not easily available before the advent of the personal computer and the Internet. A variety of assistive devices and software (see Table 10.1) make composing tasks more accessible than ever before for some students who may struggle with the physical or cognitive demands of writing.

Table 10.1. Assistive Devices and Software

Device	Affordances	Considerations for Use
Word processors	• Reduce the cognitive load of composing tasks by transferring thoughts from the mind to paper or a computer • Reduce the physical action required for writing	• Students need keyboarding skills. • Students with learning disabilities benefit from the use of a word processor because they do not need to concentrate on the process of letter formation. • Special keyboards with larger keys may be useful for some writers.
Spelling and grammar checking tools	• Alert the writer when potential errors occur	• These tools may assist writers in finding common spelling or usage errors. • Some students whose spelling is poor may find that spell checkers cannot recognize the correct word from the misspelled version that the student typed. • Teach students to adopt strategies for using spelling and grammar checkers. • Teach students to look for homonyms and generate alternative spellings using an online thesaurus.
Speech synthesis tools	• Speech synthesis software reads/voices the work that students digitally created (and other written work, too). • These tools enable students to hear how their words sound when read aloud (e.g., Davis & McGrail, 2009[a]).	• There have been few studies regarding the use of speech synthesis software that reads students' written work back to them. • Speech synthesis technology may evolve, increasing possibilities for this tool.
Word prediction tools	• These tools predict possible words that the writer may intend, and present them to the author. In typing the sentence, "Salvador wanted to buy s…," the software may present choices such as "stamps" or "sticks." The tools can be found in texting applications and spelling and grammar checking tools, for example. • As new letters are typed, word choices that do not fit are eliminated.	• Software can cut down on the number of keystrokes, which reduces the physical demands of typing. • Word prediction software may assist with spelling, too. • Some instant message programs that students use within and outside of school make use of word prediction capabilities on smartphones and e-readers.

(continued)

Table 10.1. Assistive Devices and Software (*Continued*)

Device	Affordances	Considerations for Use
Speech recognition tools	• These tools hear the author speaking and then transcribe the oral language to written text. For students with severe problems in transcription, this may be a useful alternative. • The popular Siri (www.apple.com/ios/siri) and related technologies on smartphones and e-readers are one example of speech recognition tools. • Dragon speech recognition software (www.nuance.com/dragon/index.htm) is another application that is capable of capturing and transcribing speech.	• The software might mishear the speaker and create errors that the author will have to correct later.

Note. Compiled by Wolsey and Grisham (2012)[b] from King-Sears, Swanson, and Mainzer's (2011)[c] framework and the work of MacArthur (2006).[d]
[a]Davis, A., & McGrail, E. (2009). "Proof-revising" with podcasting: Keeping readers in mind as students listen to and rethink their writing. *The Reading Teacher, 62*(6), 522–529.
[b]Wolsey, T.D., & Grisham, D.L. (2012). *Transforming writing instruction in the digital age: Techniques for grades 5–12.* New York, NY: Guilford.
[c]King-Sears, M.E., Swanson, C., & Mainzer, L. (2011). TECHnology and literacy for adolescents with disabilities. *Journal of Adolescent & Adult Literacy, 54*(8), 569–578.
[d]MacArthur, C. (2006). Assistive technology for writing: Tools for struggling writers. In L. Van Waes, M. Leijten, & C.M. Neuwirth (Eds.), *Writing and digital media* (pp. 11–20). Amsterdam, The Netherlands: Elsevier.

Although we may view writing as a single author's struggle to express his or her thoughts, writing is a social task in many ways, and technology can enhance the social aspects of the process and the product. Collaborative websites permit students to work together to plan their writing over time and at a distance. In addition, multimodal compositions leverage images, video, linguistic text, and other sources, but at times, multimodal compositions are little more than collections of words and images (e.g., Towndrow, Nelson, & Yusuf, 2013).

Young composers also need to consider the design of their composition in multimodal work especially. In the scenario at the beginning of this chapter, students sometimes realized that the online graphic organizers did not serve their communication purposes, so some groups chose to design and create new graphic organizers rather than use those they could find or generate on the Web. Graphic organizers, for example, are far more dynamic when students work asynchronously, at different times, and with tools that are no longer bounded by the standard size of a piece of paper. With time to think about their responses, students' asynchronous tasks can be both collaborative and more thoroughly considered. Figure 10.1 is a student-constructed Visual Thesaurus (www.visualthesaurus.com) representation of the term *boiling* from a science exploration based on students' reading of their text. Students used WordSift (www.wordsift.com) to help define science terms by entering their words into the box on the website. The WordSift program provided an interactive graphic organizer for the word, allowing the students to click on and explore different uses of the word. Because many words in English are polysemous (have different meanings), a tool such as WordSift affords students easy access to explore the various meanings.

It may seem that writers are working independently, but they rarely are. Most ideas are built on the ideas of others encountered elsewhere. Inspiration and creativity are the result of engaging with ideas that are often

Figure 10.1. A Student-Created Visual Thesaurus Graphic Organizer Created With WordSift

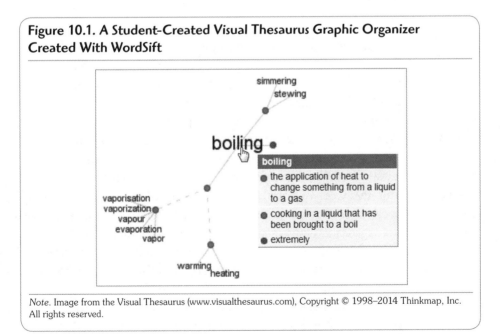

Note. Image from the Visual Thesaurus (www.visualthesaurus.com), Copyright © 1998–2014 Thinkmap, Inc. All rights reserved.

from sources, so what we write is linked to what others have done, written, or said. We draw on the ideas and guidance of teachers, written works, and model texts we've read over time, which we incorporate into our own approaches to writing. We organize our writing in a way that makes sense to us, but much of that organization is a synthesis of what we have learned from reading about writing, actually writing, and working on writing teams with colleagues who inspired us with their ideas and approaches. The content of what we write is similarly a social task. Where we employ the use of others' ideas explicitly, we attribute the source.

The big idea here is that digital environments make accessing the ideas and creative products of others relatively easy, and digital environments increase the possibility that students and other writers can engage with one another in ways that transcend the boundaries of the school walls, the school bells, and geography. A student who lives on one side of town may now work with another on the opposite side of the town, and neither need arrange for a parent to drive across town as chauffeur to make that happen.

What Do Digital Environments Change About Composing?

Asking what digital environments *add* to composing tasks is one thing, but asking what they *change* about composing tasks is quite another. Although written texts have long been accompanied by images—since the illuminated texts of the Middle Ages to the first picture book, *Orbis Pictus* (Comenius, 1658)—the capacity for creating images, using images created by others in some way, or mashing up images (and perhaps video or audio sources) from multiple sources has, arguably, never been greater. For example, mashing up content means to combine various elements (e.g., maps, addresses) to create a single, more enriched presentation. This, in itself, involves the cognitive work of composing. However, when images and text accompany, overlap, complement, or present juxtapositions of ideas, the power of both images and words seems to increase exponentially. The value of images and words together is evident in the enduring popularity of graphica, such as the comic book or graphic novel (Smetana, Odelson, Burns, & Grisham, 2009).

Recently, we had the privilege of working with a fifth-grade teacher who wanted to use generative technology (Grisham & Smetana, 2011) to advance his student's science learning, as he had recognized the limitations of the educational games loaded on the computer lab machines. You met some of Mr. Danysh's students in the opening scenario. When we use the term *generative technology*, we mean technology that is used as a tool by students to create or make—to generate ideas and learning artifacts. To illustrate the concept of technology that is generative, we worked with Mr. Danysh and 33 fifth graders on vocabulary learning, using a technology-enhanced vocabulary self-collection activity (Grisham, Smetana, & Wolsey, in press) that we call Vocabulary Self-Collection Strategy Plus (VSSPlus). Students worked in teams of three or four to identify appropriate existing images, create images, write their own definitions of important science words, compose rationales for their selections, and write scripts for audio components that were embedded in their presentations. A variety of Web-based applications support this approach, but we chose two and allowed the students to select, as a team, which of the two platforms to use. They could choose to create a PowerPoint slide or use the online tool ThingLink (www.thinglink.com). Of course, other online tools may also work for VSSPlus. (See Table 10.2 for a list of the technologies that we discuss or have used with students.)

Table 10.2. Electronic Resources to Use With Students

Resource	URL
Blogs • Blogger • Edublogs • WordPress	• www.blogger.com • edublogs.org • wordpress.com
Creative Commons licenses	• creativecommons.org/licenses
Media Education Lab at the University of Rhode Island	• mediaeducationlab.com/curriculum/materials
PowerPoint	• office.microsoft.com/en-us/powerpoint
Presentation tools	• https://delicious.com/tdwolsey/presentation
ThingLink	• www.thinglink.com
Wikis • PBworks • Wikispaces Classroom	• pbworks.com • www.wikispaces.com
WordSift	• www.wordsift.com

As students completed their work, they employed a variety of literacy skills, incorporating traditional and new literacies (cf. New London Group, 1996). One might expect that students of this age would be adept at manipulating images, finding appropriate sources, and using software and online tools. In this case, as in many others, students were not as adept as popular metaphors suggest (e.g., Wolsey & Grisham, 2011). When we asked how many students had used PowerPoint, about one third raised their hands, and the rest were unfamiliar with this application. We spoke with the teacher, who told us that the computer lab was loaded with games that were little more than digital worksheets and did not engage students' cognitive talents in any meaningful way. Although the students may be proficient users of technologies for downloading music, playing entertainment-oriented games, and so forth, they did not know how to use technology for academic purposes. This fifth-grade teacher sought to change that, and he asked us to help him.

As students worked in teams to construct their presentation, which we linked on a class wiki page (see Figure 10.2), they discussed the

Figure 10.2. Mr. Danysh's e-Dictionary for Science

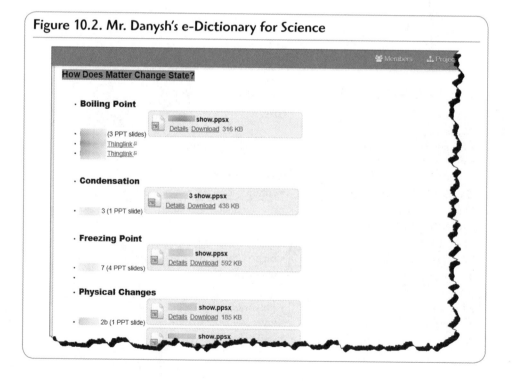

meanings of the terms as found in the context of their reading material, found additional sources to support their conclusions (e.g., glossaries in their books, online dictionaries), compared their definitions against those they found, located images that supported their understanding of the terms, and composed explanations using a variety of note-taking and scripting strategies. During the process, students also learned to use rather sophisticated features of PowerPoint that many adult users do not know are possible, and they learned to embed images, graphics, and text using ThingLink (see Figure 10.3). Although the written portions were short, the thinking and negotiating that went into the creation of the final e-dictionary entry was substantial. Students checked multiple sources of information online, consulted their textbooks, and negotiated for the final rationale, explaining the importance of the term. Students worked together to write a script, then narrated the audio podcast, which they linked to or embedded in their presentation.

What does all this have to do with composing and writing? These fifth graders learned to compose, to compare and contrast ideas among themselves and among additional sources they found, to identify key

Figure 10.3. ThingLink for the Vocabulary Term *Fever*

attributes of the material they were expected to master, to use spoken and written words to construct and convey their understanding, and to realize that they had, in fact, learned something interesting and important. Writing Anchor Standard 6 of the Common Core State Standards, for example, calls for students to "use technology, including the Internet, to produce and publish writing and to interact and collaborate with others" (National Governors Association Center for Best Practices & Council of Chief State School Officers [NGA Center & CCSSO], 2010, p. 41). The intersection of generative technologies and composition tasks put students in a position to really work with ideas and come to an understanding of content.

Writing is an act of composing, of putting ideas together, creating new ideas from existing ideas, and leveraging these for purposes of understanding the world as it is and how it might be. The students wrote notes spontaneously, without prompting from us. They wrote short texts for their presentation that represented summarization, evaluation of sources they encountered, and analysis of the task relative to their learning about the science topic, states of matter. The VSSPlus project triggered exploration of sources of information and presentation. Students talked about additional information that they had learned through one of the websites they found to obtain the meaning of the target word or phrase. They were actively engaged in the process of composing to understand science. From this experience, we emphasize three key points:

1. As we explored earlier, composing includes writing, but it may also include working with multiple sources, such as images, audio, and video.

2. Writing may include short constructions of phrases or a few sentences. The number of words, paragraphs, and pages is not as important as the understanding gained during the composing process and demonstrated in the composed product.

3. Students enhanced their communicative potential through the use of words, images, video, and/or audio components when considered as a whole.

Because the technology brought together multiple resources and afforded students the opportunity to work together, the experience of composing the dictionary entry leveraged working with images, working in collaborative groups, and working with words to come to a greater understanding than if students had simply read about the science processes in a traditional textbook.

Shared Knowledge and Processes, But Now What?

One of the things we know—actually, anyone who reads or writes knows—is that reading and writing are not mirrors of each other. They certainly share some cognitive processes, and they often draw on shared knowledge (Fitzgerald & Shanahan, 2000), but just because one can read does not mean one can write. Following this line of thought, just because one can think does not automatically translate to the notion that those thoughts are easily transformed to print in any form, digitally or on paper. Composing requires writers to do some things differently from what they do when they are reading. Thinking while reading or speaking about a topic is somewhat different from writing about it or melding visual and linguistic information in a new, creative product.

Writers must be readers, but what is the nature of the relationship between reading and writing? What students read and how much they read tends to affect their capacities as authors. Effective writers read a great deal, and they often read with the purpose of informing their own writing (Prose, 2006).

How Does Reading Inform Writing?

One of the great challenges of writing as a cognitive activity is that it is rather ill defined. For example, we can attempt to impose a five-paragraph format on student writing, but often the content and the organization that the writer intends resist that impulse. In addition, the five-paragraph essay may not be the appropriate format for the written product. We may try to think of writing in terms of food metaphors, but not all writing has a bun, condiments, and meat that fit into a neat little package, like a sandwich (e.g., Fearn, Farnan, & Grisham, 2007). Although some formats are artificial, other constraints inform the communicative nature of writing so audiences can make sense of the composition. For writers, especially those working in digital environments, constraints offer possibilities or limitations that may or may not suit the purpose for writing. For example, Robert Frost wrote that writing poetry without rhyme is like playing tennis without a net (as cited in Kennedy, 1982). He was well aware that structural constraints on his poetry helped him compose inspiring thoughts.

What we might ask is how we can assist students in the intermediate grades to learn the constraints of authentic writing, push the limits somewhat at times, and still write in such a way that understanding is constructed by the writer and by the person who reads what is composed. Some activities and domains of inquiry simply do not reduce to overly simplistic models of composition. Spiro, Feltovich, Coulson, and Anderson (1989) found that complex ideas often resisted reduction, especially if the ideas were somewhat ill defined at the start. For example, they found that medical students who thought of the vascular system in the human body as a kind of plumbing system missed key aspects of the circulatory mechanisms moving blood from one part of the body to another. The plumbing of a building is relatively static, whereas the vascular system is not. Composing processes, such as writing, are similarly resistant to oversimplification. Teachers who expect students to compose in expansive ways, to use writing to explore, inquire, and communicate important and difficult ideas, adopt a stance that does not oversimplify the task of writing coherently about a variety of topics.

Consider a common model of communication (see Figure 10.4; cf. Kinneavy, 1971). Encoders (composers, in this case) have some intention of constructing knowledge and conveying it in some way. Decoders (readers and viewers) have some intention of constructing knowledge, but that construction must be situated within the world that each decoder knows or thinks might be possible. The words have some part to play, as well, given that communication is based on some shared understandings about what words and other types of expression might mean within any given group of individuals. Even the format conveys information; for example, a poem conveys something different than does an expository text.

A complex system of communication that considers the composer, the audience, the message, and the media is challenging enough. Add to that sophisticated content, and we have a complex task that requires flexibility on our part as teachers and on the part of the student who is composing ideas for him- or herself and for others as well.

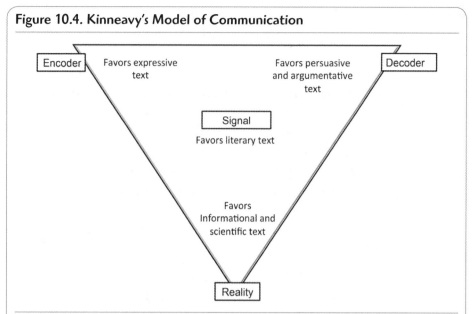

Figure 10.4. Kinneavy's Model of Communication

Encoder — Favors expressive text

Favors persuasive and argumentative text — Decoder

Signal

Favors literary text

Favors Informational and scientific text

Reality

Note. Encoders are the individuals who construct a message while the decoder receives it. In Kinneavy's model, there are several elements of communication, including the participants, the text itself (signal), and the reality to which the communication refers.

Why Might Writing With Digital Sources Present New Challenges?

Writing in digital environments requires students to navigate tricky waters. Never before has so much information been available, and never before have writers needed to evaluate and scrutinize the information they encounter online. Information is not knowledge, and knowledge is not wisdom. The task before student writers is to transform appropriate and useful information into knowledge—and sometimes into wisdom as well. Even when young writers know a great deal about a topic, they may lack the skill or strategies to transform that knowledge into a composed text and the wisdom to sieve through all the new information available to them.

Effective writers often write from their own experiences, of course. Who hasn't heard the maxim, "Write what you know?" Yet, effective writers rely on sources of information beyond their own experiences, too. This is true even in fiction writing, as Eudora Welty (1984) once discovered when her editor pointed out that in her story, she had placed Earth's moon in the wrong part of the sky. Her perceived experience did not square with the reality her readers would expect, even in a work of fiction.

One approach to accuracy in writing is to read up, ask around, and double-check (Wolsey, 2014). This strategy may assist upper-grade writers to approach writing tasks in a way that promotes authenticity and authority in their work. Reading up asks readers to read a great deal, not always with composing tasks in mind. Reading up also means that writers sometimes read with specific writing tasks in mind. For example, in writing this chapter, we read new sources that we found in the library and reread articles that we had read in the past to make sure we were aware of the most current ideas relative to accuracy in writing. Intermediate-grade writers might read to inform their writing in these ways:

- To find organizational patterns used by other authors
- To identify disconfirming evidence or alternative points of view
- To verify or classify details
- To synthesize the information from multiple sources

Asking around has never been easier. Student writers can easily and electronically ask their peers to critique their work simply by posting drafts or finished products online in a learning management system or forum (e.g., Blackboard: www.blackboard.com, Canvas: www.instructure.com, Edmodo: https://www.edmodo.com). For instance, second-grade students were asked to post their written work in an online blog, and then they were taught to ask for specific types of feedback on their work (Lapp, Shea, & Wolsey, 2011).

However, in digital environments, students may also ask experts. With appropriate guidance from their teachers, students may contact the authors of blog posts they find online, communicate with authors of articles they find in magazines, and join discussions with students at other schools across the globe to ask for more information or clarifications. One example of this took place in a school where English learners in a seventh-grade intervention class (all boys) created the Flamingo Writers Workshop online (flamingowritersworkshop.weebly.com; Grisham et al., in press). They conferred with one another and with the teacher to create and refine the products.

Finally, upper-grade writers should double-check what they have written. Of course, it is important that they proofread their work, which is one form of double-checking. But good double checkers also take a skeptical approach to their own writing. They question what they know or think they know, such as Welty's belief that the moon moved in the sky in a way it actually did not. Highly regarded news sources have entire departments dedicated to checking the facts that appear in their publications, right down to the exact title of a dignitary (see Heffernan, 2010). The *Los Angeles Times* is dedicated to accuracy in its reporting but recognizes that errors do occur. Those errors are regularly reported and corrected in a section titled "For the Record"; for instance, on page A4 of the Sunday, October 13, 2013, issue, there were three corrections noted. Double-checking in digital environments often means checking the reliability and credibility of the source (Leu et al., 2011), rereading to look for errors, asking around (see the two previous paragraphs), and citing the sources that inform the writing. Teaching students to look at reference lists and the acknowledgment sections of books and articles, online or on paper, is a good start toward helping them think about how they come to know what they know and to be skeptical of even their own ideas.

Young writers can certainly ask their peers for specific feedback. Lapp and colleagues (2011) found that second graders were very capable of providing feedback based on a system that Ms. Shea, the classroom teacher, called "pushes and praises." These second-grade writers posted their work on a blog where they could provide feedback, edit their work, and share the final pieces with their parents and family. For example, students consistently praised Bernardo for the sense of humor he displayed in his writing about his dog, Jack-Jack, whose antics resulted in a broken television. Second-grade writers also learned to push their peers to improve their writing by asking questions. Juan asked Bernardo for more details: "Where did the story take place?" Ashley pushed Bernardo to include details about the broken television. Through these digital interactions, students were able to develop a sense of the audience and what that audience might expect.

Can You Picture It?

Even if students can read up, ask around, and double-check the texts they write, we can still wonder how images fit into the digital writing environment. For that matter, we might ask how audio and video fit into the world of electronic composition. Although a full exploration of multimodal work is beyond the scope of this chapter, there is no escaping it. The pictures matter, it turns out. Young readers gain deeper and richer vocabulary meanings as they read picture books (Strasser & Seplocha, 2007). Images assist readers in interacting with words (Sipe, 2008) and making sense of unfamiliar content (Moss, 2008). Sadoski and Paivio (2007) suggest that how knowledge is encoded, via images or language, makes a difference. Two questions arise:

1. What happens when words and images are paired up or juxtaposed?
2. How do students make use of words and images when they create texts of their own?

How Do Student-Created/Selected Images and Words Work Together?

By now, you have seen our examples of how images and words complement each other in various ways. No doubt, you also can think of many examples from your own written work or the work your students do in your classroom. As students work in digital environments, they will have many opportunities to use images (and we can include video here as well) to enhance the words and sentences they use. This is also a good place to stop and mention that sometimes the process works the other way; that is, the words enhance the images. Pictures with a caption, such as the photography galleries and features that the National Geographic Society publishes, are a good example (e.g., see photography.nationalgeographic. com/photography/photogalleries). For students and their teachers, the question of how to choose the best words and the right images has new meaning in our digital age.

How Do Words Function to Anchor and Give an Interpretation of an Image?

Because this chapter focuses on writing that foregrounds the role of words, it seems appropriate to ask just how words help readers understand images that are part of digital compositions. Choo (2010) suggests that makers and composers of digital texts consider the following:

- How do words function to "relay" or contribute to the meaning of an image?
- Where will the image be placed in relation to the words and why?
- How much of the frame-space will the image occupy, compared to the words?
- Is the focal point of the text on the image or on its words, and why? (p. 172)

What About Attribution?

Students can choose to illustrate their written work using any number of online drawing tools, digital cameras, scanners, or the camera included with most cell phones. Using word-processing and publishing tools, it is easy for students at almost any age to embed an image they created into their written work. However, students often find it convenient to include images they find online in their digital compositions as well. Selecting just the right image to insert into one's writing or presentation has never been easier. However, the ease of adding images to a composition also means that students (and their teachers!) must give extra attention to crediting the source of digital and other content in their work.

Just as no teacher would be pleased to find that a student used written ideas found elsewhere without attributing the source of the ideas, images also deserve attribution (e.g., Huffman, 2010). Students enjoy some latitude in using the work of others that would not be afforded to commercial publishers, but crediting the source of the image (or audio or video) is always a good idea. What constitutes fair use of someone else's work in education can be a challenge. Copyright grants protection to the original creator of a work (including images), while fair use grants certain rights to those who wish to use others' copyrighted work. However, students who start with images that are specifically granted a license, or permission, to use the work are off to a good start. Creative Commons licenses (see creativecommons .org/licenses) provide users with some guidance as to how the work of others can be used. If you visited the link above, you probably noticed that every single license that might be assigned to an image, music file, text, and so on include an attribution component. More and more, content creators want to share their work, even for free. What most do not want is someone else to use their work without giving them credit, or attribution, for it.

Explicitly teaching students to include attribution to images in a way that follows the school or classroom guidelines and those granted by the original creator is a solid practice for teachers who want their students to compose using multimodal work that combines original words and images with those of others. Fair use of others' work in educational settings gives students new, creative ways to learn and to demonstrate their learning. To learn more about how you can help your students be good digital citizens who appropriately use others' content in their own compositions, visit the website of the Media Education Lab at the University of Rhode Island (mediaeducationlab.com/curriculum/materials). There you will find resources for learning and for teachers.

Assessment

New creative tools that incorporate images and other media offer possibilities, as well as responsibilities, for students who wish to engage the audiences of their work. Another aspect of the composing process that must be considered is the on-demand writing required by standardized assessments. The Common Core State Standards (NGA Center & CCSSO, 2010) require that technology be integrated into instructional and independent learning sequences. Research has shown that the use of technology and technology-based instruction enhances student learning (e.g., Proctor, Dalton, & Grisham, 2007).

This has been confirmed by recent NAEP (National Assessment of Educational Progress) assessments that provide a snapshot of educational progress in the United States (National Center for Education Statistics, 2012). The 2011 writing assessment was the first to use technology as part of the assessment. All eighth and 12th graders who participated in the assessment did so using a word-processing program on a computer, rather than using pencil and paper. Because of this, new scales and achievement levels were established, and although the findings could not be directly compared with past results for that reason, results indicated that students have the same strengths and weaknesses as revealed in the past by pencil-and-paper tests.

In the 2011 NAEP, the types of writing required of students were aligned with the Common Core (NGA Center & CCSSO, 2010), stressing the reinforcement of three writing capacities: persuasion (argumentation in the Common Core), explanation, and conveying an experience. Writing prompts were provided with interesting technology. On a computer screen divided vertically like the pages of a book, the left half contained the prompt with specific types of multimedia, including an audio prompt for eighth graders and a video prompt for 12th graders. For example, a prompt for conveying information asked students to describe a desert island, and the multimedia added the sound effects for the prompt. There were a number of program tools that students could elect to use as they wrote, and students' tool use was tracked and generally associated with higher scores.

Fourth graders will be assessed in the next round of the NAEP using technology. What this means is that teachers who take the time and make the effort to engage their students in working with technology will be giving their students an advantage in the testing. Beyond overall scores, there are many implications for educators that we have addressed in this chapter. One question appears to have a positive answer: The use of word-processing tools for the assessment appears to be more engaging for students. How serendipitous it is when true learning can both engage our students and prove advantageous to them.

Conclusion

Digital tools change the nature of composing tasks in significant ways; moreover, writers approach composing tasks in cognitively different ways than they approach reading tasks. As students are confronted with the challenge of composing their work by increasingly relying on sources other than their own experiences, they must learn to be accurate and thorough. Students need time to explore digital media and other sources of information prior to incorporating such sources into an assignment. Opportunities for collaboration and conversation must be incorporated into the instructional sequence.

As students make greater use of digital environments for learning, they must acquire new skills as they compose multimodal products and work with many different types of sources. Not only must students put words on a page or screen, but they must also create or choose (and provide appropriate attribution for) images that work with the words they use, and carefully consider the accuracy of their own work.

REFERENCES

Choo, S.S. (2010). Writing through visual acts of reading: Incorporating visual aesthetics in integrated writing and reading tasks. *The High School Journal, 93*(4), 166–176. doi:10.1353/hsj.2010.0002

Davis, A., & McGrail, E. (2009). "Proof-revising" with podcasting: Keeping readers in mind as students listen to and rethink their writing. *The Reading Teacher, 62*(6), 522–529. doi:10.1598/RT.62.6.6

Fearn, L., Farnan, N., & Grisham, D.L. (2007). Guest editors' note. *Action in Teacher Education, 29*(2), 3–4. doi:10.1080/01626620.2007.10463443

Fitzgerald, J., & Shanahan, T. (2000). Reading and writing relations and their development. *Educational Psychologist, 35*(1), 39–50. doi:10.1207/S15326985EP3501_5

Grisham, D.L., & Smetana, L. (2011). Generative technology for teachers and teacher educators. *Journal of Reading Education, 36*(3), 12–18.

Grisham, D.L., Smetana, L., & Wolsey, T.D. (in press). Post-reading vocabulary development through VSSPlus. In T.V. Rasinski, R. Ferdig, & K. Pytash (Eds.), *Reading and technology.* Bloomington, IN: Solution Tree.

Heffernan, V. (2010, August 20). What 'fact-checking' means online. *The New York Times Magazine* [Online]. Retrieved from www.nytimes.com/2010/08/22/magazine/22FOB-medium-t.html?_r=0

Huffman, S. (2010). The missing link: The lack of citations and copyright notices in multimedia presentations. *TechTrends, 54*(3), 38–44. doi:10.1007/s11528-010-0401-8

Kennedy, X.J. (1982). *An introduction to poetry* (5th ed.). Boston, MA: Little, Brown.

King-Sears, M.E., Swanson, C., & Mainzer, L. (2011). TECHnology and literacy for adolescents with disabilities. *Journal of Adolescent & Adult Literacy, 54*(8), 569–578. doi:10.1598/JAAL.54.8.2

Kinneavy, J.L. (1971). *A theory of discourse: The aims of discourse.* Englewood Cliffs, NJ: Prentice-Hall.

Lapp, D., Shea, A., & Wolsey, T.D. (2011). Blogging and audience awareness. *Journal of Education, 191*(1), 33–44.

Leu, D.J., McVerry, J.G., O'Byrne, W.I., Kiili, C., Zawilinski, L., Everett-Cacopardo, H., ... Forzani, E. (2011). The new literacies of online reading comprehension: Expanding the literacy and learning curriculum. *Journal of Adolescent & Adult Literacy, 55*(1), 5–14. doi:10.1598/JAAL.55.1.1

MacArthur, C. (2006). Assistive technology for writing: Tools for struggling writers. In L. Van Waes, M. Leijten, & C.M. Neuwirth (Eds.), *Writing and digital media* (pp. 11–20). Amsterdam, The Netherlands: Elsevier.

Moss, B. (2008). Getting the picture: Visual dimensions of informational texts. In J. Flood, S.B. Heath, & D. Lapp (Eds.), *Handbook of research on teaching literacy through the communicative and visual arts* (Vol. 2, pp. 393–398). Newark, DE: International Reading Association; New York, NY: Routledge.

National Center for Education Statistics. (2012). *The Nation's Report Card: Writing 2011* (NCES 2012-470). Washington, DC: National Center for Education Statistics, Institute of Education Sciences, U.S. Department of Education. Retrieved from nces.ed.gov/nationsreportcard/pdf/main2011/2012470.pdf

National Governors Association Center for Best Practices & Council of Chief State School Officers. (2010). *Common Core State Standards for English language arts and literacy in history/social studies, science, and technical subjects.* Washington, DC: Authors.

New London Group. (1996). A pedagogy of multiliteracies: Designing social futures. *Harvard Educational Review, 66*(1), 60–92.

Proctor, C.P., Dalton, B., & Grisham, D.L. (2007). Scaffolding English language learners and struggling readers in a universal literacy environment with embedded strategy instruction and vocabulary support. *Journal of Literacy Research, 39*(1), 71–93.

Prose, F. (2006). *Reading like a writer: A guide for people who love books and for those who want to write them.* New York, NY: HarperCollins.

Reinking, D., McKenna, M.C., Labbo, L.D., & Kieffer, R.D. (Eds.). (1998). *Handbook of literacy and technology: Transformations in a post-typographic world.* Mahwah, NJ: Erlbaum.

Sadoski, M., & Paivio, A. (2007). Toward a unified theory of reading. *Scientific Studies of Reading, 11*(4), 337–356. doi:10.1080/10888430701530714

Sipe, L. (2008). Young children's visual meaning making in response to picture books. In J. Flood, S.B. Heath, & D. Lapp (Eds.), *Handbook of research on teaching literacy through the communicative and visual arts* (Vol. 2, pp. 381–391). Newark, DE: International Reading Association; New York, NY: Routledge.

Smetana, L., Odelson, D., Burns, H., & Grisham, D.L. (2009). Using graphic novels in the high school classroom: Engaging deaf students with a new genre. *Journal of Adolescent & Adult Literacy, 53*(3), 228–240. doi:10.1598/JAAL.53.3.4

Spiro, R.J., Feltovich, P.J., Coulson, R.L., & Anderson, D.K. (1989). Multiple analogies for complex concepts: Antidotes for analogy-induced misconception in advanced knowledge acquisition. In S. Vosniadou & A. Ortony (Eds.), *Similarity and analogical reasoning* (pp. 498–531). New York, NY: Cambridge University Press. doi:10.1017/CBO9780511529863.023

Strasser, J., & Seplocha, H. (2007). Using picture books to support young children's literacy. *Childhood Education, 83*(4), 219–224. doi:10.1080/00094056.2007.10522916

Towndrow, P.A., Nelson, M.E., & Yusuf, W.F.B.M. (2013). Squaring literacy assessment with multimodal design: An analytic case for semiotic awareness. *Journal of Literacy Research, 45*(4), 327–355. doi:10.1177/1086296X13504155

Welty, E. (1984). *One writer's beginnings.* Cambridge, MA: Harvard University Press.

Wolsey, T.D. (2014). Accuracy in digital writing environments: Read up, ask around, double-check. *Voices From the Middle, 21*(3), 49–53.

Wolsey, T.D., & Grisham, D.L. (2011). A nation of digital immigrants: Four principles [Editorial]. *The California Reader, 44*(2), 1–9. Retrieved from www.californiareads.org/res/TCR_editorial-44-2.pdf

Wolsey, T.D., & Grisham, D.L. (2012). *Transforming writing instruction in the digital age: Techniques for grades 5–12.* New York, NY: Guilford.

CHILDREN'S LITERATURE CITED

Comenius. (1658). *Orbis pictus.* Nuremberg, Germany.

Thomas DeVere Wolsey teaches graduate courses at the University of Central Florida, Orlando, USA, and has authored books and articles on literacy intersections with technology. He worked in public schools for 20 years teaching English and social studies at the secondary level. Thomas is interested in how school spaces affect learning, how technology changes and intersects literacy instruction, and how writing in the disciplines is best taught. You can contact him at tdwolsey@msn.com.

Dana L. Grisham currently teaches graduate courses in literacy at National University in San Diego, California, USA. She has taught literacy and pedagogy courses at the University of California, Berkeley; Washington State University; San Diego State University; and California State University, East Bay (in Hayward), from which she retired in 2010. Over the course of her career, she has taught college-level courses related to literacy, technology, and the needs of English learners, in addition to teaching for a decade at the elementary and middle school levels. Dana has published more than 80 scholarly works—articles, book chapters, and books—including *Transforming Writing Instruction in the Digital Age: Techniques for Grades 5–12* (Guilford, 2012), coauthored with Thomas DeVere Wolsey. She currently serves as a coeditor of *Reading & Writing Quarterly* and is one of the authors of Literacy Beat (literacybeat.com), a scholarly blog on literacy and technology.

Linda Smetana is a professor of educational psychology at California State University, East Bay (in Hayward), USA, where she teaches graduate courses in the teacher preparation, special education teacher preparation, and graduate reading programs. In addition, she has 30 years of experience in public school teaching, from preschool through continuation high school. Linda currently maintains a connection with teachers and students in her role as a literacy and learning specialist in an urban school district, as the public school setting provides opportunities for action research. She has published numerous articles in the areas of literacy, teacher preparation, Response to Intervention, and technology. Her coauthored article (with Dana Grisham) on generative technology was named the Outstanding Article of the Year by the *Journal of Reading Education*.

INDEX

Note. Page numbers followed by *f* and *t* indicate figures and tables, respectively.

G

Gallagher, K., 37
Ganske, K., 67, 171
GarageBand, 141
generative technology, 182–183, 186
Genovese, M., 141
genre-based curricula, 69
genres: choice of, 66–69; genre-specific
    strategies for stories example, 28*t*;
    humor/jokes, 127; non-genre-specific
    studies, 68, 69*t*. *See also* multigenre
    projects (grades 4–6)
geography graphic organizer example, 137*f*
Gilbert, J., 18
Glover, M., 61, 62, 69
Glutting, J.J., 98
goals: of essay writing, 101; establishment
    of, 29; how to accomplish, 8–9;
    for multigenre projects, 158–159;
    overcoming negative perceptions about
    writing, 93
Good Clean Jokes Sites, 127
Google, 82
Google Docs, 144–146
Google Earth, 142
grades 4–6. *See* multigenre projects (grades
    4–6)
Graham, S., 5, 8, 10, 11, 18, 19, 20, 21,
    22, 23, 24, 25, 26, 27, 28, 29, 30, 88,
    89, 91, 92*t*, 157, 174
grammar checkers, 179*t*
grammar skills, 26
graphic organizers: collaborative use
    of, 181; geography example, 137*f*;
    persuasive essay example, 107*f*; for
    POW + TREE, 100*f*; student-created
    visual thesaurus example, 181*f*
Greenwald, E.A., 73
Grimes, N., 48
Grisham, D.L., 180*t*, 182, 183, 184, 187,
    194
guided analysis, 10

H

Hagaman, J.L., 91, 92*t*
Hammer, C.S., 98
handwriting skills, 25*t*

Hannigan, K., 50, 50–51*f*
Harris, K.R., 11, 22, 24, 25, 26, 27, 28,
    29, 30, 88, 89, 91, 92, 92*t*, 94, 98, 107,
    108
Hawthorne, J., 75*f*
Hebert, M., 5, 8, 25, 88, 157
Heffernan, V., 191
Hicks, T., 146
high-quality texts, 9–10
Hill for Literacy, 92*t*
Hillocks, G., Jr., 18
Historic Map Works, 162*t*
hook, 50*f*
Hoose, H., 171
Hoose, P., 79, 80, 171
Hosta, D., 49
Houston, J.D., 98
"How ASIMO Works" example, 83–84
How to Make a Book (student example),
    54, 55*f*
Huffman, S., 193
humor, 126–127, 129
Hundal, N., 40
Hurley, M.M., 88

I

iBooks Author, 141, 142*f*
images in digital writing: how to use, 191–
    192; interpretations of, 192–193; student-
    created, 192; student's experience of
    using, 177–178
immersion model, 61
immigration research resources, 167*t*
iMovie, 140–141
independent performance, 97*t*, 102–103,
    104–105, 106
independent writing example, 107*f*
information: explanation of presentation
    of, 84; integration by grade level of, 7;
    learning how to summarize and compare,
    9; sensitizing students to, 8; student
    expression of, 7–8
informational texts: online, 128–129;
    reading aloud, 99; Reading Standards for
    Literature and Informational Text, 6–7;
    resources for, 76. *See also* Self-Regulated
    Strategy Development

informational writing scoring guidelines, 122–123

InsectIdentification.org, 161*t*

Institute for Education Science, 91

instructional designs, 54. *See also* K–3 writing workshop (vision and choice); writing instruction

Integration of Knowledge and Ideas reading category, 7

International Reading Association, 151

interviewing skills, 168–169

iPad apps, 136, 141

IRIS Center, 92*t*

iTunes U, 141

J

Johnston, T., 46–47

jokes, 126–127, 129

journal articles, 167*t*

judgment, comparative, 7

K

K–3 writing workshop (vision and choice): barriers to choosing a topic, 64–66; choice of genre, 66–69; choices for boys, 121–122; choosing a topic, 62–64; developing the vision, 57–60; impact of choice, 62; importance of vision, 56–61; organizational choices, 38, 70; reading like a writer, 60–62; terminology for, 57. *See also* digital writing in K–3

KeepVid, 143

Kennedy, X.J., 188

Key Ideas and Details reading category, 6

Kidspiration 3, 136–137, 137*f*

Kieffer, R.D., 178

kindergarten class's shared writing example, 144*f*

King-Sears, M.E., 180*t*

Kinneavy, J.L., 188, 189*f*

Kittle, P., 56

Kiuhara, S., 11

knowledge: shared, 187; transfer of, 125–126

knowledge bases, 5

Kotthoff, H., 127

Koyen, J., 163

Krashen, S., 169

Krensky, S., 47

L

Labbo, L.D., 178

Laminack, L.L., 50–51*f*

Lane, K.L., 92*t*

Langer, J.A., 18

language arts education trends, 119

Lapp, D., 190, 191

Laud, L., 88

learning: activities for promoting, 31*t*; progression of, 15; using writing to promote, 30–32

learning environment, digital, 152–153

learning management systems, 190

Leitner, D., 145

LetterSchool app, 136

letter to firefighters example, 148*f*

Leu, D.J., 191

Levinson, C., 80

Lexia, 136

Library of Congress, 161, 162*t*, 169

literacy, 115, 120. *See also* boys' literacies

literature: cultural knowledge in, 10; on immigration, 166–167*t*

Little, A., 92*t*

long jokes, 126–127, 129

Los Angeles Times, 191

Lunsford, A.A., 77

M

MacArthur, C., 180*t*

MacLachlan, E., 39, 40

MacLachlan, P., 39, 40

magazines as mentor texts, 58–59

Mainzer, L., 180*t*

make (use of term), 57

Maliszewski, D., 169

manageability of digital tools, 149, 151–152

Mannis, C.D., 172

Martino, G., 3

Mason, L.H., 91, 92*t*, 98, 103, 107

Mathias, R., 92*t*

Mazzeo, J., 73

McCloud, S., 169

Reid, R., 91, 92*t*
Reinking, D., 178
reluctant writers, 37, 49–51, 50*f*, 93
research on reading and writing: Common
	Core standards for, 5; federal support for,
	4; writing about text, 8
research projects: on assigned topics,
	77; online/digital tools for, 142–143;
	partnered, 153; standards by grade for, 7
resources/tools/websites: assessment of
	digital tools, 194–195; assistive devices
	and software, 179–180*t*; for conducting
	research, 143; electronic, 183*t*;
	informational texts, 76; iPad apps, 136,
	141; jokes/humor sites, 127; literature
	on immigration, 166–167*t*, 169; online,
	128–129, 144–146, 180; rules followed
	by online texts, 123; science and social
	studies, 161–162*t*; scriptwriting, 171; for
	Self-Regulated Strategy Development,
	92*t*; software, 134, 140*f*; student
	access to, 160–161; teaching critical
	use of, 83; using 21st-century writing,
	29–30; writing support, 162–163; for
	younger students, 142. *See also* digital
	environments and tools
response groups, 165*f*
revisions, enhancing skills for, 27–29
Reynolds, P.H., 137
Rideout, V.J., 73
Roberts, D.F., 73
Rowe, C., 163
Rowling, J.K., 41
Ruszkiewicz, J.J., 77

S

Sadoski, M., 191
Salahu-Din, D., 88
Sandler, M.W., 80
Sandmel, K., 88, 92*t*
Santangelo, T., 22, 24, 25, 26, 27, 28, 29,
	30, 89
Scardamalia, M., 88
Schertle, A., 46
Science Buddies, 161*t*
Scieszka, J., 79
scriptwriting, 171, 172*f*

self-image of writers, 60
self-monitoring of writing performance,
	101, 102*f*
Self-Regulated Strategy Development,
	87; description and use of, 91–95;
	framework, stages, and instructional
	process of, 95–97; resources for, 92*t*;
	stages of instruction, 96–97*t*; uses of, 28.
	See also POW + TREE + TWA model
self-statements example, 102*f*
sensory descriptions, 45–46
sentence construction, 26, 40, 41, 123
Seplocha, H., 191
Shanahan, T., 4, 5, 7, 8, 9, 187
shared/guided writing, 51*f*, 144–147
shared knowledge and processes, 187
sharing work, 143–146, 149
Shea, A., 190
Sheinkin, S., 80
short stories as mentor texts, 58
sieve metaphor, 115
similes, 47
Sipe, L., 191
Skype, 147
slang, 123, 171
Slate magazine, 122
slide show example, 134*f*
SMART Board, 149
Smarter Balanced Assessment Consortium,
	4, 74
Smetana, L., 182, 183
Smith, M.W., 115, 119, 120, 121, 125
Society for Science and the Public, 161*t*
sources, attribution of, 193–194
source texts, 98, 103
speech recognition tools, 180*t*
speech synthesis tools, 179*t*
spelling checkers, 179*t*
Spinelli, E., 39
Spiro, R.J., 188
stacks of texts, 58, 59, 61, 70
standards: by grade level, 5, 6, 7; inclusion
	of writing, 4; new versus old, 5;
	Reading Standards for Literature and
	Informational Text, 6; shifts from past
	writing assessment, 7–8
Stationery Studio, 136–137, 137*f*

Stolley, K., 80
stories: digital tools for creating, 137–141; genre-specific strategies example, 28t
story page example, 139f
Strasser, J., 191
Strickland, D.S., 83, 171
Strickland, J., 75f, 83–84
study units, 61
subliterature, 120
summaries, 84
supportive environment, 23–24, 56, 97t, 102–103
Swanson, C., 180t
Swinburne, S., 45

T
teaching writing. *See* writing instruction
technology. *See* digital environments and tools
template-driven writing, 74
templates for writing, 9f, 12–13, 13f
text, writing about, 5; comparison chart example, 9f; comparisons, 8; high-quality texts, 9–10; increasing challenge level of assignments, 14–15; introducing appropriate text models, 10–11; providing explicit instruction, 11–14; template for writing about similarities and differences, 13f
texting, 126
text markup example, 105f
texts: conversational, 126; introducing appropriate models, 10–11; types and purposes of, 26–27
text-to-speech resources, 141–142
text transcription skills example, 25t
ThingLink, 185, 185f
Thinkmap, 181f
Tierney, R., 5
Time for Kids, 76
Todd, M., 163
tools. *See* digital environments and tools; resources/tools/websites
topics: barriers to choosing, 64–66; choices offered, 76–77, 121; choosing, 56, 62–64; collecting readings and media around, 75; researching, 169

topic sentence, 90f
Toulmin guidelines for argument construction, 80–82
Towndrow, P.A., 180
transcription skills, 25t
transfer of knowledge, 125–126
Turkle, S., 75f
Turner, K.H., 126

U
understanding, using writing to promote, 30–32
United States Census Bureau, 162t
units of study, 61
University of Connecticut, 147
Urban Programs Resource Network, 161t

V
Vague but True, 127
verbs, 49–50, 50–51f
vision in using mentor texts, 56–62. *See also* K–3 writing workshop (vision and choice)
Visual Thesaurus, 181, 181f
Vocabulary Self-Collection Strategy Plus, 182–183, 186

W
Walters, K., 77
warrants, 81
Watson, E.P., 163
Weida, S., 80
Welty, E., 189
White, E.B., 46
Wigfield, A., 120
Wikimedia Foundation, 82
Wikipedia, 82–83, 122
wikis, 128, 143, 144, 184–185
Wikispaces Classroom, 143
Wilhelm, J.D., 115, 119, 120, 121, 125
Wilkinson, B., 88
Willems, M., 136
Wilson, C., 122
Wilson, W.S., 3
Wisconsin Fast Plants Program, 161t
Wolsey, T.D., 180t, 183, 184, 190
Wood, A., 60

word choice, 123–124, 192
word functions, anchoring/interpreting images, 192–193
word prediction tools, 179t
word processing software, 29–30, 124, 139, 179t, 195
WordSift, 181
World Book Online for Kids, 142
writers: challenges for, 93; effective, 189–190; guidelines for receiving feedback, 165f; individualizing instruction for, 94; motivational state of, 20; reluctant, 49–51, 50f; self-image of, 60
writer's notebooks, 43
writing: about reading, 5–8; about what is read, 7; accuracy strategy, 190; elements of good, 20–21, 44; evidence-based practices, 20–22; how writing informs, 187–188; independent, 51f, 97t; shared knowledge and processes of, 187; source for recommended practices, 22–23; tools for publishing, 156; types of, 84; use of term, 178
writing instruction: art of, 71; assumptions underlying, 30; Coiro's lessons for, 151; constraints of, 188; enhancing planning, revising, and editing, 27–29; facilitating maintenance and generalization of, 94–95; foundational skills, 24–26, 120; genre-specific strategies for stories example, 28t; neglect of, 88; providing guidance, 12; reasons for focusing on, 87–89; removing guidance, 13; source for, 22–23; state requirements, 5, 14–15; time spent on, 18; topic choice, 121; using 21st-century writing tools, 29–30; using model texts for, 10; using writing to promote understanding and learning, 30–32; Your Turn lessons, 41–44, 50–51f. See also Common Core State Standards; evidence-based writing instruction; model texts
writing interventions, testing of, 21–22
writing process, 88
writing standards, 4. See also Common Core State Standards
Writing Study Group of the NCTE Executive Committee, 18
writing workshops. See K–3 writing workshop (vision and choice)

Y

Yang, W., 141
Yolen, J., 40
Young, G., 136
Young, J.R., 75f
Youngs, S., 157
Your Turn lessons, 41–44, 50–51f
Yusuf, W.F.B.M., 180

Z

zines, 160, 162–163, 164–165, 167–168, 168f, 173f